- Refines the definition of "counterinsurgency" as comprehensive civilian and military efforts designed to simultaneously defeat and contain insurgency and address its root causes.

- Introduces tenets and precepts of counterinsurgency.

- Adds Chapter VI, "Assessing Counterinsurgency Operations."

- Emphasizes that understanding grievances is key to addressing root causes of insurgency and creating durable stability.

- Renames "dominate narrative" to "counterinsurgency narrative" and updates the discussion on narrative development and dissemination.

- Articulates that US counterinsurgency efforts should provide incentives to the host-nation government to undertake reforms that address the root causes of the insurgency.

- Reduces redundancies and improves continuity between Joint Publication (JP) 1, *Doctrine for the Armed Forces of the United States,* and JP 3-0, *Joint Operations.*

- Removes appendices on provincial reconstruction team, insurgent approach indicators, and insurgency and crime. The provincial reconstruction team appendix was incorporated into JP 3-08, *Interorganizational Coordination During Joint Operations.*

- Adds appendices on civil military operations, authorities in counterinsurgency operations, example counterinsurgency qualification standards outline, and precepts for counterinsurgency.

TABLE OF CONTENTS

EXECUTIVE SUMMARY
COMMANDER'S OVERVIEW

- **Provides an Overview of Counterinsurgency Operations**

- **Explains the Nature, Prerequisites, and Objects of an Insurgency**

- **Presents the Fundamentals of Counterinsurgency**

- **Discusses the Operational Environment During Counterinsurgency Operations**

- **Covers Planning for Counterinsurgency Operations**

- **Describes Assessing Counterinsurgency Operations**

- **Addresses Supporting Operations for Counterinsurgency Operations**

- **Discusses Building Governance to Counterinsurgency Operations**

Overview

Insurgency is the organized use of subversion and violence to seize, nullify, or challenge political control of a region.

Insurgency uses a mixture of subversion, sabotage, political, economic, psychological actions, and armed conflict to achieve its political aims. It is a protracted politico-military struggle designed to weaken the control and legitimacy of an established government, a military occupation government, an interim civil administration, or a peace process while increasing insurgent control and legitimacy—the central issues in an insurgency.

Counterinsurgency is a comprehensive civilian and military effort designed to simultaneously defeat and contain insurgency and address its root causes.

Counterinsurgency (COIN) is primarily a political struggle and incorporates a wide range of activities by the host nation (HN) government of which security is only one, albeit an important one. The HN government in coordination with the chief of mission (COM) should lead the COIN efforts. When the operational environment (OE) is not conducive to a civilian agency lead for the COIN effort within a specific area, the joint force commander (JFC) must be cognizant of and able to lead the unified action required for effective COIN.

Approach to Counterinsurgency	The joint force needs to adapt approaches based on the following considerations: political control, the population-centric nature of COIN, assessing relevant actors, and understanding the OE.
Governance and Legitimacy	The authority to govern is dependent upon the successful amalgamation and interplay of four factors: mandate, manner, support and consent, and expectations. When the relationship between the government and those governed breaks down, challenges to authority may result.
Insurgent Narrative versus Counterinsurgency Narrative	Insurgents often try to use the local narrative to gain popular support and recruits for their cause. COIN planners must reinforce the credibility and legitimacy of the HN and US COIN efforts and compose a unifying message, called the COIN narrative, that exploits the negative aspects of the insurgent efforts.

Insurgency

Nature of Insurgency	Insurgent groups adopt an irregular approach because they initially lack the resources required to directly confront the incumbent government in traditional warfare. By adopting an irregular approach, insurgencies avoid decisive battles in which the incumbent government can apply its superior combat power. Over time, insurgencies work to force governments to the negotiating table, trigger their collapse to seize control, or grow until their forces can directly confront and defeat the government security forces and physically take over the seat of government.
Prerequisites for Insurgency	Historically, lack of government control, vulnerable populations, and revolutionary leadership available for direction have been identified as the prerequisites for an insurgency to occur. Contemporary analysis suggests a somewhat different approach that more properly identifies the prerequisites to be viewed as opportunity, motive, and means.
Insurgent Objectives	Insurgent objectives can be generally categorized as reform, revolution, secession, nullification, and resistance. However, these categories are archetypes, and many insurgencies exhibit characteristics of more than one category, often as a result of the alliance building.
Insurgent Narrative, Strategy, and	The strength and success of an insurgency depends in large part on its ability to shape the behavior of its ranks and the

Organization	population whose compliance or outright support it requires. Insurgent strategies are composed of interdependent political and military dimensions. The relative emphasis on each of those aspects and exactly how they are linked is shaped by the combination of opportunity/motive/means factors, and the nature of the insurgent objectives. Insurgent organizational and operational approaches are directly related to the strength of the HN government.
Stages and Outcomes of Insurgency	The stages of insurgency are pre-conflict stage, inception, open conflict, and resolution. Outcomes of insurgency may be an insurgent victory, a negotiated settlement, or a government victory.

Fundamentals of Counterinsurgency

Counterinsurgency Mindset	Warfare that has the population as its focus of operations requires a different mindset and different capabilities than warfare that focuses on defeating an adversary militarily. In COIN operations this means an adaptive and flexible mindset to understand the population, anticipate insurgent actions, be comfortable among the population, and appreciate the comprehensive approach of unified action.
Tenets of Counterinsurgency	The tenets of COIN are understand the OE, develop the COIN narrative, synchronize and integrate lines of effort, and unity of command and unity of effort.
United States Government Involvement in Counterinsurgency	The context for US involvement in COIN is based on three possible strategic settings: assisting an established HN government; as an adjunct to US major combat operations; or US operations in an ungoverned area.
Operational Approaches	Framed by the strategy of a comprehensive approach to COIN, the JFC's operational approach is largely based on the JFC's understanding of the OE and the specific insurgency. Successful development of the operational approach requires continuous analysis, learning, assessment, dialogue, and collaboration between commander and staff, as well as other subject matter experts including other interagency and multinational partners in unified action.
Employment Considerations	As joint land operations tend to become decentralized, mission command becomes the preferred method of command and control. The nature of insurgency requires

that the commander's operational approach be flexible enough to adapt specific tactical activities to local conditions. In a COIN environment, tasks will often need to be carried out in ways generally requiring specialized training and sometimes requiring development of new tactics, techniques, and procedures.

The Operational Environment

Understanding the Operational Environment

An understanding of the OE enables the development of a COIN approach that includes realistic, achievable objectives, and properly aligns ends, ways, and means. Understanding of the OE is accomplished through tailoring the joint intelligence preparation of the OE and assessment requirements for a COIN environment.

Operational Environment in Counterinsurgency

The various components of the OE provide a lens through which a COIN force may gain an understanding of the decision making and associated behavior of the relevant actors. The COIN OE encompasses the relevant actors and the physical areas and factors within the physical domains and the information environment.

Tools and Methods for Understanding the Operational Environment

Many tools and methodologies have been developed that are worthy of consideration by the JFC for understanding the OE for a COIN operation. These include traditional intelligence approaches; intelligence, surveillance, and reconnaissance; sociocultural analysis; analytical frameworks; network analysis; social science; information management and information technology; and identity intelligence.

Planning

Joint Operation Planning

COIN plans and orders should integrate and synchronize operations, forces, and capabilities in a manner that addresses the root causes of insurgency and neutralizes insurgents. In the complex COIN environment, it is impossible to accurately view the contributions of any individual organization, capability, or the area in which they operate in isolation from all others. Commanders and staff must work with the COM and country team to develop mechanisms to synchronize the operation or campaign plan and achieve civil-military synergy in operations.

Military Operational Considerations for

Within the context of operating in a given HN, there are several operations, programs, and activities that may be

Counterinsurgency	conducted as a part of or simultaneously with COIN, including negotiation and diplomacy, security cooperation (foreign internal defense, security force assistance, and security assistance), unconventional warfare, counterterrorism, counterguerrilla operations, stability operations, and peace operations. Other key operations related to COIN are civil-military operations (CMO), information operations, military information support operations, maritime security operations, and counterdrug operations.
Additional Operational Options for Counterinsurgency	There are several options to consider when conducting COIN operations: generational engagement; limited support/light footprint; identify, separate, isolate, influence, and reintegrate; attack the network operations; partnering; and shape, clear, hold, build, and transition. Each option offers a different but complementary avenue and must be weighed against the OE and the actors involved and may be used individually or in conjunction with each other.
Termination (End State), Transnational Military Authorities, Reconciliation, Reintegration, and Political Reform	Effective COIN planning cannot occur without a clear understanding of the military end state and the conditions that must exist to end military operations. To plan effectively for termination, the supported JFC must have a shared understanding with the COM, and they must understand how the President and Secretary of Defense intend to terminate the joint operation and ensure that its outcomes endure. In some cases a transitional military authority may be required in ungoverned areas, occupied territory, or an allied or neutral territory liberated from enemy forces, including insurgent or resistance movement. A transitional military authority is a temporary military government exercising the functions of civil administration in the absence of a legitimate civil authority. If established, the transitional military authority will eventually relinquish control of the OE, with activities assumed by the HN or another authority. It is important to plan transition from the start of the operation. Reconciliation and reintegration of insurgent forces can be achieved through the stabilization framework provided in Department of Defense Instruction 3000.05, *Stability Operations*, and associated Service documents. Once the insurgent political infrastructure is destroyed and local leaders begin to establish themselves, necessary political reforms can be implemented. These

aspects of COIN should ideally be led by civilian agencies, intergovernmental organizations, or nongovernmental organizations, with the military in a supporting role.

Assessing Counterinsurgency Operations

Operation assessment offers perspective and insight, and provides the opportunity for self-correction, adaptation, and thoughtful results-oriented learning.

COIN operation assessment requires an integrated approach to support commander and policy maker decisions regarding the implementation and resourcing of operations to accomplish strategic objectives. Effective assessment is necessary for counterinsurgents to recognize changing conditions and determine their significance to the progress of the COIN operation. It is crucial to the JFC's ability to identify anticipated and unanticipated effects and successfully adapt to the changing situation.

The Assessment Process and Assessment Plan

Relevant factors for assessments in COIN are rarely uniform across regions and operational phases. To account for the differences between various locations within a given operational area, COIN operations require decentralized command structures. This principle extends to the operation assessment planning for COIN. Operation assessment in COIN relies on those with the most in-depth knowledge of specific locations within the operational area, usually subordinate units, to identify and assess factors relevant to their localities. The joint force should structure the assessment plan to incorporate the reporting and assessments of subordinate commands without being prescriptive as to what information is collected or how it is analyzed. The assessment process operates during the planning and execution cycle. This process supports the clear definition of tasks, objectives, and end states, and gives the staff a method for selecting the commanders' critical information requirements that best support decision making. Assessment plans link the intelligence estimates of the current OE conditions to information about friendly force status and actions.

Operation Assessment Methods

Operation assessment methods include contextual assessments and stage-based assessment plans. For contextual assessment, commanders at each echelon determine what is important to help them describe progress toward achieving objectives and attaining end states through a reporting period (typically a month or a quarter of a year). A stage-based assessment plan uses sets of basic criteria to establish a common framework, with an emphasis on identifying key issues and potential means of addressing them, along with risk to the operation or campaign if they are not addressed.

Supporting Operations for Counterinsurgency

Integrating Operations to Support the Strategic Narrative

Failure to incorporate the strategic narrative into actions through the operational level down to the individual counterinsurgent will do greater harm more quickly than almost any action in COIN. If done correctly, operations nested with a strategic narrative are strengthened through sense of purpose, unity of effort, and the ability to gain and maintain initiative against insurgents.

Cyberspace Considerations in Support of Counterinsurgency Operations

Cyberspace operations provide security within the environment and help to isolate insurgents within the affected area or separate them from external support secured through cyberspace. Carefully planned cyberspace operations are capable of creating the effects to deny the enemy freedom of action and maintain US and joint forces freedom of maneuver in support of COIN operations.

Considerations for Air Operations in Counterinsurgency

Air forces and capabilities may provide considerable asymmetric advantages to counterinsurgents, especially by denying insurgents secrecy and unfettered access to bases of operation. If insurgents assemble a conventional force or their operating locations are identified and isolated, air assets can respond quickly with joint precision fires or to airlift ground forces to locations to accomplish a mission.

Space Capabilities

Space contributions to COIN include intelligence collection, satellite communications, and positioning, navigation, and timing. Monitoring areas of interest from space helps provide information on enemy location, disposition, and intent; aids in tracking, targeting, and engaging the adversary.

Maritime Considerations in Support of Counterinsurgency Operations

The expeditionary character of maritime forces may provide access when access from the other operational areas is denied or limited. Maritime forces may provide direct support to the joint force that does not include combat operations, to include logistic support, intelligence/communication sharing, humanitarian relief, and CMO in the form of maritime civil affairs, and expeditionary medical aid and training.

Conventional Ground Force Considerations in

Conventional ground forces bring capabilities that play an important role in the military contribution to COIN

Support of Counterinsurgency Operations	operations. These forces and capabilities are especially critical for successful counterguerrilla, intelligence, humanitarian, and informational efforts.
Special Operations Considerations in Support of Counterinsurgency Operations	Special operations forces may conduct a wide array of missions with HN security forces or may be integrated with US conventional forces. They are particularly important when the joint force is using an indirect approach to COIN.
Detainee Operation Considerations in Support of Counterinsurgency Operations	How counterinsurgents treat captured insurgents has immense potential impact on insurgent morale, retention, and recruitment. Humane and just treatment may afford counterinsurgents many short-term opportunities as well as potentially damaging insurgent recruitment. Abuse may foster resentment and hatred, offering the enemy an opportunity for propaganda and assist potential insurgent recruitment and support.
Counter-Improvised Explosive Device Operations	Insurgents have traditionally relied on improvised explosive devices (IEDs) as a means of delivering fires against friendly forces and civilians. IEDs have the capability, if not countered and neutralized, of not only hindering the operational momentum of a COIN effort, but also creating the effects of terrorism and insecurity that can erode legitimacy of the HN government and the will to fight the insurgents.
Counter Threat Finance	Counter threat finance (CTF) operations may be conducted to disrupt and deny finances or shut down networks. CTF operations are often planned and conducted by the cooperating members of the international community and reach from the strategic to the tactical level.
Public Affairs	Public affairs supports the commander's COIN objectives and helps shape the OE through the timely, truthful, and accurate informing of and interaction with internal and external audiences. HN and US information, the media's reporting, insurgent propaganda, and other contributors to the information environment influence how the populace perceives the combined COIN effort, the insurgency, and the HN's legitimacy.
Identity Intelligence Operations	Identity intelligence operations activities assist US forces, the HN, and partner nations to positively identify, track, characterize, and disrupt threat actors conducting and facilitating insurgent activities in the OE.

Building Governance to Support Counterinsurgency

Principles of Governance	Supporting indigenous governance is often an important COIN tool to counter insurgent efforts to seize, nullify, or challenge governing authorities. Governance consists of the rules, processes, and behavior by which interests are articulated, resources are managed, and power is exercised in a society. These rules and processes must be seen as predictable and tolerable in the eyes of the population to be deemed legitimate. They are manifested in three core functions: representation, security, and welfare.
Encouraging Political Reform	Part of finding a political solution may involve political reform of HN governance institutions and structures. Political reform in support of COIN objectives should be focused on fostering changes that will degrade the insurgents' ability to build their narrative around perceived political grievances. Such efforts must be based on local populations' expectations of what acceptable governance should look like.
Building Effective Governance	HN structures must be seen to be delivering effective governance. Whenever possible, support to indigenous governance should be channeled by, with, and through HN personnel and structures.
Security Sector Reform	Security sector reform is primarily a means to strengthen the capabilities, capacity, and effectiveness of the HN security apparatus, which in turn improves the capabilities of the security forces to secure and protect the population from insurgent/terrorist violence.
Criminal Justice System Reform	Effective and acceptable delivery of justice is an essential governance function; it allows for nonviolent dispute resolution. To enhance HN legitimacy, justice reform should build upon the existing legal frameworks in the HN. This may include common law, civil law, criminal codes, traditional or religious law, and international law.
Disarmament, Demobilization, and Reintegration	Disarmament, demobilization, and reintegration (DDR) attempts to stabilize the OE by disarming and demobilizing insurgents and by helping return former insurgents to civilian life. DDR efforts during an active conflict focus on inducing insurgent defection and using former insurgents to undermine the insurgency.

Economic and Infrastructure Development

Economic and infrastructure development have frequently featured as the main nonlethal lines of effort in recent COIN operations. Often, such efforts have featured Western templates to determine priorities and have struggled to secure the local population's buy-in. Economic and infrastructure development in support of COIN should be based on local expectations, capabilities, and capacities to ensure sustainability. Fulfilling local expectations in terms of service delivery can help bolster the legitimacy of HN governance structures, while undermining the insurgency.

CONCLUSION

This publication provides joint doctrine for the planning, execution, and assessment of COIN operations.

CHAPTER I
OVERVIEW

"In the aftermath of wars in Iraq and Afghanistan, the United States will emphasize nonmilitary means and military-to-military cooperation to address instability and reduce the demand for significant US force commitments to stability operations. US forces will nevertheless be ready to conduct limited counterinsurgency and other stability operations if required, operating alongside coalition forces whenever possible. Accordingly, US forces will retain and continue to refine the lessons learned, expertise, and specialized capabilities that have been developed over the past ten years of counterinsurgency and stability operations in Iraq and Afghanistan."

Secretary of Defense Leon J. Panetta
Sustaining US Global Leadership: Priorities for 21st Century Defense,
January 2012

1. Introduction

a. **Insurgency is the organized use of subversion and violence to seize, nullify, or challenge political control of a region.** Insurgency uses a mixture of subversion, sabotage, political, economic, psychological actions, and armed conflict to achieve its political aims. It is a protracted politico-military struggle designed to weaken the control and legitimacy of an established government, a military occupation government, an interim civil administration, or a peace process while increasing insurgent control and legitimacy—the central issues in an insurgency. Each insurgency has its own unique characteristics but they have the following aspects: a strategy, an ideology, an organization, a support structure, the ability to manage information, and a supportive environment. It is these aspects that set an insurgency apart from other spoilers and present a significant threat. Typically, insurgents will solicit, or be offered, external support from state or non-state actors.

b. Insurgencies will continue to challenge security and stability around the globe in the 21st century. While the possibility of large scale warfare remains, few nations are likely to engage the US, allies, and partner nations. Globalization, numerous weak nation-state governments, demographics, radical ideologies, environmental concerns, and economic pressures are exacerbated by the ease of interaction among insurgent groups, terrorists, and criminals; and all put both weak and moderately governed states at risk. Today, a state's failure can quickly become not only a misfortune for its local communities, but a threat to global stability and US national interests.

c. Long-standing external and internal tensions tend to exacerbate or create core grievances within some countries, which can result in political strife, instability, or, if exploited by some groups to gain political advantage, even insurgency. Moreover, some transnational terrorists with radical political and religious ideologies may intrude in weak or poorly governed states to form a wider, more networked threat.

d. The United States Government (USG) has supported numerous allies and partner nations to prevent or disrupt threats to their stability and security through foreign assistance and security cooperation (SC) activities as part of geographic combatant commanders' (GCCs') theater campaign plans in conjunction with other USG efforts. The Department of Defense's (DOD's) efforts can include counterterrorism (CT) operations and foreign internal defense (FID) programs supported by stability operations tasks. If a friendly nation appears vulnerable to an insurgency, and it is in the best interest of the USG to help the host nation (HN) mitigate that insurgency, the USG would support the affected nation's internal defense and development (IDAD) strategy and program through a FID program. When an HN government supported by a FID program appears to be overwhelmed by internal threats, and if it is in the national security interests of the USG, then the third category of FID, US combat operations, may be directed by the President. **Those US combat operations would be in the form of counterinsurgency (COIN) operations, whether in conjunction with the HN forces, or in place of them, until the HN has the necessary capability and capacity to take on combat operations.** However, the HN must retain responsibility for dealing with the insurgency even though US forces may temporarily be conducting COIN operations.

e. **COIN is a comprehensive civilian and military effort designed to simultaneously defeat and contain insurgency and address its root causes.** COIN is primarily a political struggle and incorporates a wide range of activities by the HN government of which security is only one, albeit an important one. Unified action is required to successfully conduct COIN operations and should include all HN, US, and multinational partners. The HN government in coordination with the chief of mission (COM) should lead the COIN efforts. When the operational environment (OE) is not conducive to a civilian agency lead for the COIN effort within a specific area, the joint force commander (JFC) must be cognizant of and able to lead the unified action required for effective COIN.

2. Approach to Counterinsurgency

Because a COIN operation is in essence a civil-military operation, it differs in many respects from a traditional military force-on-force operation and requires a special mindset. It is the population-centric nature of COIN that distinguishes it from most traditional military force-on-force operations. In COIN success means that the population assents to be governed by the HN government and the insurgents have either reconciled through a peaceful political process or suffered total military defeat. US participation in COIN operations is typically led by a COM in conjunction with a JFC and requires significant interagency coordination in the application of the instruments of national power. A complete analysis of the populace's grievances and the interconnected social, economic, informational, physical, and governing structure is required for the full application of military capabilities. COIN operations will take time. It is unlikely that there will be a decisive battle that will determine the outcome of the conflict. Successful COIN operations adapt to changes in the OE and the adversary's strategy, operations, and tactics. The joint force needs to adapt approaches based on the following considerations:

a. **Political Control. COIN is an armed struggle for legitimacy of all or part of the HN.** COIN requires the integration of elements of security, economic development, and information through a **political strategy** that establishes and sustains the **control** that reinforces legitimacy and effectiveness of an HN government while reducing insurgent influence over the indigenous population. The USG's nonlethal actions in support of the HN are often just as important to the COIN effort as the JFC's lethal actions. COIN is not nation building, and the JFC and COM strengthen the legitimacy of the HN government through understanding and continuously assessing the nature of the conflict, and then tailoring only those resources and capabilities necessary to enable the HN government to provide a secure, *predictable,* and *tolerable* living environment for the population that the HN government seeks to control. Because of sociocultural factors, USG normally should not be concerned with transforming the HN government into a mirror image of a Western-style democracy, although some democratic principles are universal and may be valuable in establishing a base level of HN government legitimacy, and adherence to certain human rights standards is required by US statutes to qualify for US foreign assistance.

(1) **Insurgency** is a struggle for some form of political power, whether that power is sought through reform, revolution, secession, nullification, or resistance. Political power is nearly always the *end,* not the *method,* of the insurgent's strategy and tactics. Thus, the JFC should not confuse the various methods used by insurgents with the end or goal of their struggle. The methods used by the insurgent to gain political power are a mix of raw intimidation and violence, religious extremism, political ideology, and exploitation of local grievances that occur outside the accepted political process. People support an insurgency because they perceive it is in their best interest. They support an insurgency because the insurgent leadership has spun a compelling narrative (the insurgent narrative) that the HN government and/or a foreign occupier or supporting country are collectively responsible for their woes (e.g., their psychic, physical, or economic insecurity), and the people would be better off actively, or at least passively, supporting the insurgency. Narratives are complex and may draw on mix of ideology, identity, history, and religion. When that narrative is tied to actual persecution, disenfranchisement, or other structural grievances related to a particular ethnic, religious, sectarian, or regional group, it is all the more powerful. This means that the HN must address these grievances and institute positive change to undermine the insurgent narrative and gain the initiative. This is often the major challenge that the US will face with assisting an HN that is resistant to dealing with fundamental need to change. The basis for an insurgency is typically the nexus of opportunity, motive, and means.

(2) The **USG COIN strategy** is based on supporting the HN COIN strategy. It is designed to simultaneously protect the population from insurgent violence; strengthen the legitimacy and capacity of the HN government; and isolate the insurgents physically, psychologically, politically, socially, and economically. All efforts are pursued for the purpose of addressing the *perceived* and actual *political imbalance that the insurgent leadership has exploited.* The USG never intends to remain engaged in a COIN effort with an HN government indefinitely and wants to responsibly end its COIN operation. Thus, the COM and JFC ensure that the HN government can maintain a secure and stable environment expected by the population.

b. **COIN Is Population-Centric.** The development of a proper COIN approach starts with the acceptance of the people as important to COIN operation. However, the HN may be fully capable of securing the population. The US may play an enabling role with capabilities such as direct action (DA) or logistical support. Moreover, each conflict is unique. One should not assume the population is the center of gravity (COG) in COIN. It could be a range of factors, from an external actor to core leadership. Success in COIN depends on a counterinsurgent's ability to motivate various people, sometimes referred to herein as actors, toward behavior that supports an outcome of the operation consistent with the USG's desired political end state. In traditional warfare, success is achieved primarily by destroying the enemy's means to sustain military operations and occupying its territory. In COIN, the defeat of the enemy's military capabilities is just one component of what is ultimately a broader struggle for control over a target population that requires a balanced mix of both lethal and nonlethal actions by the JFC. The cumulative effects created by all COIN activities must enable the greater affiliation or allegiance of the population and other actors to the HN government rather than support for the insurgency or even ambivalence. In turn, supportive behavior by the population supports HN government legitimacy and control.

c. **Assessing Relevant Actors.** Traditional warfare tends to focus primarily on the adversary's means, especially military and technological capacity. In a COIN operation, the JFC simultaneously targets the opportunity, the motive, and the means that serve as the basis for the insurgency. The perceptions and behavior of relevant actors, especially the relevant populations, can influence all three of these factors. In COIN, the relevant actors always include the insurgency, the indigenous population, host-nation security forces (HNSF), and the HN government. Actors are dynamic and many will belong to more than one category at the same time or move from one category to another over time. As operational and political conditions change, some actors may shift their allegiances to protect or pursue their own interests. COIN requires continuous assessment of the relevant actors, both directly and indirectly, to maintain an objective understanding of their opinions and strengths of their affiliations/allegiance. See Chapter II, "Insurgency," paragraph 3, "Prerequisites for Insurgency," for the discussion regarding opportunity, motive, and means being the basis for insurgency.

d. **Understanding the OE**

(1) The OE is the composite of the conditions, circumstances, and influences that affect how the JFC uses available capabilities and makes decisions. Understanding the OE involves understanding the relevant actors, the physical domains, and the information environment. It requires a holistic view of insurgent, neutral, and friendly political, military, economic, social, information, and infrastructure (PMESII) systems. Understanding the OE requires understanding the decision making, mental disposition, and behavior of significant actors, especially the public opinion of the relevant populations. Their natures and interactions will affect how the JFC plans, organizes for, and conducts COIN operations. Understanding the OE requires a continuous understanding of the dynamics of the insurgency, and its effects on the population, the insurgents, and the counterinsurgents. Given that the success of an insurgent often depends upon the support of the local population, commanders should pay particular concern to that aspect of the OE. In traditional force-on-force operations, the JFC should think like the adversary, but for a COIN effort, the JFC should analyze not only how the insurgents think, but also how the local population thinks. The JFC should have the ability to objectively analyze the effect of all the lethal and nonlethal activities undertaken by the joint force and its interagency and multinational partners on local perceptions and determine whether those activities support

the COIN narrative, or whether they inadvertently feed into the insurgent's narrative. Refer to Chapter IV, "The Operational Environment," for a full discussion of the OE.

(2) In an environment with an insurgency, tasks and activities often need to be carried out in dramatically different ways, generally requiring specialized training and sometimes requiring development of new or modification of extant capabilities. The targeted application of security, diplomatic, development, and information resources in a COIN environment typically is fraught with the risk of unintended consequences and requires a sophisticated understanding of sociocultural factors in the local context. Integration of resources and capabilities will likely need to be tailored for the purposes of stabilization, normally with coordination between the JFC and the COM. For military forces, COIN operations often involve a wider range of tasks and capabilities than those required in traditional warfare. Similarly, interagency initiatives in a COIN environment often differ in important respects from traditional diplomacy and development. Armed forces that are optimized for major combat operations will usually require specific training, in particular on how they interact with diplomacy and development actors, and perhaps even structural reorganization to meet the unique requirements of COIN operations.

3. Governance and Legitimacy

a. **Governance.** Governance is the ability to serve the population through the rules, processes, and behavior by which interests are articulated, resources are managed, and power is exercised in a society. A state's ability to provide effective governance rests on its political and bureaucratic willingness, capability, and capacity to establish rules and procedures for decision making and on its ability to provide public services in a manner that is predictable and tolerable to the local population. In an ungoverned area (UGA), the state or the central government is unable or unwilling to extend control, effectively govern, or influence the local population. A UGA can also indicate where a provincial, local, tribal, or otherwise autonomous government does not fully or effectively govern. UGA is a broad term that encompasses under-governed, misgoverned, contested, and exploitable areas, characterized by the traits of inadequate governance capacity, insufficient political will, gaps in legitimacy, the presence or recent presence of conflict, or restrictive norms of behavior.

b. **Governance and Legitimacy.** The authority to govern is dependent upon the successful amalgamation and interplay of four factors: mandate, manner, support and consent, and expectations. When the relationship between the government and those governed breaks down, challenges to authority may result. If a significant section of the population, or just an extreme faction, believes it cannot achieve a remedy through established political discourse, it may resort to insurgency.

(1) **Mandate.** The perceived legitimacy of the mandate that establishes a state authority, whether through the principles of universal suffrage, a recognized or accepted caste/tribal model, or authoritarian rule.

(2) **Manner.** The way in which those exercising that mandate conduct themselves, both individually and collectively in meeting the expectations of the local population(s).

(3) **Support and Consent.** The extent to which local populations consent to, or comply with, the manner/authority of those exercising the mandate. Consent may range from active support, passive support, or indifference, through unwilling compliance.

(4) **Expectations.** The relative quality or amount of support that local populations expect from their government.

c. **Support to HN Government.** Successful COIN operations require an HN government that is capable and willing to counter the insurgency and address its root causes. Typically this involves a mix of political reform, improved governance, and/or targeted economic development initiatives. COIN involves a careful balance between constructive dimensions (enhancing the capacity of the HN government to address the root causes of insurgency) and destructive dimensions (destroying and marginalizing the insurgency's political and military capabilities). In some situations the USG may need to take the lead for the HN government, especially in the early stages of a COIN effort. However, COIN activities should be transitioned back to an HN-led effort as soon as possible. This is especially true when the HN government may have suffered a crisis in legitimacy and governance, which will be bolstered by increased responsibilities, capabilities, and capacity. The political will of the HN government to carry out such activities is, therefore, critical.

d. **Legitimacy.** Many governments rule through a combination of consent and influence, and in some cases, coercion. Legitimacy is a significant indicator of the extent to which systems of authority, decisions, and conduct are accepted by the local population. Political legitimacy of a government determines the degree to which the population will voluntarily or passively comply with the decisions and rules issued by a governing authority. Governments described as legitimate rule primarily with the consent of the governed; those described as illegitimate tend to rely heavily on coercion. Citizens obey illegitimate governments because they fear retribution, rather than because they voluntarily accept its rule. While a legitimate government may employ limited coercion to enforce the rule of law, most of its citizens voluntarily accept its authority. **Legitimacy determines the transaction costs of political and governmental power:** low legitimacy may breed contempt on the part of the population and may require extensive prodding and incentives, or in extreme cases threats and intimidation, by the government to secure compliance of the population; high legitimacy generally invites compliance by the population and therefore requires less effort by the government to ensure compliance. The latter normally fosters allegiance of the governed to the government, and legitimate governance is inherently more stable. The societal support it engenders allows it to adequately manage internal problems, change, and conflict.

(1) **Legitimacy in COIN.** The struggle for legitimacy with the relevant population typically is a central theme of the conflict between the insurgency and the HN government. The HN government generally needs some level of legitimacy among the population in order to retain confidence of the populace and an acknowledgment of governing power. The insurgency will attack the legitimacy of the HN government while attempting to develop its own legitimacy with the population. The COIN effort must reduce the credibility of the insurgency while strengthening the legitimacy of the HN government. In a COIN environment high legitimacy of the HN government magnifies the resources/capabilities of the COIN effort (through such means as a populace willing to report on insurgents) and

allows the HN to concentrate finite resources on targeting the insurgency. In dealing with an enemy like the insurgents, who are drawn from segments of the population, it is often a particular challenge for the HN to be seen as legitimate in public opinion. Legitimacy of the HN government can be undercut when an outside force like the USG is engaged by the HN to aid in the fight against the insurgent.

(2) **Drivers of Legitimacy.** Legitimacy is achieved by the HN government through being perceived as effective and credible and by providing an environment for the population to maintain predictable and tolerable living conditions. In some situations the provision of security and some basic services may be enough for citizens to see a government as legitimate. Some elements of the population may only ask of their government that they be kept safe and left alone to live their lives with little interaction with the HN government. In other cases, the population may expect more extensive services from the HN government. The key is that legitimacy is ultimately decided in the minds of the population. Therefore, the goal of COIN is to ensure that the HN government meets the baseline expectations of the population to solidify its legitimacy.

4. Insurgent Narrative versus Counterinsurgency Narrative

Insurgents typically have a strategic narrative as the central mechanism through which their ideologies, policies, and strategies are expressed and absorbed. Counterinsurgents should also develop a strategic narrative both to contrast and counter the insurgent narrative.

a. **Insurgent Narrative.** Narratives are central to representing collective/group identities, particularly the collective identity of religious sects, ethnic groupings, and tribal elements. Insurgents often try to use the local narrative to gain popular support and recruits for their cause. They typically emphasize certain collective/group identity themes and selective interpretation of religious beliefs to contextualize local grievances as an element of the insurgent cause. Like terrorist groups, insurgents will exploit populations whose social narrative and norms are similar to or can be manipulated by the insurgent group. Stories about a community's history provide models of how actions and consequences are linked. Stories are often the basis for strategies and actions, as well as for interpreting others' intentions. Whenever possible, the USG should identify all insurgent narratives.

b. **COIN Narrative.** COIN planners must reinforce the credibility and legitimacy of the HN and US COIN efforts and compose a unifying message, called the COIN narrative, that exploits the negative aspects of the insurgent efforts. The COIN narrative overshadows and counters the insurgents' narrative and propaganda. It is vital for counterinsurgents to analyze, advertise, and exploit the differences between accepted HN cultural norms and the insurgent narrative and propaganda. The COIN narrative must be the result of a meticulous effort using unified action. Because it has to be culturally authentic, this requires close collaboration among the HN government, COM, and JFC. It should appeal to a wider audience, yet must be shaped and adapted to appeal to the cultural perspective of the population. The COIN narrative strikes a balance between simplicity and explaining an often complex situation. It also must be adaptive and deeply rooted in local culture, or it will fail or even be counterproductive. The COIN narrative must explain to the population what they stand to gain from supporting the COIN forces, HN government, and US. It must also

---

EXAMPLE OF A COUNTERINSURGENCY (COIN) NARRATIVE

Protecting the people is the mission. The conflict will be won by persuading the population, not destroying the enemy. The International Security Assistance Force will succeed when the Government of the Islamic Republic of Afghanistan earns the support of the people.

The host-nation government and US forces mission is to protect the people and establish a stable, safe, and productive environment for the population of Afghanistan. When the diverse ethnicities and tribes of Afghanistan put aside their differences and choose to work together, Afghanistan can prosper, as the population can then work to rebuild the nation and engage in commerce freely. The people will benefit by enjoying safety, and can profit from the uninterrupted basic services (power, clean water, and communications) and opportunities to exploit the natural resources in ways that cannot be done while fighting continues, as well as benefiting from a fair and just legal system.

Supporting the insurgents is strongly against the best interests of all Afghans. The insurgents are simple bullies who seek to use fear to control the population. They kill and terrorize to force the people to follow their will, they seize the people's goods and wealth for themselves in the name of their cause, and provide no services in return beyond the dubious promise to not harm those who cooperate. Under the insurgents, Afghans will never prosper: they can only hope to survive another day. The terrorists lie that they fight to "liberate" Afghanistan from foreign invaders, but they fight only to enrich themselves.

The US interest in Afghanistan is simply in stabilizing the region. The US benefits from the denial of Afghanistan as a safe haven for violent terrorists; Afghanistan makes a valuable ally in an important region of the world; and US industry benefits from a stable Afghanistan, as it opens the opportunity to establish joint ventures with the people of Afghanistan. Free trade of Afghan mineral wealth and American manufactured goods is to the benefit of both Afghans and Americans.

Various Sources

explain to the population what the US stands to gain from supporting the HN government. By clearly stating US goals, it prevents insurgents from portraying US forces as invaders with hidden motives. Finally, the COIN narrative assists in managing both expectations and information. When faced with more than one significant insurgent narrative (e.g., that developed by indigenous insurgents, by transnational terrorists, and/or by a major criminal enterprise), more than one COIN narrative may be required.

For additional discussions about the insurgent narrative and COIN narrative, see Chapter II, "Insurgency," paragraph 5, "Insurgent Narrative, Strategy, and Organization," and Chapter III, "Fundamentals of Counterinsurgency," subparagraph 3b, "Develop the COIN Narrative," respectively.

CHAPTER II
INSURGENCY

"This is another type of war, new in its intensity, ancient in its origin—war by guerrillas, subversives, insurgents, assassins, war by ambush instead of by combat; by infiltration, instead of aggression, seeking victory by eroding and exhausting the enemy instead of engaging him. It is a form of warfare uniquely adapted to what has been strangely called 'wars of liberation,' to undermine the efforts of new and poor countries to maintain the freedom that they have finally achieved. It preys on economic unrest and ethnic conflicts. It requires in those situations where we must counter it, and these are the kinds of challenges that will be before us in the next decade if freedom is to be saved, a whole new kind of strategy, a wholly different kind of force, and therefore a new and wholly different kind of military training."

President John F. Kennedy
Remarks at West Point Graduation
June 6, 1962

1. Overview

a. Insurgency is the organized use of subversion and violence to seize, nullify, or challenge political control of a region. The conflict often begins long before it is recognized, allowing the insurgency to spread and develop a covert organization within the HN until it reveals its presence through overt subversive acts and violence. Recent operations indicate that insurgencies in the 21st century often may attract transnational terrorists in addition to covert or overt external support. Also, the increasing influence of commercial, informational, financial, political, and ideological links between previously disparate parts of the world has created new dynamics that further shape insurgencies and other irregular forms of conflict. The interaction of these dynamics with local politics makes modern insurgencies distinct and complex challenges for HNs, multinational partners, and the USG, especially when using the military instrument of national power.

b. The objective of insurgency is to gain political control of a population or a geographic area, including its resources. Unlike traditional warfare, nonmilitary, nonlethal means are often the more effective elements, with military forces still fulfilling a major security requirement and playing a larger enabling role in creating nonlethal effects to attain USG and HN objectives. Political power is the central issue in insurgencies, and insurgencies are designed to weaken government control and legitimacy while increasing insurgent control and influence, especially with the relevant populations. Insurgencies are typically protracted conflicts of 10 to 20 years and add to long-term regional instability that is normally contrary to US national interests. Insurgencies often end through a negotiated settlement involving political reform by the incumbent HN government.

2. Nature of Insurgency

a. Insurgent groups adopt an irregular approach because they initially lack the resources required to directly confront the incumbent government in traditional warfare. In some cases an irregular approach may also suit the geographic terrain and/or sociopolitical context of the OE. By adopting an irregular approach, insurgencies avoid decisive battles in which the incumbent government can apply its superior combat power. This allows the insurgent to exploit the terrain and population as cover and concealment for their operations. Insurgents typically begin and organize in a covert if not clandestine manner.

b. Insurgents challenge government forces only to the extent needed to attain their political aims: their main effort is not just to engage HN military and other security forces, but instead to establish a competing system of control over the population, making it impossible for the government to administer its territory and people. Insurgent strategy involves selecting targets and striking when, where, and how it will best support their political or operational objectives. Employing a mixture of force, propaganda, subversion, intimidation, and political mobilization, insurgents seek to exhaust and discredit the governing political authority, undermining its support and breaking its will without necessarily decisively defeating its military forces. Insurgencies rely on propaganda of the deed throughout their activities to reinforce their strategic narrative. Often this strategy relies on cumulative effects of operations over a protracted period of time to gradually undermine the credibility and legitimacy of the government in the eyes of the population. In many cases this is accompanied by a corresponding attempt to supplant government administration with insurgent "shadow" government in more and more areas. Over time, insurgencies work to force governments to the negotiating table, trigger their collapse to seize control, or grow until their forces can directly confront and defeat the government security forces and physically take over the seat of government.

c. Insurgencies driven by commercial or criminal objectives (e.g., drug cartels) are an exception, because they typically have little interest in fully displacing the government and assuming the entire responsibility for governing the population. Rather, they focus on dominating the state's security apparatus through bribery and fear and intimidation by extreme violence, so it will not impinge on their illicit activities, and they often rely on the rest of the government's administrative capacity to address the population's expectations for essential services. For powerful criminal enterprises, it is an acceptable cost of doing their business.

3. Prerequisites for Insurgency

Fundamental to COIN is understanding why and how an insurgency begins. Historically, lack of government control, vulnerable populations, and revolutionary leadership available for direction have been identified as the prerequisites for an insurgency to occur. Contemporary analysis suggests a somewhat different approach that more properly identifies the prerequisites to be viewed as opportunity, motive, and means (see Figure II-1).

a. **Opportunity.** Similar to the historical prerequisite of "lack of government control," opportunity alludes to the emergence of significant gaps in the ability of the national government or local allies to provide security for its territory and population. Specifically, the government must have the capability and capacity to detect the early stages of insurgency—organization and mobilization—a challenge that typically requires a certain awareness and the cooperation of a significant portion of the population, or the establishment

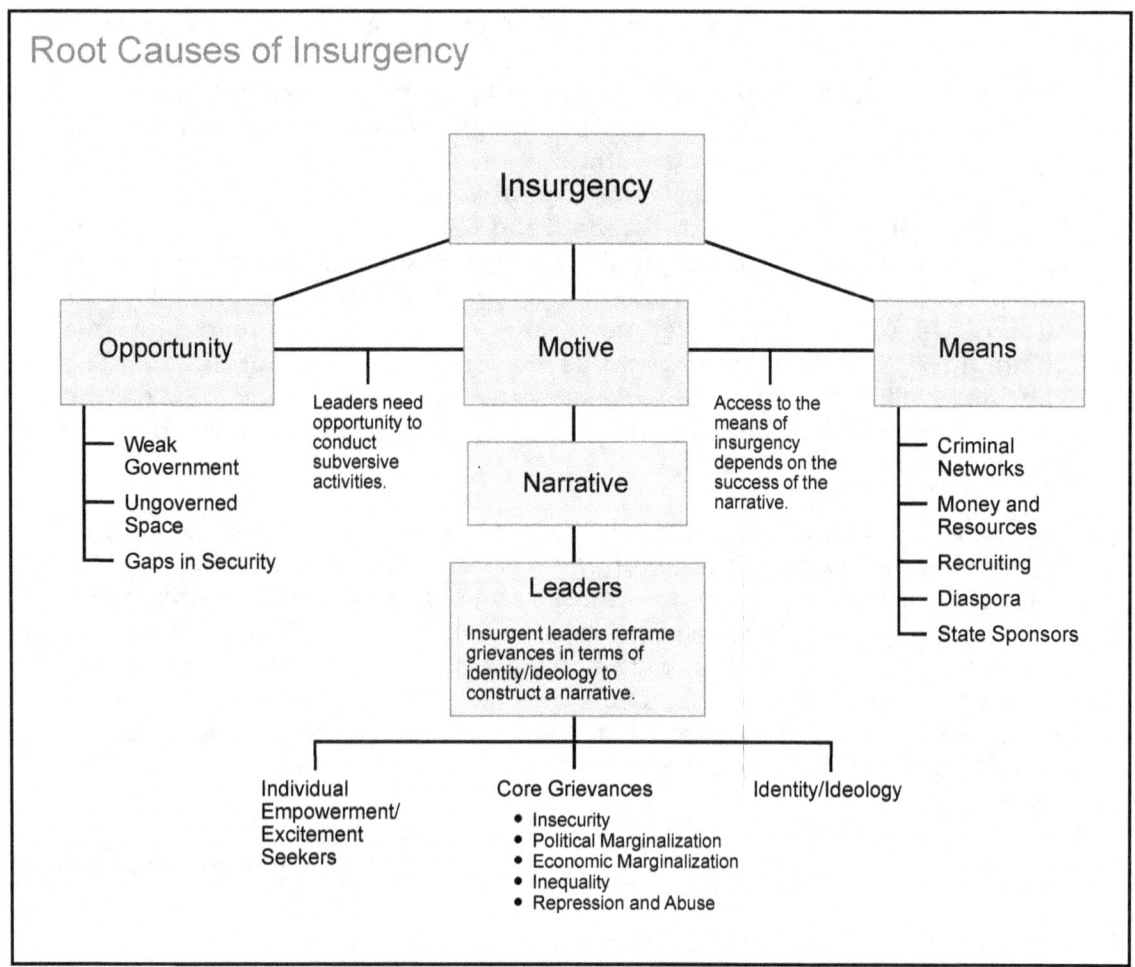

Figure II-1. Root Causes of Insurgency

of a program of domestic surveillance that if perceived as too extensive could result in what may be referred to as a police state. Moreover, the government must be capable of suppressing the insurgency in a way that deters other potential rebels while not feeding the insurgent narrative (i.e., not fostering perceived public grievances) and not provoking wider resistance to the government. Whether urban or rural, physically definable, or a matter of popular perception, opportunity arises when there is a gap in government control that provides an incipient insurgency with sufficient freedom to begin organizing and maneuvering politically and militarily. This gap also may be seen as a result of security forces either overreacting or appearing to engage in punitive violence not specifically linked to insurgent conduct. Understanding how the gap arose and how the nascent insurgency has exploited it to begin mobilizing an organized resistance provides insights to inform an effective COIN strategy and a planned operational approach. Gaps in government control can stem from insufficient capacity of government security forces, demographic changes, falling government revenues, or eroding legitimacy of governance and declining allegiance among segments of the population.

b. **Motive.** COIN doctrine has focused on grievances of the relevant population as a key cause (i.e., motive) for insurgency. A rigorous examination of the evidence has

STRATEGY OF PROVOCATION

Throughout history, insurgents and propagandists have sought to provoke political regimes into overreactions, attempting to discredit government forces or their allies. Often the strategy involves ambushes or attacks in heavily populated areas to produce firefights putting civilians at risk. The Irish Republican Army, Al Qaeda, and Hamas are three notorious practitioners of this approach. Against less professional forces, provocation can induce indiscriminate retaliation against civilians. Sometimes, the strategy is used to ignite ethno-sectarian conflict, consolidating one community behind the insurgents as the only way to secure itself. The February 2006 bombing of the Al Askariya mosque—one of the most sacred sites in Shi'ite Islam—by Sunni Al Qaeda extremists in Iraq provides one of the clearest recent examples.

The lesson for counterinsurgents is clear: selective police or military action against insurgents bolsters government credibility. By demonstrating the ability to accurately identify culprits and punish specific behavior, counterinsurgents establish more effective deterrence while reinforcing that compliance and cooperation will be rewarded. Conversely, indiscriminate violence where punishment is not clearly linked to conduct in the eyes of the population is likely to generate only wider resistance as civilians see no benefit—and particularly no improvement in security—to compliance with the HN government.

Various Sources

demonstrated that the existence of grievances does not in and of itself cause an insurgency. Poverty, unemployment, economic inequality, inadequate essential services, political marginalization, and repression are unfortunately commonplace, and exist in many places where insurgency does not. Basic physical and economic security—the absolute necessities to survive—are the only grievances that are inherently political. There must be a compelling motive to organize an insurgency, because insurgents are generally treated as violent, traitorous criminals by the security forces, government authorities, and potentially some segments of the indigenous population. The motive may be a complex combination of the following:

(1) **Compelling Narrative.** It takes dynamic and intelligent leadership to build a compelling narrative that links grievances to a political agenda and mobilizes the population to support an unlawful subversive and violent social movement. That narrative explains who is to blame for the grievances, how the grievances will be addressed, how the population will benefit under the insurgent's ideology, and how the population and insurgency should work together to accomplish that goal. The compelling aspect of the narrative is not only in its content, but how it is presented (i.e., promoted and publicized) to the target audience, which normally requires ideological leaders. It is consistently reinforced through communication and through propaganda of the deed. Insurgents often frame grievances in terms of local identities, such as religious, ethno-sectarian, or regional groupings. A compelling narrative is often spun around the marginalization of a particular community, region, or class by the government.

(2) **Leadership.** Established and aspiring leaders are present in most societies: where opportunity and motive (grievances) intersect, revolutionary or transformational figures emerge to attempt to mobilize segments of the population to follow them. The degree to which emerging insurgent leaders are successful at crafting and delivering a narrative that links grievances to a political vision is a key determinant of their subsequent ability to gain popular support and resources (means) and eventual success. Also, managing the tensions among local allies and their conflicting agendas is often one of the main challenges for insurgent leaders, and a critical focal point for designing COIN strategy and operations.

(3) **Adopting Grievances.** While grievances on their own are not sufficient to cause an insurgency, they are relevant to understanding its origins, evolution, and dynamics. Moreover, COIN approaches and negotiated settlements that fail to adequately address the underlying grievances rarely create a durable stability. The grievances driving the insurgency evolve over time and are transformed by the dynamics of the conflict itself. Political alignments are reshaped as power shifts between different groups, and as the insurgent and counterinsurgent interact with communities over time. This highlights a critical challenge for both insurgents and counterinsurgents: co-opting local grievances and political agendas into a broader movement. In many ways, insurgency is fundamentally an alliance-building process, in which leaders with a broad political vision seek to knit together a patchwork of communities, interest groups, and influential elites. Co-option can be complex and operates in both directions: just as insurgents seek to leverage local grievances, locals also seek to co-opt insurgents and counterinsurgents as allies to win disputes and settle scores with their rivals. Historically, most insurgencies occur in agrarian societies, where disputes over land tenure and water rights are typically among the most important drivers of conflict. This can give rise to a checkerboard effect, in which the decision by one side in a local conflict to ally with insurgents can lead their rivals to side with the government. One key variable in that evolution is whether the relevant communities believe their existence would be threatened by the victory of one side or the other.

(4) **Failed Security.** A failure by government security forces to provide security is also a common driver of instability. This frequently leads communities to look to other groups to fill the gap. Such groups may be concerned solely with securing their own communities when they emerge, but evolve to challenge the state's authority as their legitimacy and ambitions grow.

(5) **Abusive Behavior.** Beyond failing to provide security, the government may itself become a source of insecurity for the population. Some insurgencies actually create or exacerbate grievances, such as by deliberately provoking retaliation by HNSF against the insurgents' own constituency for the anticipated polarizing effect. Abusive behavior by government officials, security forces, or their local supporters can become one of the most potent grievances, and often contributes to the emergence of insurgencies. While often linked to disputes over political power and/or economic interests, sometimes corruption and abuses are the consequence of other structural drivers, a lack of professionalism, or other institutional shortcomings. Even where it is linked to other disputes, abusive behavior can rise to the level of a grievance in its own right when it severely transgresses cultural norms.

INDIVIDUAL MOTIVES AND TALIBAN RECRUITMENT IN HELMAND PROVINCE, AFGHANISTAN

The motivating factors for young men to join the Taliban were diverse, frequently highly complex, and not amenable to resolution through the application of reconstruction money. Young men joined the Taliban because they were mobilized through kinship groups, wanted self-protection in a dangerous environment, could not attain status through traditional tribal mechanisms, wanted support for claims to disputed land or resources, and for religious reasons. Religion appeared to play a role in mobilizing some young men, but largely because it legitimized other grievances, such as the lack of support for and from the government and negative perceptions of the actions and presence of foreign forces.

Stuart Gordon, Winning Hearts and Minds? Examining the Relationship Between Aid and Security in Afghanistan's Helmand Province (April 2011).

(6) **Elites' Agendas.** Elite attitudes tend to reflect both community-wide grievances as described above, and a discrete set of concerns about their status, such as elitism often trumping the rule of law. Elites may oppose government or commercial initiatives that could undermine their positions of authority, even if the program would benefit the community. In some cases, it is competition among elites that provides an opening for insurgents to co-opt communities by backing one competitor against others.

(7) **Individual Empowerment.** Reference to communal grievances as a reason for joining an insurgency sometimes masks (or may be mixed with) a simpler desire for adventure, opportunity, or sense of control over one's own destiny. Particularly where traditional social systems have broken down or fail to provide avenues for social advancement for youth, insurgent movements may offer an attractive escape from boredom and stagnation. Becoming an insurgent offers a boost in status and a sense of purpose. That sense of empowerment can be enough to motivate some to take up arms, even as they rhetorically reference other more conventional grievances.

(8) **Social Mobilization.** An insurgency relies on social mobilization over time, which includes picking a side (insurgency or government). The process typically draws on existing ethnic, religious, racial, socioeconomic, geographic, and/or political identities, and the symbols associated with them, which is why the narrative is a key element for social mobilization. However, individuals and communities typically are members of multiple overlapping groups with whom they may be identified. The degree to which their behavior is shaped by membership in any of these groups depends on multiple factors, but important factors in determining which identity will define the primary loyalty of both individuals and communities are which side is perceived as best to advance their interests, the ease of switching sides, and which side they expect to win. Switching does not necessarily imply abandoning fundamental social ties to family, friends or community, but more often it involves a shift in the political and/or military alliances through which a group seeks to advance its interests, and a corresponding redefinition of loyalties and politics.

(9) **Community Allegiance.** If a community (i.e., family, clan, tribe, or village) believes it has the option to side with either the insurgency or the government, then in most cases allegiance follows control and security. That is, the populace is likely to comply with whomever it perceives has established durable control in their area. This pattern of shifting allegiance to ensure survival tends to emerge over the course of the conflict and hold true regardless of what a community's political preferences were when the violence began. In this case, "control" means establishing predictable and tolerable conditions for the population: a clear set of rules that are consistently enforced under which they feel they can reasonably survive. The failure to publicize or consistently enforce those rules, or the use of arbitrary punishment, tends to generate opposition among civilians who will then perceive that compliance will not guarantee their basic interests and survival. The effects of shifting allegiance may be extremely difficult and have an unpredictable debilitating effect on the community. For example, when a community believes that one side's victory will lead to the community's complete destruction or marginalization, it is unlikely to see any alternative to fighting to the bitter end. If an insurgency has promoted this belief—as in the case of a security dilemma—proving otherwise can be critical for counterinsurgents. Also, the dilemma of community allegiance may have to be faced dozens and dozens of times throughout the operational area.

c. **Means.** It takes considerable resources to mount a subversive and violent challenge to the incumbent government authorities, and the ways an insurgency goes about securing those resources determines a great deal about its behavior. The leaders of emerging insurgencies must assemble and organize personnel, funds, weapons, and systems of secure communications and logistics—all covertly.

(1) **Recruiting.** The first variable to consider is recruitment, as it has an impact on all the others. Here the degree to which insurgent leaders can leverage pre-existing strong social networks is critical. Social networks may be defined by village, clan, tribe, ethnicity, language, socioeconomic status, or membership in sports clubs, military units, professional associations, or criminal groups. Where those networks exist and insurgent leaders successfully draw on identities and grievances to mobilize them, recruitment is easier and faster. Moreover, where recruits are bound together by preexisting social ties, unit cohesion and reciprocal loyalty are often stronger. Finally, the ties between insurgents and their communities provide an integral support base from which insurgents can draw other types of resources as well.

(2) **Social Networks.** Typically only insurgent leaders who are members of the relevant community possess the required internal legitimacy to mobilize social networks. Where leaders lack that legitimacy, or where they seek to activate networks beyond their own community, the relationship between recruits and resources is reversed: leaders require access to resources to attract and equip recruits. In some cases, insurgents exploit lootable natural resources, such as alluvial diamonds, lumber, or minerals. Other groups rely on more conventional criminal activities, such as kidnapping, smuggling, drug trafficking, human trafficking, counterfeiting, and money laundering. Still others receive support from transnational terrorist organizations through funding, recruitment, training, and propaganda. Reliance on social networks constrains insurgent freedom of action by potentially anchoring the insurgency in a well-established set of social norms. If they fail to conform to those

norms insurgent leaders risk undermining the very legitimacy that facilitated recruitment and organization, and they open themselves up to criticism or challenge from other members of the community.

(3) **Forced Recruitment.** Some insurgent groups also use forced recruitment to bolster their ranks, which often includes the illegal recruitment of children. This approach is typically associated with insurgent groups more focused on resource exploitation and enrichment than on altering or replacing the governing authorities. In extreme cases, forcible recruitment becomes intertwined more fundamentally with the strategy, ideology, and survival of the insurgent group. In most cases, forcible recruitment occurs alongside voluntary participation. Insurgents may seek to forcibly co-opt a social network by coercing its members to join their ranks. In doing so, insurgents may secure the neutrality or even the support of the rest of the kin-group or community. Often participation is characterized as a duty based on the identity or narrative promoted by the insurgents. In such cases, social pressure may be used to try to cajole recruitment, but is often reinforced by brutal retaliation against those who resist.

(4) **Diasporas.** Ethno-sectarian conflicts are often supported by diaspora communities living in other parts of the world. Similar to transnational terrorist organizations, diasporas can assist with funding and recruitment. In contrast to transnational terrorist networks, diaspora groups are generally better positioned to favorably influence the public opinion and policies of their country and the attitudes of global media toward the insurgents.

(5) **External Sponsors.** State sponsorship offers advantages well beyond those available through transnational sources or the exploitation of illicit economies. Supporting nations can provide insurgents with a larger scale and broader variety of resources and training, and even more valuable, an external sanctuary to organize or prepare for future activities. However, while each of these sources provides advantages, they also have drawbacks. First, the recruits attracted by the prospect of individual material rewards are likely to be less dedicated to the cause, and therefore less disciplined and loyal, particularly in the face of setbacks. Insurgencies that rely on resources rather than social networks to recruit tend to be more violent toward civilians. This further undermines their already low legitimacy and can inhibit their efforts to widen their political support. Insurgent groups can mitigate this issue if they are patient and use the resources provided by outside sources to build a political base before launching military operations. External sponsors can also include transnational sympathizers. Contemporary insurgents are able to use the Internet to build transnational networks which sympathize with them but may not have an ethnic or sectarian affiliation. These networks can provide funds, legitimacy, connections, information, and potentially recruits. Transnational sympathizers can also include transnational criminal organizations and gray market organizations which link to insurgents and provide an outlet for natural resources exploited by insurgents and a source of weapons and other assets.

(6) **Resourcing Risks.** While necessary, recruitment carries risks for insurgent groups. Recruitment activities can alert authorities to the presence and extent of an insurgent group before it is ready to act. Recruitment also carries the operations security risks that can

arise through the indiscipline of new recruits, and/or infiltration by agents of the incumbent government. Many of the most successful and resilient insurgent groups have invested heavily in operations security and counterintelligence procedures to mitigate the risks associated with recruiting, including extensive vetting and information compartmentalization. The resource base can overtake insurgent politics in terms of defining insurgent organization, strategy, and objectives. Deepening involvement in illicit economies can transform insurgent organizations into criminal enterprises as accruing resources becomes an end in itself. Diaspora politics and priorities can diverge significantly from those in the theater of operations, creating tensions between the local population, insurgents, and their geographically removed backers. State sponsors have their own agendas and a degree of influence or even outright control over insurgent operations, but this is often the price of access to key resources.

4. Insurgent Objectives

a. Insurgent objectives can be generally categorized as reform, revolution, secession, nullification, and resistance. However, these categories are archetypes, and many insurgencies exhibit characteristics of more than one category, often as a result of the alliance building. Moreover, insurgent goals often evolve during the course of the conflict.

b. In some conflicts, multiple insurgent groups may operate simultaneously, either competing with one another or setting aside the fact that they may have differing views on post-conflict governance to form temporary alliances against the government. The motivations of individual fighters may differ from that of the group in general, and the chaos of insurgency provides ample opportunity to pursue personal agendas under the cover of insurgent action. Likewise, both deviant individuals and criminal organizations often exploit conflict to pursue their own goals through violent means. This complexity can give the insurgency a more chaotic, less organized quality and create a challenge for analysts trying to distinguish between various overlapping patterns of violence. Nevertheless, at the broadest level, the goals of an insurgency most often fall into one of five categories.

(1) **Reform.** Some insurgencies do not aim to change the existing political order but, instead, seek to compel the government to alter its policies or undertake political, economic, or social reforms. The scope of those reforms may range from relatively modest changes in policy to more significant changes to the structure and characteristics of the government. However, typically insurgents envision deeper changes to the sociopolitical structure of society as occurring through more moderate or gradual political processes rather than direct coercion.

(2) **Revolution.** Revolutionary insurgents seek to overthrow and radically reshape the political system, socioeconomic structure, and sometimes even the culture of the nation. Revolutionaries often want to change the fundamental sources of political legitimacy around which government and political authority are organized.

(3) **Secession.** Secessionist insurgencies seek complete political autonomy for a geographically defined area which may lie within a country's existing national boundaries.

(4) **Nullification.** Some insurgents seek to roll back governmental authority—particularly coercive local authority—in a geographically defined area. In some cases, warlords or powerful criminal groups may seek greater freedom of action to pursue illicit economic activities. In others, insurgents may seek to nullify state control of a region in order to create a sanctuary in support of insurgency or terrorism elsewhere. Often, the HN government mistakenly dismisses the early stages of other types of insurgencies as just criminal activities. Conversely, objectives of other categories can shift over time toward nullification (e.g., Revolutionary Armed Forces of Colombia and drug trafficking).

(5) **Resistance.** Some insurgencies seek to compel an occupying power to withdraw from a given territory. The drivers and dynamics of resistance movements are more complex than typically understood. The concept of "foreign forces" is entirely context dependent: remote, semiautonomous, or sociopolitically distinct areas within a nation state may regard HNSF from other areas or even the national capital as outsiders. In some cases, forces from more distant countries may even be preferable in the eyes of locals if they are regarded as more impartial and trustworthy than neighbors or countrymen with whom there is a history of conflict or tensions. Although autonomy and self-determination are powerful themes for insurgent narratives, actual participation by individuals and communities in a resistance insurgency is often driven by more tangible grievances against the occupying force or pragmatic calculations about the distribution of political power in a post-conflict regime. The grievances often arise from a failure to establish predictable and tolerable conditions for the civilian population; the manipulation of the occupying force by its local allies to target rival communities; a failure to accommodate elites and communities from the losing side in the new political order; or a combination of all three. In other words, **the emergence of resistance movements is typically tied to the conduct of the occupying power.** Where foreign forces avoid these pitfalls as they are regarded as playing a constructive or necessary stabilizing role, they are generally well tolerated on an interim basis.

5. Insurgent Narrative, Strategy, and Organization

a. **Insurgent Narrative.** The strength and success of an insurgency depends in large part on its ability to shape the behavior of its ranks and the population whose compliance or outright support it requires. Social mobilization depends in large part on the credibility of the insurgent narrative. A narrative is an organizational scheme expressed in story form. Narratives are central to representing identity, particularly the collective identity of religious sects, ethnic groupings, and tribal elements. They provide a basis for interpreting information, experiences, and the behavior and intentions of other individuals and communities. Stories about a community's history provide models of how actions and consequences are linked. Thus narratives shape decision making in two ways: they provide an interpretive framework for a complicated and uncertain environment and offer idealized historical analogies that can serve as the basis for strategies.

(1) In the context of insurgency, the narrative is a tool to shape how the population perceives circumstances and events. The narrative is used to link conditions-based grievances to the nature or behavior of the incumbent regime and articulate an alternative political vision that will address those grievances. It provides an explanation and

justification of how insurgents will align ends, ways, and means to achieve their political objectives and frames how insurgent and counterinsurgent actions are interpreted. Perhaps most important, insurgents try to create self-reinforcing narratives about which side is most likely to win and therefore influence whose side civilians should follow.

(2) The credibility of an insurgent narrative depends on how the population interprets a mixture of indicators and cues about the nature of the insurgency, its likelihood of success, and the consequences of its failure. The likelihood of insurgent success is based in large part on assessments of insurgent political and military strength. Such assessments are typically grounded in direct experience or observation of insurgent operations and activities. The uncertainty inherent in insurgency coupled with the competition between insurgent propaganda and counterinsurgent information operations (IO) often generates wild rumors and distorted perceptions of particular incidents. Populations can often only assess that strength in their immediate vicinity, generating wildly different perceptions of the broader national environment in different parts of the operational area.

(3) Another set of cues relates to how successfully insurgents invoke culturally relevant symbols and concepts. As described above, individuals and communities typically identify with multiple groups, each one associated with an ideology, codes of behavior, and historical narratives. In most competitions for political power, all sides selectively invoke those identities to justify their pragmatic calculated decision making in pursuit of their interests. However, identities are not infinitely malleable, and the degree to which they resonate with experiences and circumstances of particular communities varies. **To successfully rally the population around a particular identity, insurgents have to articulate their message in a way that is internally consistent with the narratives associated with that identity and the experiences of the target population. It must offer a plausible link between history, myth, and current conditions.**

(4) Demonstrating the credibility of its narrative also creates an imperative for action on the part of the insurgents. Making the argument is not sufficient. Insurgents need to continually demonstrate that events reinforce their narrative. This requires words, in the form of propaganda, and deeds, in the form of attacks against the government, enforcement of rules on civilians, and in some cases, provision of alternative governance. The ability to portray the words and deeds of counterinsurgents as confirming the insurgent narrative is equally important.

b. **Strategy.** Insurgent strategies are composed of interdependent political and military dimensions. The relative emphasis on each of those aspects and exactly how they are linked is shaped by the combination of opportunity/motive/means factors, and the nature of the insurgent objectives. Strategy is also shaped—in some cases constrained—by the identities around which the insurgent narrative is constructed. Those identities often include deeply rooted cultures of war and codes of conduct that create expectations about how the conflict will be waged that are contrary to American ideas of what is "normal" or "rational." They may also include deeply rooted historical social grievances which the insurgent narrative co-opts to mobilize support.

(1) **Protracted Popular War.** Although the fundamental challenges for insurgents have remained relatively constant, insurgent strategies have evolved along with the changing character of war. The period of modern insurgency is generally regarded as beginning with Chinese Communist insurgency that began in the 1920s. The protracted popular war strategy is designed to be flexible, with shifts between phases occurring at different times in various parts of the operational area. Where insurgents encounter setbacks or defeats, they can regress to an earlier phase in order to allow the insurgency to survive and regenerate. The strategy also emphasizes patience and the value of protracting the conflict to exhaust the HN's will and resources over time: insurgencies may remain in one phase for years if necessary. Mao Tse-Tsung emphasized the importance of the political base as a foundation for military operations. As explained in his theory of **protracted popular war,** this strategy involves three phases:

(a) Phase I is characterized by insurgents operating clandestinely through subversion, propaganda, and intimidation to build support among the population. Insurgents promote a narrative that links grievances to a political program of change to mobilize the population, either co-opting existing identities or forging a new one (e.g., raising "class consciousness" among landless peasants). Phase I insurgents seek to infiltrate key government organizations and civilian groups. The objective in this phase is to enlist the population to provide recruits, intelligence, and materiel, and to organize for future guerrilla operations. Insurgents avoid major combat and typically limit violence to terrorism and sabotage during this early phase of the operation or campaign.

(b) Phase II involves a shift to guerrilla operations in which insurgents step up the scale and intensity of terrorism and sabotage and begin directly launching ambushes and limited attacks on the HNSF. Such attacks are designed to erode both the control of the HN government and its ability to provide services to the population, damaging both its coercive apparatus and its basis for legitimacy. Insurgents may also employ a strategy of provocation anticipating security forces will overreact and thereby alienate the government from the population. The combination of continued political action and military operations creates gaps in state control and administration that insurgents often fill with alternative or "shadow" governance, demonstrating their ability to address the grievances of the population. As phase II progresses, insurgents expand their ranks and procure additional armament in preparation for phase III.

(c) Phase III only occurs once the insurgency has grown significantly in strength and is marked by a transition from asymmetric or guerrilla operations to operations conducted during traditional warfare. Insurgent forces begin operating in large formations, in conjunction with guerrilla operations, and seek open battle with the HNSF. Shadow governance begins operating openly in areas controlled by the insurgent forces.

(2) **Focoism.** Focoism is another strategy that contends that rather than mobilizing the population through clandestine political action and subversion, small groups of armed insurgents could accomplish the same goal through military action. Under this theory, attacks by small insurgent militias against the government would inspire a wider uprising among the population. Narrative remains important, but is promoted through military operations rather than propaganda and clandestine organization. Focoism is more a theory

than a proven strategy, because the Cuban Revolution largely conformed to the Maoist approach and benefitted enormously from the heavy-handed government responses to guerrilla attacks. Focoist strategies subsequently failed in Congo, Bolivia, and Argentina, and remain widely discredited, but they are sometimes conflated with other approaches that do not rely on political mobilization as a precursor to military operations. Such insurgencies typically involve groups with access to significant resources through state sponsorship or exploitation of lootable natural resources, and their access to resources does not depend significantly on the support of the population. Being less dependent on building a political base, they tend to rely heavily on coercion for recruitment—in Sierra Leone for example, nearly 90 percent of Revolutionary United Front fighters were abducted and compelled to join the insurgent group.

(3) The Algerian Front de Libération Nationale (FLN) demonstrated a variation on the Maoist approach that combined protracted war in rural areas with urban terrorist tactics, and introduced the use of IO at the strategic level. Between 1954 and 1962, the FLN waged an insurgency against France to gain independence for Algeria. Initially based in remote rural areas, the FLN invested heavily in political mobilization and waged an extensive guerrilla campaign against French forces, benefiting from sanctuary and materiel support from neighboring countries. In1956 it launched a campaign of terrorist bombings in the capital, Algiers. Despite adopting a compartmentalized cellular structure for its urban operations, the FLN organization in Algiers was defeated by February 1957. However, the FLN strategy of provocation was effective: widespread torture and extrajudicial killings by French forces undermined support for COIN operations in France and damaged French legitimacy internationally. By 1960 the French had largely defeated the FLN militarily, but **the political impact of its COIN tactics made it impossible for France to achieve its strategic objective:** retaining control of Algeria. The Algerian war illustrated both the potential of **compound strategies** that combine rural and urban insurgent approaches, and the overwhelming importance of narrative and perception in contemporary insurgencies.

(4) The Irish Republican Army (IRA) is an example of another variation on insurgent strategy: **subversion.** In short, subversion involves the simultaneous, coordinated employment of insurgent violence and participation in the established political system to undermine the government from within. In the case of Northern Ireland, Sinn Fein acted as the political wing of the IRA and participated in the government. Even as the IRA waged a sophisticated and resilient protracted urban insurgency, it leveraged civil disobedience (such as labor strikes, demonstrations, sit-ins, hunger strikes) and Sinn Fein's voice in the political system to attempt to discredit the British government at home and internationally. More recently, US forces and their multinational partners encountered similar challenges in Iraq, where political parties like the Supreme Council for Islamic Revolution in Iraq constituted the political wings of militant organizations, participating in the government even as they contested its control on the ground.

(5) Although most insurgent groups seek to defeat and replace the government of the territory they are contesting, Hezbollah represents an important exception to this rule. From its origins as a Syrian and Iranian-backed Shi'a terrorist organization in the Lebanese civil war, it has employed a sophisticated blend of grassroots service provision, political organization, combat, and a strategy of provocation to expand its influence. Through

systematic institutionalization, large-scale funding, and the provision of weapons by its state sponsors, Hezbollah became the most powerful paramilitary force in Lebanon, far outstripping the official Lebanese Armed Forces. A participant in the formal Lebanese government, it leverages its military power to exert control, but avoids taking over the government. Hezbollah is an example of a group that uses asymmetric tactics with state-like capabilities. Although often presented as ideal types, each of these strategies is linked to the emergence and evolution of a specific insurgency in response to its particular political, sociocultural, geographic, economic, technological, and geopolitical context. Insurgents are adaptive and often innovative adversaries that often combine elements of these strategies in new and confounding ways to defeat an HN government, evolving over the course of the conflict to avoid defeat and capitalize on opportunities.

c. **Organization.** While each insurgency will have its own unique organization that may change over time, there are shared general organizational characteristics that provide a general framework for analysis of insurgencies.

(1) Insurgencies develop operational approaches from the interaction of various factors and various networks. Insurgencies will develop and adapt their operational approaches and organizational structure to the current conditions of the OE. More specifically, insurgent organizational and operational approaches are directly related to the strength of the HN government. If the HN is strong, the insurgency will have to be more secretive and selective. Conversely, the insurgency can be bolder if the HN is weak. So an insurgency may begin organized in cells linked by leaders and may evolve into more of a hierarchical organization as it grows and gains popular support.

(a) **Politically organized** insurgencies develop a complex political structure before or at the same time that they begin undertaking military operations against the government. These groups stress consolidating control of territory through the use of shadow governments rather than through military power. The military component of politically organized insurgencies is subordinate to the political structure.

(b) **Militarily organized** insurgencies emphasize military action against the government over political mobilization of the population. The insurgents calculate that military success and the resulting weakening of the government will cause the population to rally to the insurgents' cause. Militarily organized insurgencies begin with small, weak, ill-defined political structures, often dominated by military leaders. However, a military organized insurgency does not imply that all its members are fighters.

(c) **Traditionally organized** insurgencies draw on preexisting identities through tribal, clan, ethnic, or religious affiliations. Established social hierarchies—a system of chiefs and sub-chiefs, for example—often substitute for political and military structures in traditionally organized insurgencies.

(d) **Cellular organized** insurgencies develop and are centered in urban areas. These insurgencies lack hierarchical political and military leadership structures, instead organizing around small, semiautonomous cells. Urban-cellular insurgencies generally rely more heavily on terrorism than do other types of insurgency. Their cellular structure and reliance on terrorism can limit their ability to mobilize popular support.

(2) **Political and Military Components.** Insurgent structure may be generally broken down into two wings: political and military. Insurgent sociocultural factors, approaches, and resources tend to drive its organization, and most insurgencies. Figure II-2 depicts them in any activities that these two wings may perform, from exploiting root causes to overt guerrilla operations. Progression up the diagram does not have to be linear; insurgencies can perform many of these activities at any time, in any order or combination.

(a) **Political Wing.** Insurgencies will have some form of political wing, although some may only require an emerging political wing. The political wing is primarily concerned with undermining the legitimacy of the HN government and its allies while building up support for the insurgency. This may be accomplished by participation of members of the political wing in legitimate elections and political processes in order to infiltrate the government and undermine it from within. The political wing of the insurgency builds credibility and legitimacy for the insurgency within the population and potentially with the international community. The political wing may downplay insurgent violence and subversion, some to the point of outright deception.

<u>1</u>. **Shadow Government.** An insurgency and its political wing may become strong enough to not only challenge the HN government, but it may act as an alternative government. It may provide some or all of the functions or services of a government, for example food distribution, health care, security, and education. Normally the shadow government will attempt to satisfy grievances in local areas first. They may attempt to transfer blame for any residual issues to foreign presence or the HN government in order to facilitate popular support.

<u>2.</u> **Supportive Parties.** While not part of the insurgency, an existing legal political party may come to support the insurgency or may form a legal political party that supports the insurgency. These legal political parties may become the insurgents' conduit for diplomacy and political reconciliation. In some cases, the political party may consist of former insurgent strategic leaders and cadre. Efforts should be made to open and maintain these avenues for reconciliation.

(b) **Military Wing.** The military wing of the insurgency conducts violent criminal activities and ultimately some forms of combat operations. Most insurgencies may initially have few combatants; however, military-focused insurgencies will focus on this wing and build their guerrilla force (military) capability and capacity over time and may execute overt operations and go back into hiding to survive. As the insurgency grows in relative strength, however, its military wing will likely form a larger guerrilla force and may be able to operate continuously in an overt fashion. Guerrilla forces usually start with paramilitary operations, but advanced insurgencies may transition to more traditionally planned and organized military operations. Thus, if security is ineffective or the insurgency has grown powerful relative to the HN government, the military elements may exist openly. If the state maintains a continuous and effective security presence, some part of the military wing will likely maintain a secret existence.

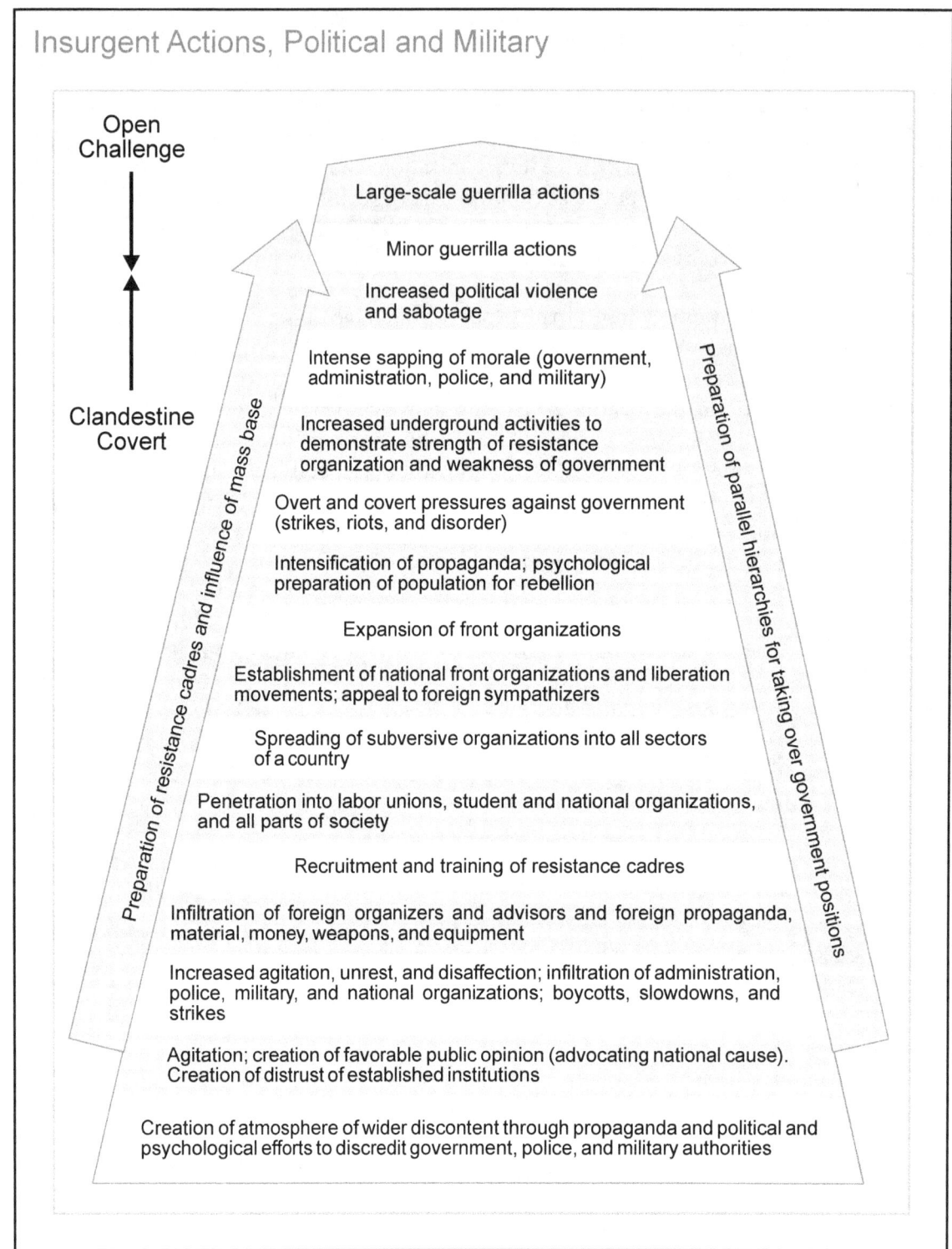

Figure II-2. Insurgent Actions, Political and Military

(3) **Elements.** Insurgent organizations are often composed of different elements that perform complementary but distinct roles. Some elements openly challenge the government through public actions and guerrilla and terrorist attacks. Other elements operate through covert or clandestine methods, subverting existing political and civil

institutions to support the insurgency or damage the legitimacy of the HN government. The proportion or presence of each element relative to the larger organization depends on the strategic approach the insurgency uses and the opportunity, motive, means factors. In many cases, these categories overlap and individuals may shift between them as the conflict and the insurgency evolve. This is especially true where insurgencies are based on existing social networks such as tribes and clans. The following categories should be regarded as illustrative; each insurgency should be carefully analyzed to identify the overt and covert elements within its organizational structure.

(a) **Political and Military Leadership.** Leaders provide overall direction in more organized insurgencies. These leaders are the "key idea people" or strategic planners and are responsible for developing the insurgent narrative. They usually exercise leadership through some mixture of force of personality, the power of ideology, public esteem, or personal charisma. In some insurgencies, they may hold their position through religious, clan, or tribal authority. The leaders of movements based on religious extremism may also be religious figures. In loosely organized insurgencies, authority may be distributed across the leaders of multiple smaller groups that share similar or overlapping goals, such as expelling an occupier. Within an insurgent group, responsibility for political and military leadership may be consolidated in a single chain of command, or be divided across different people or elements of the insurgent organization. Political leaders—historically referred to as a cadre—develop, spread, and enforce insurgent ideology. They seek to widen support domestically and internationally through IO and propaganda, and may function as a shadow government or government-in-exile. Political leaders play a key role in coordinating guerrilla operations with other subversive or violent activities to promote the insurgent narrative.

(b) **Underground.** The underground is that element of the insurgent organization that conducts operations in areas normally denied to the auxiliary and the guerrilla force. The underground is a cellular organization within the insurgency that conducts covert or clandestine activities that are compartmentalized. This secrecy may be by necessity, by design, or both, depending on the situation. Most underground operations are required to take place in and around population centers that are held by counterinsurgent forces. Underground members often fill leadership positions, overseeing specific functions that are carried out by the auxiliary. The underground and elements provide coordinated capabilities for the insurgent movement. The key distinction between them is that the underground is the element of the insurgent organization that operates in areas denied to the guerrilla force. Members of the underground often control cells used to neutralize informants and collaborators from within the insurgency and the population.

(c) **Guerrillas.** Guerrillas conduct the actual fighting and provide security. They support the insurgency's broader agenda and maintain local control. Guerrillas protect and expand the counter state, if the insurgency establishes such an institution. They also protect training camps and networks that facilitate the flow of money, instructions, and foreign and local fighters. Guerrillas include any individual member of the insurgency who commits or attempts an act of overt violence or terrorism in support of insurgent goals. Guerrilla leaders are considered part of the combatant element for analyzing insurgencies.

(d) **Support Base.** Sometimes referred to as the auxiliary, the insurgency's support base typically conceals its involvement with the movement. Ranging from sympathetic individuals who store weapons or warn of COIN force activities to major providers of finances or materiel, these supporters are critical to the insurgency but generally do not participate in combat operations. Typical activities include running safe houses; storing weapons and supplies; acting as couriers; providing intelligence collection; giving early warning of counterinsurgent movements; providing funding from lawful and unlawful sources; and providing forged or stolen documents and access or introductions to potential supporters. COIN forces face key challenges in distinguishing between voluntary supporters and those who have been coerced into cooperating with insurgency; understanding the complex motives of supporters; and neutralizing or co-opting them without appearing oppressive to the broader population that is unaware of their activities.

6. Stages and Outcomes of Insurgency

a. Shaped by its context and objectives, every insurgency develops differently, but some general patterns can be observed. Insurgencies may evolve through subversion and radicalization, popular unrest, civil disobedience, localized guerrilla activity, and widespread guerrilla operations to open, armed conflict by large formations of insurgences. Alternatively, they may wither away to dormancy if they are effectively countered or if they fail to capture sufficient popular support.

b. One or more different stages may appear in different areas simultaneously in a country affected by insurgency. Similarly, different insurgent groups or different factions of the same group operating in a given country may be at different stages or even evolving through different operational approaches.

c. An insurgency may actually succeed in overthrowing the government (historically a rare event), may force the government into political accommodation (a more common outcome), may be co-opted by the government and cease fighting (also common), or may be crushed. In general, insurgencies are typically protracted conflicts.

d. Insurgencies may be co-opted by domestic or transnational terrorist groups, morph into criminal networks, or wither into irrelevance. Measures that succeed against incipient insurgencies often differ greatly from those that are effective against mature or declining insurgencies. Exhaustion and errors by either side can push the conflict toward resolution, either on the battlefield or through negotiation. Thus, planners and decision makers should clearly understand the stages the insurgency has reached to develop appropriate responses or to thwart its overall progression.

(1) **Pre-Conflict Stage.** An insurgency in the pre-conflict stage is difficult to detect because most activities are conducted covertly by the underground and guerrillas, and the insurgency has yet to make its presence felt through the use of acknowledged acts of violence. Moreover, some actions conducted in the open can easily be dismissed as nonviolent political activity. During this stage, an insurgent movement is beginning to organize: leadership is emerging, and the insurgents are mobilizing around a grievance and a group identity, beginning to recruit and train members, and stockpiling arms and supplies.

(2) **Incipient.** An insurgency enters the incipient conflict stage when the insurgents begin to use violence. Often these initial attacks provide analysts the first alert to the potential for an insurgency. The target government, however, may frequently dismiss insurgent actions as the work of bandits, criminals, or terrorists, which increases the risk that the government will employ counterproductive measures. The incipient stage is the most dangerous phase for insurgents; they have made their presence known through violent activities, but are still weak and in the process of organizing. Insurgents must balance the need to demonstrate their viability, publicize the insurgent cause, rally supporters, gain illicit funding, and provoke government overreactions while limiting their exposure to government security forces. During this phase, insurgents may emphasize highly asymmetric and terrorist tactics, such as kidnappings, small bombings, assassinations, and acts of intimidation such as "night letters" where the target is provided a written warning to cease an activity or suffer consequences. Understanding the characteristics, capabilities, and actions of both the insurgents and the government can help analysts assess whether an incipient conflict is likely to sputter out or expand into an open conflict.

(3) **Open Conflict Stage.** At this stage, there is no doubt that the government is facing an insurgency. Politically, the insurgents are overtly challenging governing authorities and attempting to exert control over territory. Militarily, the insurgents are staging more frequent attacks, which have probably become more aggressive, violent, and sophisticated and involve larger numbers of fighters. As the insurgency becomes more active, external support for the insurgents probably becomes more apparent, if it exists.

(4) **Resolution.** Some insurgencies progress steadily through the life cycle stages; many grow in fits and starts, occasionally regressing to earlier stages; and others remain mired in one stage for years. In theory, an insurgency will eventually reach a conclusion, either an insurgent victory, a negotiated settlement, or a government victory. At least 130 insurgent conflicts have occurred since World War II—estimations vary widely and go as high as nearly 300 insurgent-government conflicts—and at least two dozen were ongoing as of late 2011. Of the insurgencies that have ended:

(a) About 36 percent concluded with an insurgent victory after an average duration of about 10 years.

(b) Almost 28 percent had mixed outcomes, generally because the belligerents reached a compromise that required all to make significant concessions. These insurgencies lasted an average of about 8 years.

(c) Approximately 36 percent resulted in a government victory after an average duration of almost 12 years.

e. **Insurgent Victory.** An insurgent victory is the only potential outcome that is likely to be clear cut, marked by the insurgents seizing control of the government, expelling a foreign occupier, or gaining independence. Nevertheless, an insurgent victory may spark another insurgency by the ousted regime's supporters or by a subgroup excluded from the new government. The final collapse of the government will probably appear in retrospect to have been rapid, but the signs of imminent insurgent victory may be difficult to see as they are occurring. Signs that insurgents may be on the verge of obtaining their goal include:

(1) Withdrawal of support for the government by specific, critical segments of the domestic population, possibly even including elites aligned with the government leaving the country.

(2) Evidence that the population increasingly views the government as illegitimate.

(3) Insurgent co-optation, incorporation, or elimination of other major groups opposed to the government.

(4) Withdrawal of support for the government from critical foreign allies, pressure from those allies to overhaul the government's policy to address insurgent grievances, or increasing international support or recognition for the insurgents.

(5) Rapid growth of insurgent forces or significant expansion of insurgent control of territory and population.

(6) Severe weakening of the national economy, possibly including departure of multinational corporations, as a result of the insurgency.

(7) Reports of military plots, coup attempts, massive desertion, defection, or surrender of security forces.

(8) Evidence of a sudden government willingness to seek a negotiated settlement with the insurgents.

f. **Negotiated Settlement.** Negotiated settlement is a progressive process involving a number of steps. A negotiated settlement is likely to have many false starts, delays in implementation, and attempts by spoilers to undermine the agreement. Moreover, the risk of renewed violence—either by the original insurgent organization protesting perceived government duplicity or by splinter groups unsatisfied with the terms of the settlement—will probably persist for several years after fighting has officially ended. Recognizing sincere efforts to reach a negotiated settlement can be difficult because insurgents often engage in negotiations to buy time to recover from setbacks and to prepare for the next round of fighting. If the conflict has been protracted, the insurgents' expectations of a purely military victory will probably be tempered, and they then will be more likely to seek genuine compromise. The insurgents are unlikely to reach this conclusion until they have been fighting for some time, suggesting that sometimes an insurgent conflict needs to run its course for a while before serious negotiations are possible. The first part of the process usually starts with a stalemate. There must also be acceptance by the HN that the insurgent is a legitimate negotiator. From this a ceasefire may occur and may be routinely broken. A negotiated settlement will have intermediate agreements, concessions, ascensions of moderate leaders, and a third-party guarantor. Indicators that insurgents are sincere include:

(1) Reports that neither side believes it can win militarily.

(2) Reports that the insurgents believe they can win an election or otherwise achieve their goals through legal political participation.

(3) A moderation of insurgent goals. Incorporation into the government's negotiating position of a liberal amnesty offer and mechanisms for former insurgents to participate in the legal political process.

(4) A dramatic and unexpected battlefield victory by one of the belligerents that is quickly followed by overtures to negotiate. Neither party wants to negotiate from a position of weakness, and a belligerent on the decline may seek a symbolic victory to improve its bargaining position.

(5) Evidence that foreign patrons or allies are cutting off support or are pressing the insurgents or the government to negotiate.

(6) A change of government that brings to power a strong leader whom the insurgents view as personally committed to resolving the conflict and capable of ensuring the compliance of other government elements.

(7) Willingness of both sides to accept third-party mediation and monitoring of a cease-fire and the eventual implementation of an agreement.

g. **Government Victory**

(1) A government victory is likely to be a protracted process marked by gradual decline in violence as the insurgents lose military capabilities, external assistance, and popular support. Low-level violence may persist for years, and, lacking a climactic final battle, the end will probably be indistinct.

(a) As the government succeeds in reducing the number of insurgents and the size of their infrastructure, the insurgents become harder to find and to eliminate.

(b) If the conflict has lasted a long time, insurgency may have become a way of life for many fighters, and the violence may continue long after the insurgents have abandoned any hope of achieving their goals. The conflict is even more likely to persist if the insurgents have become heavily involved in criminal activities such as drug trafficking or resource plunder, which can become the insurgency's primary reason for existence.

(2) Signs of an impending government victory would probably be ambiguous and seem more like atmospherics than specific indicators. Evidence of daily life returning to normal, government services and administration fully functioning, and government forces operating nationwide probably suggest the government has effectively defeated the insurgency. Other specific signs that can signal a government victory include:

(a) Commercial activity increases, markets reopen, and businesses remain open after dark.

(b) Civilians feel safe enough to leave their homes at night.

(c) Refugees or internally displaced persons voluntarily return to their homes.

(d) Civilians openly interact with officials or security force personnel.

(e) Civilians promptly alert security forces to the presence of insurgents.

(f) Officials can travel with minimal security and can spend their nights in areas that formerly were unsafe.

(g) Government offices are open and functioning normally.

(h) Security forces—even in small units—are able to operate throughout the country, including in formerly insurgent-held areas.

(i) The police reclaim responsibility for security, and the military largely returns to base.

CHAPTER III
FUNDAMENTALS OF COUNTERINSURGENCY

"In small wars, caution must be exercised, and instead of striving to generate the maximum power with the forces available, the goal is to gain decisive results with the least application of force. In small wars, tolerance, sympathy, and kindness should be the keynote of our relationship with the mass of the population. Small wars involve a wide range of activities including diplomacy, contacts with the civil population, and warfare of the most difficult kind."

Small Wars Manual
United States Marine Corps, 1940

1. Overview

a. COIN is the blend of comprehensive civilian and military efforts designed to simultaneously defeat and contain insurgency and address its root causes. The goal of COIN operations is to enable the HN government to exercise political control over its population territory via system of legitimate governance. Therefore, COIN is fundamentally an armed political competition between a government and its partners on the one hand, and insurgents and their supporters on the other. Military operations to kill or capture insurgents, degrade their capabilities, and disrupt their organizations are generally a critical element of a broader comprehensive approach. However, COIN is a complex protracted effort that often requires the integration of capabilities, typically associated with peace operations (PO), foreign humanitarian assistance (HA), stability operations, FID, and CT with those of numerous interagency partners to help the HN government marginalize insurgents and win the support of the population. Governments often severely underestimate the financial, political, military, and human costs required to prevail in COIN.

(1) COIN approaches must be adaptable and agile. Strategies will usually be focused primarily on the population rather than just the insurgents and will seek to reinforce the legitimacy of the affected government while reducing insurgent influence. This can often only be achieved in concert with political reform to improve the quality of governance and address underlying grievances, many of which may be legitimate.

(2) Since US COIN operations will normally involve engagement in support of a foreign government (either independently or as part of an intergovernmental organization [IGO] or multinational force), success will often depend on the willingness of that government to undertake the necessary political changes, if applicable. However great its know-how and enthusiasm, an outside actor (e.g., USG) cannot fully compensate for lack of will, incapacity, or counterproductive behavior on the part of the supported HN government.

b. The existence of a robust insurgency demonstrates that a substantial part of the population views the HN government as illegitimate. Every insurgency is unique and reestablishing HN legitimacy and control requires a coherent, realistic political strategy that is focused on addressing the opportunity, motive, and means at the root of the insurgency. Likewise, a COIN campaign to implement that strategy must be carefully aligned to the particular nature of the insurgency; the physical, economic, political, and human dimensions of the OE; and the nature of the HN government and its security forces.

c. In many cases, the most effective and legitimate forms of HN governance will differ significantly from Western models. They may involve decentralized authority, a blend of formal and informal governance systems, and/or very different expectations about the role of the state in the lives of its citizens. There is no universal model: to succeed, both the politico-military strategy and the operational approach to COIN must be adapted to local conditions.

d. All governments rule through a combination of consent and coercion. Governments described as legitimate rule primarily with the consent of the governed and strictly limit their use of coercion against their citizens. Those described as illegitimate tend to rely more heavily on coercion to maintain control and suppress peaceful political contention. Citizens of the latter obey the state for fear of the consequences of doing otherwise, rather than because they voluntarily accept its rule. While even a legitimate government may use coercion to enforce the rule of law, most of its citizens voluntarily accept its authority to govern. Legitimate governance is inherently more stable. The societal support it engenders allows it to adequately manage internal problems, change, and conflict.

e. The struggle for legitimacy in the eyes of the relevant population typically is a central theme of the conflict between the insurgency and the HN government. Insurgents exploit the HN government's loss of legitimacy with one part of the population to launch an operation or campaign to extend their influence and control over the rest of the populace. Insurgencies employ a mixture of violence, subversion, and governance to establish a system of competitive control, undermine the legitimacy of the HN government, and buttress their own legitimacy. The COIN effort must reduce the credibility of the insurgency while strengthening the legitimacy of the HN government. The joint force must normally establish and maintain legitimacy with both the HN government and the indigenous population, and strive to ensure that its actions garner favorable public opinion by the US population. USG actions must be just and worthy to maintain support and facilitate sustained COIN operations. Counterinsurgents achieve this objective by undertaking appropriate actions and striving for a balanced application of both lethal and nonlethal means as dictated by the local circumstances.

(1) **Legitimacy in the Local Context.** Legitimacy is achieved by the HN government through being seen as effective and credible. The HN government achieves this by providing predictable and tolerable living conditions to the population. Legitimacy is ultimately decided in the minds of the population, and therefore, the COIN operation works to ensure that the HN government meets the baseline expectations of the population in order to solidify its legitimacy. Different cultures may see acceptable levels of development, corruption, and political participation differently. Additionally, the importance of security in situations where violence has escalated cannot be overemphasized. Establishing security can win the people's confidence, gain credibility, and enable the HN government to develop legitimacy in other areas. If the local population considers genocide or the exclusion of some ethnic minorities as legitimate, the joint force will face a particular challenge in working with the HN government to change these perceptions.

(2) **Indicators of Legitimacy.** There are seven possible indicators of legitimacy that can be used to analyze threats to stability. The key indicator of legitimacy is the ability to provide security for the populace, including protection from internal and external threats. Second, the selection of leaders in a manner considered just and fair by a substantial majority of the populace, normally as established in a constitution or similar document. Other indicators of legitimacy include: a level of popular participation in or support for national and local political processes that are consistent with local expectations; an acceptable balance between governmental corruption and transparency; a culturally acceptable level and rate of political, economic, and social development; the existence and acceptance of laws or legal system that is predictable and tolerable to the local population; and a high level of acceptance of the pillars of government by major social institutions.

f. **Success in COIN.** A COIN operation may be deemed successful when the following conditions are met:

(1) The affected HN government is able to exercise control over its population and territory via legitimate systems of governance that meet the population's expectations.

(2) The HN government has adequate capacity and willingness to address the root causes of insurgency (opportunity, motive, and means); government corruption is reduced and good governance increases.

(3) HNSF establish positive relations with the population, especially in the area of conflict, and have the quality not just quantity of sufficient strength to counter the insurgents. Insurgent violence has been reduced to a level that is manageable by the civilian authorities (i.e., law enforcement and security forces) of the HN government.

(4) Nonindigenous elements of the counterinsurgent force (i.e., US forces) can terminate combat operations and transition to indirect and/or direct support FID categories, as required by the HN, without the resurgence of the insurgency beyond the capabilities of the HN. HN forces are dominating the offensive. Simultaneously external military support for the insurgency is waning.

(5) The HN government's legitimacy is established by several factors and support by external actors.

g. **Impediments to Success.** It should not be assumed that both the government and the insurgents want a definitive end to the insurgency. Over time, both the government and the insurgents develop a vested interest in the continuation of an insurgency based conflict. For the insurgents, it becomes a way of life. In some insurgencies like Colombia there are third and fourth generation insurgents. The more time and effort insurgents give to the insurgency, the less time they have to develop marketable skills. In addition, a "war economy" develops in which insurgents, criminals, and even corrupt elements of the HN profit from the conflict through illicit activities (such as smuggling, kidnapping, black market, etc.) and/or the influx of external assistance (development assistance, Commanders' Emergency Response Program spending, economic investment). Moreover, for the government, a continuing insurgency can be a source of outside assistance but might also provide an alibi for poor domestic performance. The government might face lower expectations for economic development, promotion of rights, etc. Hence the government benefits from continuation of an insurgency that does not threaten to overthrow it.

2. Counterinsurgency Mindset

a. COIN is distinguished from traditional warfare due to the focus of its operations—a relevant population—and its strategic purpose—to gain or maintain control or influence over, and the support of that relevant population through political, psychological, and economic methods. Warfare that has the population as its focus of operations requires a different mindset and different capabilities than warfare that focuses on defeating an adversary militarily. In COIN operations this means an adaptive and flexible mindset to understand the population, anticipate insurgent actions, be comfortable among the population, and appreciate the comprehensive approach of unified action. As a COG for the HN government and often a COG for insurgents, the population is typically the critical aspect of successful COIN. Counterinsurgents should learn to think like the local population and to understand how local perceptions are formed in order to better appreciate the impact that the lethal and nonlethal actions will have on HN government and USG legitimacy. This requires an intimate knowledge of the grievances the insurgency has co-opted and the narrative it has used to mobilize support. A second aspect of the COIN mindset is being able to understand the insurgent strategy and narrative in order to anticipate and counter their operations. Finally, counterinsurgents must understand that the military instrument is only one part of a comprehensive approach through unified action for unity of effort. In addition to the security situation, the joint force may have to be flexible enough to execute tasks that other organizations are better suited to conduct.

b. The core of a COIN effort is the political strategy, which should articulate how the HN will address the root causes (opportunity, motives, and means) that drive the insurgency. The strategy provides a framework around which all other programs and activities are organized. Depending on the root causes of the insurgency, the strategy may involve a mixture of political reform, reconciliation, popular mobilization, economic development, and governmental capacity building. In general terms, a COIN operation is only as good as the political strategy it supports and only as good as the HN's motivation to enact the above political reforms and capacity building. Where the political strategy is vague, unrealistic, or lacking in support from domestic or international stakeholders, the operation is unlikely to succeed, whatever the merit of individual programs. An effective political strategy focuses on strengthening the government's capability, capacity, and willingness to respond—and be perceived as responding—to the expectations of its people.

c. The existence of a robust insurgency demonstrates that an HN government has lost legitimacy with a substantial part of its population. Regaining that legitimacy will almost always require a degree of political reform to successfully address the root causes that gave rise to insurgency in the first place. In many cases factions of the HN government may prove reluctant or unwilling to adopt those reforms because they threaten powerful political or economic interests. However, HN governments are not monolithic: the USG should thoroughly assess its HN partners to understand the perspectives and interests of different individuals and networks. Based on that detailed analysis, supporting nations should structure their assistance to the HN government in ways that promote reform and empower moderates.

d. **Comprehensive Approach.** COIN requires unified action through interagency and interorganizational coordination of the instruments of national power to support an HN's political, security, economic, and information components that reinforce the legitimacy of the HN government and its effective control of the OE. By doing this, the population will support the HN government rather than the insurgency (see Figure III-1). Theater and operational strategies should emphasize those functions for shaping and executing a COIN effort. To be effective, officials involved in COIN must address two imperatives—political action and security—with equal urgency, recognizing that insurgency is fundamentally an armed political competition. Effective security through military activities, although unlikely to deliver success alone, will almost always be critical to the political resolution. Security operations conducted in support of a COIN strategy, coordinated with economic development, and integrated with information-related capabilities, will provide security for the population and improve the overall political situation at the local level. This should increase acceptance of the HN government and, in turn, popular support for the HN and USG COIN operation. COIN functions therefore include informational, security, political, and economic and development components, all of which are designed to support the overall objective of establishing and consolidating control by the HN government. The sociocultural factors of the HN must be taken into account when developing the political strategy that will frame the application of the functional components of the comprehensive approach.

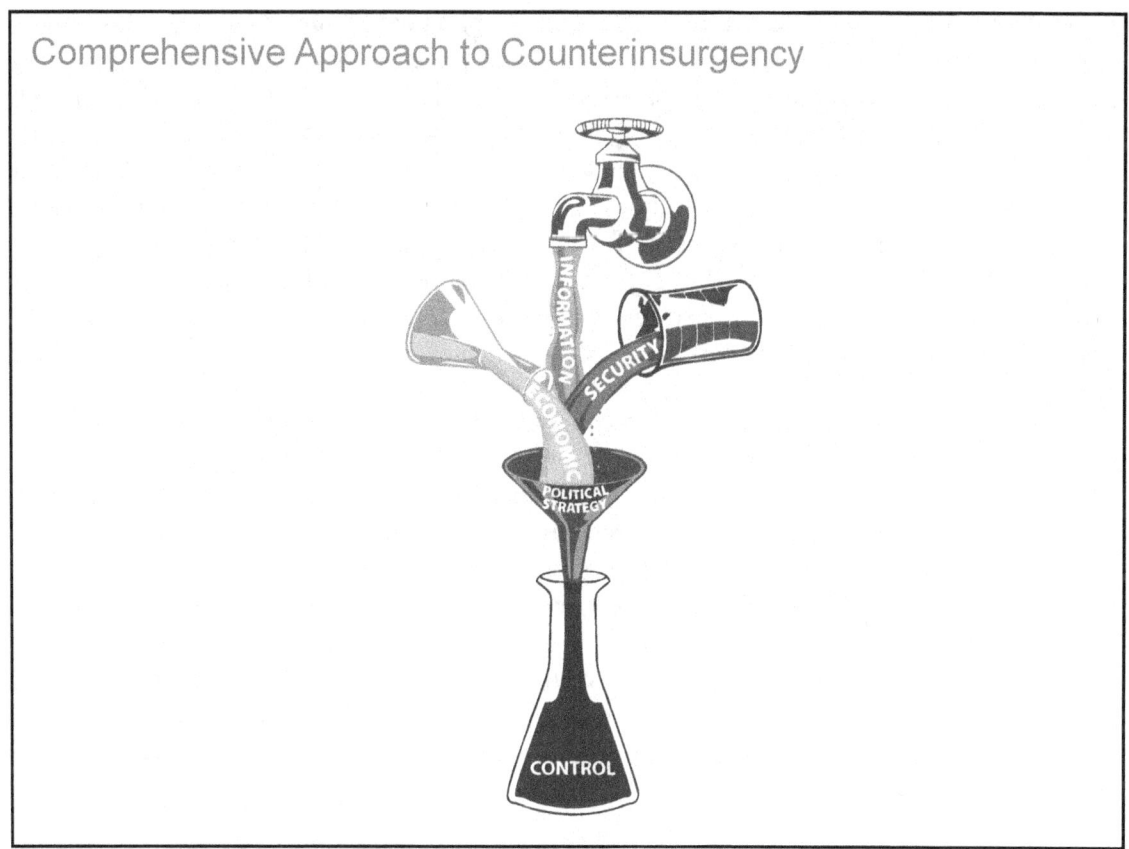

Figure III-1. Comprehensive Approach to Counterinsurgency

(1) **Political Strategy.** This is the core of a COIN effort, because it provides a framework around which all other programs and activities are organized. As described above, depending on the root causes of the insurgency, the strategy may involve elements of political reform, reconciliation, popular mobilization, and governmental capacity building. COIN efforts are only as good as the political strategy they support. Tactical civil and military efforts cannot compensate for a strategy that does not match the political and operational realities on the ground or lacks support from key stakeholders. Effective strategies address both the actual capability, capacity, and willingness of the HN government to meet the expectations of its citizens and how it is perceived by the population. It cannot be overstated that the political strategy must account for the sociocultural factors of the HN population. The existence of a robust insurgency demonstrates that the behavior of the HN government has failed to meet the expectations of a substantial part of its population and is no longer viewed as legitimate. In almost all cases, regaining that legitimacy will require a degree of political behavior modification (substantive political reform, anticorruption and governance improvement) to successfully address the root causes that gave rise to insurgency in the first place. Supporting nations may be able to assist the HN in these reforms.

(2) **Security.** In COIN operations, the term security is frequently used to refer to the degree to which the HN government can suppress insurgent activity in an area. However, the concept of "human security" is a more comprehensive approach which can only be measured through the collation of individual perceptions across a community. The paramount concern is the absence of physical violence, but other relevant factors may include maintenance of laws, the protection of human rights, freedom to conduct economic activity, public safety (fire, ambulance, etc.), and public health (such as safe drinking water and sanitation) that also are essential services, which are part of the economic functional component. The expectations and priorities of the population define which factors are relevant and what constitutes acceptable conditions, and not necessarily to Western standards or assumptions. The emphasis on physical security in COIN does not imply disregard for other aspects of human security—only prioritization. The end state of providing human security should be implicit in the wider efforts to improve the standard of governance down to the local level. In some areas, the sequencing is reversed, and addressing other aspects of human security—such as rule of law and security of livelihoods—may be a prerequisite to establishing a security presence capable of defending the population from insurgent violence.

(3) **Economic Function.** The economic function in COIN includes immediate humanitarian relief and the provision of essential services such as safe water, sanitation, basic health care, livelihood assistance, and primary education. In COIN, economic initiatives should be carefully tailored to respond to the economic grievances that insurgents exploit in their narrative. Longer term programs for development of infrastructure to support agricultural, industrial, educational, medical, and commercial activities will not necessarily be part of the economic function in COIN unless they support the political strategy and can be used to counter the insurgent narrative. In all cases, economic initiatives must be tailored to the affected government's willingness to undertake key reforms, capacity to absorb support, reduce dependency of foreign donors to sustain stability, and ability to manage its outcomes.

(4) **Information.** In COIN, the information flow can be roughly divided into that information which the USG requires to guide its politico-military approach (i.e., knowledge of local conditions) and that information which the USG wishes to disseminate in order to influence populations. At the same time, counterinsurgents also seek to impede the information flow of insurgent groups—both their intelligence collection and their ability to influence relevant actors.

(5) **Control.** The four functions (information, political, security, and economic) contribute to the overall objective of enabling the affected government to control its environment. This implies the ability to contain insurgent activity (the tempo of operations, level and intensity of violence, and degree of instability that it engenders) such that the population will, in the long run, support the government against the insurgents—noting that this balance can differ from one society to the next.

e. **Unified Action in COIN.** Unified action that includes all HN, US, and participating multinational forces and agencies, normally requires the COM, in conjunction with the designated JFC, to lead the overall USG COIN effort in coordination with the HN government. The COM typically provides the JFC coordinating authorities to interact with the HN government and its military/security forces depending on the specific situation. Military participation in COIN also may be focused on support to a USG FID program, including security sector reform (SSR), or support to an HN IDAD program. Both FID and SSR may be supported through security force assistance (SFA); and both would support the HN government eventually taking over the combat operations of the COIN operation and supporting other stabilization efforts as required. In some hostile or unpredictable OEs, the JFC should be prepared to lead the COIN effort until a COM can assume that responsibility. The JFC would focus military operations as part of a comprehensive approach.

3. Tenets of Counterinsurgency

The operational tenets of COIN are to provide guideposts for the joint force. These tenets complement the principles of joint operations and provide focus on how to successfully conduct COIN. The tenets of COIN are further supported by the tactical precepts of COIN.

For additional information on the principles of joint operations, see Joint Publication (JP) 3-0, Joint Operations, *and for information on the precepts of COIN, see Appendix D, "Precepts for Counterinsurgency."*

a. **Understand the OE.** Because each COIN operation is different, significant time and resources are devoted at the outset to develop a robust understanding of the nature of the conflict, the insurgency, and a holistic understanding of the OE where the COIN effort will take place (see Chapter IV, "The Operational Environment," for an explanation of understanding the OE in COIN). It is through this understanding that the JFC can decipher the true nature of the problem the joint force operation is meant to resolve; develop realistic end states and intermediate goals; identify an operational approach that is relevant to the nature of the conflict, and appropriate for the local context of the operational area, and determine feasible operations based on available resources; consider relevant aspects of the

OE during the planning of lethal and nonlethal missions and activities for increased chances of success; and determine potential second- and third-order effects. By clearly understanding the nature of the challenge, the COIN force can align forces, capabilities, missions, and goals. All members of the COIN force work to develop and maintain a common understanding of key aspects of the conflict and the OE. This common understanding helps drive coordination and synchronization of the efforts of all COIN partners during the planning and execution of operations. COIN operations are dynamic, and the situation within the OE can change rapidly, requiring the joint force to constantly monitor, evaluate, and assess the nature of the conflict and the operationally relevant aspects of the OE.

(1) **Sociocultural Knowledge.** Sociocultural knowledge is essential to successful COIN. American ideas of what is "normal" or "rational" are not universal. To the contrary, members of other societies often have different notions of rationality, appropriate behavior, level of religious devotion, political organization, social order, and norms concerning gender. What may appear abnormal or strange to an external observer may appear as self-evidently normal to an HN group member, and vice versa. US counterinsurgents—especially commanders, planners, and small-unit leaders—should strive to avoid imposing their ideal of normalcy on a foreign culture. On the other hand, US personnel should keep in mind that cultural norms and traditions are often linked to political agendas and ideologies, may vary considerably across the HN society, and may be heavily contested. In some cases, disputes over cultural traditions may be an element of the root causes of the insurgency, or part of the narrative insurgents craft to mobilize support. Service forces should receive appropriate cultural awareness training before joining specific COIN operations.

(2) **Understanding HN Partners.** While improving the capacity of the HN government to control its territory and population is key, addressing the core grievances is also necessary to end the insurgency. External counterinsurgents will often have to cajole or coerce HN governments and entrenched elites to recognize the legitimacy of those grievances and address them. Reforms that threaten the political and financial interests of those elites are most likely to generate resistance. Therefore, external counterinsurgents have to put as much effort into understanding and shaping the behavior of their HN partners as they do into countering the insurgents. This typically requires a critical assessment of the motivations and interests of factions and individuals within the HN government. See Chapter IV, "The Operational Environment," for more detail.

(3) **Prepare for a Long-Term Commitment.** Insurgencies are protracted by nature, and history demonstrates that they often last for years or even decades. Thus, COIN normally demands considerable expenditures of time and resources, especially if they must be conducted simultaneously with operations in a protracted war combining traditional and irregular warfare (IW). The relevant population may prefer the HN government to the insurgents; however, people do not actively support a government unless they are convinced that the counterinsurgents have the means, ability, stamina, and will to win—credibility. The insurgents' primary battle is against the HN government, not the US; however, US support can be crucial to building public faith in that government's viability. The population must have confidence in the staying power of both the US counterinsurgents and the HN government. Insurgents and the relevant population often believe that a few casualties or a few years will cause the US to abandon a COIN effort. Constant reaffirmations of

commitment, backed by deeds, can overcome that perception and bolster US credibility. Even the strongest US commitment, however, will not succeed if the population does not perceive the HN government as having similar credibility. US forces must help create crucial HN capabilities and capacities to sustain the HN's credibility and legitimacy. It is also important to note that US support to an HN's COIN efforts can decrease or even cease while the HN's COIN efforts are still fighting an insurgency. This normally is because the HN can successfully deal with the insurgency.

(4) **Preparation.** Preparing for a protracted COIN effort requires establishing headquarters and support structures designed for long-term operations. Planning and commitments should be based on sustainable operating tempo and personnel tempo limits for the various components of the force. Even in situations where the US goal is reducing its military force levels as quickly as possible, some support for HN institutions usually remains for a long time. US preparatory actions for long-term support must come at the public request of the HN and be focused on supporting the IDAD strategy.

(5) **US Public Support.** US public opinion should be considered as part of the OE, just as the indigenous population opinion is essential to the COIN effort, because USG COIN efforts must prove worthwhile to the US public. At the national strategic level, gaining and maintaining US public support for a protracted deployment is critical. Demonstrating incremental success is essential to maintaining support.

(6) **Learn and Adapt.** Counterinsurgents may develop situational awareness of the OE as the COIN operation is executed. Counterinsurgents assess and adjust the operation's design and plan throughout the operations.

b. **Develop the COIN Narrative.** Fulfilling military objectives is only part of the COIN effort: the key is to demonstrate to the relevant actors that the HN government and its allies are not only winning, but that their cause is just and irresistible. This is accomplished through the development of a COIN narrative to directly compete with the insurgent narrative. The COIN narrative should contextualize what the population experiences, legitimizing counterinsurgent actions and delegitimizing the insurgency. It is an interpretive lens designed to help individuals and groups make decisions in the face of uncertainty where the stakes are perceived as life and death. The COIN narrative should explain the current situation and describe how the HN government will defeat the insurgency. It should invoke relevant cultural and historical references to both justify the actions of counterinsurgents and make the case that the government will win.

(1) The COIN narrative provides an operational framework for integrating IO with the full range of lethal and nonlethal military and civilian operations in order to shape the perception of relevant actors, particularly the insurgents and the population. The COIN narrative operationalizes the concept of "propaganda of the deed," which recognizes that actions have significance beyond their direct or immediate consequences. Actions signal an actor's intentions and indicate its credibility to follow through on promises and threats; they constitute a critical form of communication to local audiences. Every action takes on a symbolic meaning that is interpreted through the lens of the narrative. Simply assuming that relevant actors will interpret counterinsurgent actions the way they were intended leaves

them vulnerable to misinterpretation or deliberate distortion by insurgents. Conversely, intentional exploitation of this phenomenon can magnify the impact of counterinsurgent actions on the population and the insurgency.

(2) The COIN narrative should be based on the counterinsurgents' politico-military strategy and be developed in conjunction with the military operational approach. At the tactical level, the COIN narrative should help units and any civilian partners interpret operational-level guidance and select the most appropriate tools and methods to address specific local-level COIN challenges. Choosing approaches that are both effective at solving the immediate challenge and consistent with COIN narrative helps ensure that tactical successes amount to more than the sum of their parts, shaping the perceptions of insurgents and population and achieving operational objectives over time.

(3) US forces committed to supporting COIN are there to assist an HN government. The long-term goal is to leave a government able to stand by itself, which is also normally the goal even if the US begins COIN in an area that does not have an HN government. Regardless of the starting conditions, the HN ultimately has to win on its own. Achieving this requires development of viable local leaders and institutions. US forces and USG departments and agencies can help, but HN elements must accept responsibilities to achieve real victory. While it may be easier for joint forces to conduct operations themselves, it is better to work to strengthen local forces and institutions and then assist them. HN governments have the final responsibility to solve their own problems. Eventually all foreign armies are seen as interlopers or occupiers; the sooner the main effort can transition to HN institutions, without unacceptable degradation, the better.

(4) **Manage Expectations.** The US and its HN partners must take steps to proactively manage the expectations of the local population and other relevant actors. This process involves encouraging and reinforcing reasonable expectations, setting counterinsurgents up for success when they prove able to deliver on promises. Counterinsurgents trying to build enthusiasm for their efforts should avoid making unrealistic promises. At best, a failure to deliver promised results may undermine the credibility of the counterinsurgents, and at worst be interpreted as deliberate deception rather than good intentions gone awry. Conversely, consistently meeting reasonable expectations can increase the population's patience with the inevitable inconveniences and uneven progress typical in COIN operations.

c. **Primacy of Politics.** At the beginning of a COIN operation, military actions may appear predominant as security forces conduct operations to secure the populace and kill or capture insurgents. However, USG and HN political objectives guide the COIN approach. Commanders must consider how operations contribute to strengthening the HN government's legitimacy and achieving US goals—the latter is especially important if the HN is very weak, whether failing or recovering. This means that political and diplomatic leaders must actively participate through all aspects (planning, preparation, execution, and assessment) of a COIN effort. The political and military aspects of insurgencies are so bound together as to be inseparable: military action is valuable only where it supports the political strategy. Resolving most insurgencies requires a political solution, whether or not facilitated by significant military activities. Moreover, most insurgency solutions involve some sort of political compromise and are rarely a "winner take all" situation. In COIN, the relationship between military operations and achieving political objectives is more complicated than in traditional warfare. Traditional adversaries invest in building conventional military capabilities that are distinct from the population and take significant time and effort to regenerate if destroyed. In contrast, the low resource requirements of insurgent groups allow them to generate military strength directly through mobilization of segments of the population. If the root causes of the insurgency—the opportunity, motive, and means factors—are left unaddressed or are exacerbated by combat operations, insurgent forces often prove able to regenerate or even expand their political appeal and military strength. Consequently, counterinsurgent military operations must be carefully designed to support the political strategy at the strategic, operational, and tactical levels. COIN often requires a mixture of aggressive lethal operations to degrade insurgent capabilities and disrupt insurgent networks, and nonlethal operations to begin addressing core grievances. However, both lethal and nonlethal efforts should be guided primarily by their potential to influence the perceptions of the insurgents and the population. In COIN, both the objectives and the way they are achieved affect the perceptions of the population: actions executed without properly assessing their political effects at best result in reduced effectiveness and at worst are counterproductive. Therefore, political considerations inform all aspects of operational art, including the prioritization and sequencing of operations, the employment of forces, and guidance regarding tactics, techniques, and procedures (TTP). Avoid excessive collateral damage and disproportionate use of force. The COIN force needs to avoid collective punishment of the population within the contested area and escalating repression. Forces that engage in coercion and intimidation are placed at an operational disadvantage. As the OE changes so must the operational approach.

d. **Secure the Population.** The most important concern for the population caught in the midst of a COIN is security. The centrality of the population to success in COIN makes population security the foundation for all other efforts and a prerequisite for lasting stability. Civilians tend to cooperate with whichever side proves capable of providing a predictable and tolerable environment. Although the conditions that constitute predictable and tolerable vary across different contexts and societies—and may vary within the operational area—they boil down to a clear set of rules that are consistently enforced under which the population feels it can reasonably survive. In many cases, civilians will cooperate with the side that establishes effective control over their area even if it contradicts their political preferences. However, understanding and addressing the population's security concerns can prove challenging.

(1) **Human Security and Prioritization.** To effectively secure the population, the concept of security has to be expanded beyond the suppression of insurgent activity and protection from physical violence to include the full range of issues that affect individual and community survival. While physical security is the first priority, other critical factors can include access to dispute resolution, the protection of human rights, access to critical community resources (migration routes, grazing land), and access to essential services. **The expectations and priorities of the population define which factors are relevant and what constitutes acceptable conditions, not Western standards or assumptions.** Those expectations may vary enormously across different parts of the operational area or the population (urban versus rural areas; mining communities versus nomads). Providing human

security should be integral to efforts to expand HN control at the local level. In some areas, the sequencing is reversed: addressing other aspects of human security—such as rule of law and security of livelihoods—may be a prerequisite to establishing a security presence capable of defending the population from insurgent violence.

(2) **Physical Security.** Insurgent violence against the population shapes the populations behavior in three key ways. It undermines the government's credibility and legitimacy as a provider of security in return for cooperation; it isolates the population from the government by punishing those seen to be collaborating; and it establishes a rival system of control/governance over the civilian population. If insurgents are able to establish a more credible and consistently enforced set of rules than the government, the population is more likely to cooperate irrespective of whether they agree with the insurgents' goals. Since insurgents require secrecy, anonymity can be stripped from key persons of interest via the application of biometrics and biometrics-enabled intelligence. Thus it is critical that the COIN force provide adequate levels of security for the population in order to retain its support and cooperation. Those efforts should align with the overall politico-military strategy, but to be effective they must address the full range of security concerns of the population, which may extend well beyond the insurgents and not be captured in standard military threat assessments. Particularly where the HN government or security forces have a history of human rights violations, or insurgent violence has effectively intimidated the populace into silence, COIN forces may have to make a concerted effort to understand how the population perceives the security environment.

(a) COIN forces may be a source of insecurity for the population as well. There is balance to be struck between two competing objectives: being as close as feasible to the population to bring security, and ensuring that such proximity does not have the unintended effect of endangering the population by placing a military objective in their midst. Abusive, corrupt, or predatory behavior by elements of the security forces can taint the entire COIN operation, undermine the legitimacy of the HN government, and push the population to support the insurgency. This is particularly true if the population interprets such abuses as evidence of a broader struggle for survival between different identity groups. Even one or two incidents, if captured in video or as still images, can undermine the entire COIN strategic narrative. In such cases, abuses have the potential to inflame a security dilemma and play into the insurgent narrative.

(b) **Law Enforcement Use of Force.** The perception of legitimacy with respect to the use of force is also important. If the HN police have a reasonable reputation for competence and impartiality, it is better for them to execute urban raids, as the population is likely to view that application of force as more legitimate than military action. This is true even if the police are not as well armed or as capable as military units. However, local circumstances affect this decision. If the police are seen as part of an ethnic or sectarian group oppressing the general population, their use may be counterproductive. Effective counterinsurgents thus understand the character of the local police and popular perceptions of both police and military units. This understanding helps ensure that the application of force is appropriate and reinforces the rule of law.

(3) **Rule of Law.** Access to effective mechanisms to resolve disputes without resorting to violence and in accordance with a consistent set of rules is fundamental to ensure that the population feels secure. The rule of law should govern the conduct of COIN forces, transparently and consistently following its own rules to demonstrate the political credibility of the HN government and its allies to the population and the insurgents.

(4) As with governance systems in general, the legal systems deemed most effective and legitimate in the eyes of the local population may differ greatly from Western models, and may vary across the operational area (e.g., the capital city versus remote rural areas). JFCs should endeavor to support locally appropriate systems while adhering to US and international human rights standards.

(5) Even carefully targeted military operations against insurgents can create risks for the population. The security of the population may require offensive operations against insurgents to seize the initiative and neutralize the threat. In some contexts, populations have proven tolerant of increased civilian casualties as a result of aggressive offensive operations against insurgents when those operations helped produce a significant overall improvement in civil security. In other contexts, every civilian casualty resulting from COIN operations has undermined support for the government and its allies. COIN forces should carefully assess the political, cultural, and security context through the eyes of the population in order to develop an effective approach to managing this dilemma. Normally, counterinsurgents can use rules of engagement (ROE) to minimize potential loss of life. ROE should address lesser means of force and nonlethal means when such use is likely to create the desired effects, and joint forces can do so without endangering themselves, others, or mission accomplishment. Escalation of force procedures do not limit the right to use deadly force when such force is necessary to defend against a hostile actor demonstrating hostile intent. Commanders should provide training on the rules for the use of force and ROE. Even precise and tailored force must be executed legitimately and with consideration for consequent effects. Overwhelming effort may prove necessary to destroy an opponent, especially extremist insurgent combatants. However, counterinsurgents should carefully calculate the type and amount of force and who applies it, regardless of the means of applying force. An operation that kills five insurgents is counterproductive if collateral damage leads to the recruitment of 50 more insurgents. Thus, careful targeting is required to weigh the potential effects and perceptions of the relevant population, the US population, the multinational partner populations, and international opinion.

(6) **Isolate the Insurgency.** Insurgents must be isolated from the population, their cause, and support. While it may be required to kill or capture insurgents, it is more effective in the long run to separate an insurgency from the population and its resources, thus letting it die. Confrontational military action, in exclusion, is counterproductive in most cases; it risks generating popular resentment, creating martyrs that motivate new recruits, and producing cycles of revenge.

(a) **Expropriating the Insurgent Cause.** Skillful counterinsurgents can deal a significant blow to an insurgency by expropriating its cause. Insurgents often exploit multiple causes, however, making counterinsurgents' challenges more difficult. In the end, any successful COIN operation must address the legitimate grievances insurgents exploit to generate popular support. These may be different in each local area, in which case a complex set of solutions will be needed. A mix of usurpation and direct refutation may also be used. Counterinsurgents may champion portions of the insurgents' cause while directly refuting others. This approach may be especially useful when stated insurgent goals are clearly disproportionally beneficial to one group. Counterinsurgents may be able to also "capture" an insurgency's cause and exploit it. For example, an insurgent ideology based on an extremist interpretation of a holy text can be countered by appealing to a moderate interpretation of the same text. When a credible religious or other respected leader passes this kind of message, the counteraction is even more effective.

(b) **Cutting Logistics.** Counterinsurgents must cut off the flow of arms and ammunition into the area and eliminate their sources. An effective weapon in denying logistics to an insurgency is populace and resource control. These two controls are distinct, yet linked, normally a responsibility of indigenous civil governments. They are defined and enforced during times of civil or military emergency.

1. Populace control provides security for the populace, mobilizes human resources, denies personnel to the enemy, and detects and reduces the effectiveness of enemy agents. Populace control measures include curfews, movement restrictions, travel permits, registration cards, and relocation of the population.

2. Resource control regulates the movement or consumption of materiel resources, mobilizes materiel resources, and denies materiel to the enemy. Resources control measures include licensing, regulations or guidelines, checkpoints (for example, roadblocks), ration controls, amnesty programs, and inspection of facilities.

(c) **Reducing Finances.** Counterinsurgents can exploit insurgent financial weaknesses. Controls and regulations that limit the movement and exchange of materiel and funds may compound insurgent financial vulnerabilities. These counters are especially effective when an insurgency receives funding from outside the state. Additionally, effective law enforcement can be detrimental to an insurgency that uses criminal means for funding. Department of the Treasury designations and other diplomatic tools outside the scope of DOD are key to countering threat finance. The JFC must work closely with the COM to identify and target counter threat finance (CTF) sources, and may even consider the creation of interagency and threat finance cell (TFC) to enhance the collection, analysis, and dissemination of intelligence to support and strengthen US, multinational, and HN efforts to disrupt and eliminate key insurgent financial network nodes.

(d) **Momentum.** As the HN government increases its legitimacy, the populace begins to assist it more actively. Eventually, the people marginalize and stigmatize insurgents to the point that the insurgency's claim to legitimacy is destroyed. However, victory is gained not when this isolation is achieved, but when legitimate government functions are maintained by and with the people's active support and when insurgent forces lose legitimacy.

e. **Synchronize and Integrate Lines of Effort (LOEs).** In COIN, lethal and nonlethal activities cannot be designed and implemented in isolation. They are carefully synchronized at the operational and tactical levels to reinforce each other and support the COIN narrative. From planning through execution, the efforts of joint interagency, multinational, and HN participants are integrated toward a common purpose. Insurgent opportunities, motives, and means typically cut across the spectrum of LOEs, so that failure to integrate will at best render the COIN effort less effective and at worst lead to counterproductive impacts across different LOEs. Counterinsurgents will therefore have to prioritize efforts while remaining cognizant of the linkages and effects these operations will have in other areas.

f. **Unity of Command and Unity of Effort**

(1) **Unity of Command.** Military unity of command is the preferred method for achieving unity of effort in any military operation. Military unity of command is achieved by establishing and maintaining formal command or support relationships. Unity of command should extend to all military forces engaged in COIN (US, HN, and other multinational forces). The purpose of command relationships is for military forces, police, and other security forces to establish effective control while attaining a monopoly on the legitimate use of violence within the society.

(2) **Unity of Effort.** Many participants in a COIN effort may not be subject to unity of command, so unity of effort must be present at every echelon of a COIN operation. Otherwise, well-intentioned but uncoordinated actions can conflict or provide vulnerabilities for insurgents to exploit. Usually, JFCs work to achieve unified action through liaison and interorganizational coordination with the leaders of a wide variety of government and multinational agencies, including those of the HN and the US. Whether there is a single chain of command or not, there must be a single mission, which is COIN. The military contribution to COIN is coordinated with the activities of USG interagency partners, the operations of multinational forces, and activities of various HN agencies (to the extent they are all participants in the COIN operation) to be successful. Nongovernmental organization (NGO) activities cannot and will not be integrated with military plans. For further details on US military and NGO relations, see *Guidelines for Relations Between US Armed Forces and Non-Governmental Humanitarian Organizations in Hostile and Potentially Hostile Environments.* It is not helpful to assign military actors with a security mission and civilian actors with a governance and development mission.

(3) **Coordination with NGOs.** Governmental participants in COIN will likely need to coordinate with NGO actors as well. Most NGOs will not allow their activities to be integrated with military plans in order for NGOs to maintain impartiality and independence in their operations, acceptance for their role among the conflict-affected population, and the ability to operate securely.

(4) **Intelligence Drives Operations.** Effective COIN is enabled by timely and reliable intelligence, gathered and analyzed at all levels and disseminated throughout the force. A cycle develops where operations produce intelligence that contribute to the conduct of subsequent operations. Reporting by units, members of the country team, and information derived from interactions with civilian agencies is often of equal or greater importance than reporting by specialized intelligence assets. This reporting may be both solicited and unsolicited information from the relevant population or insurgency defectors. In all cases

corroboration of the information retains significant importance to prevent acting upon false, misleading, or circular reporting. These factors, along with the need to generate a favorable operational tempo, drive the requirement to produce and disseminate intelligence at the lowest practical level. The perishable nature of some intelligence requires commanders to establish organizational architectures that provide operations-intelligence fusion at the lowest possible tactical level. Also, units should deploy analytical capacity as far forward as possible, so that the analyst is close—in time and space—to the supported commander.

4. United States Government Involvement in Counterinsurgency

a. **Context for USG Involvement in COIN.** The context for US involvement in COIN is based on three possible strategic settings: assisting an established HN government; as an adjunct to US major combat operations; or US operations in a UGA. Support for an existing government is the most common, and constitutes one variety of FID, in which US policy makers and the HN government can jointly decide on the appropriate level of US involvement through the development of an IDAD strategy. Depending upon the strength, legitimacy, and effectiveness of capabilities available to the affected government, the USG may play a subtle role in countering an incipient insurgency or may intervene more forcefully. The USG selects the most appropriate, most indirect, and least intrusive form of intervention that will achieve the desired end state and protect the sovereignty of the HN government. It is often the case that the less intrusive and more indirect the approach selected, the more likely it is to succeed, though this may depend on the maturity of the insurgency. An incipient insurgency can often be more easily addressed by a small-scale US response with greater emphasis on non-military US resources than a mature insurgency. However, most affected nations will only seek US assistance when the insurgency has developed sufficient maturity to pose a real threat, by which time the smaller scale response options may no longer be effective. Where US COIN efforts follow major combat operations or occur in a UGA, US forces will typically be the only ones available to conduct combat operations, and the joint force may be called upon to play a role in governance and civil administration until civilian counterparts can deploy, or a new indigenous government can be established. (See Chapter VIII, "Building Governance to Support Counterinsurgency.")

b. **Levels of USG Involvement.** USG involvement can take the form of indirect support, direct support without combat operations, or combat operations. A variety of tools and approaches are available for each level of involvement, and can be mixed and matched to suit the specific challenges of each insurgency. An expert advisor, who may be either a civilian or a military officer, will be sent directly to the staff of the HN government. One is most successful when the selected advisor possesses cultural and language skills appropriate to the HN, is paired with an effective indigenous leadership team, and can deploy for an extended period of time.

(1) **Indirect Support.** This approach emphasizes HN self-sufficiency and focuses on building strong national infrastructures through economic and military capabilities. Indirect support is typically implemented through the existing US country team, sometimes augmented through the deployment of a team of specialists with relevant expertise. The US military contribution to this type of support is derived from SC guidance and provided

primarily through security assistance (SA), supplemented by multinational exercises, exchange programs, and selected joint exercises (see Chapter V, "Planning," paragraph 3b, "SC.")

(2) **Direct Support Not Involving Combat Operations.** Under this approach, the US personnel are directly engaged in providing assistance to the HN civil administration, security forces, and/or civilian populace. Direct support operations are normally conducted when the HN has not attained self-sufficiency and is faced with social, economic, or military threats beyond its capability to handle. Assistance may take the form of SFA, direct participation in civil-military operations (CMO) (primarily, the provision of services to the local populace), military information support operations (MISO), communications and intelligence cooperation, mobility, and logistic support. In some cases, the provision of new equipment may be authorized as well. The scale of direct support can vary considerably, ranging from a single expert advisor seconded to the HN government, to an extensive training program for HN security forces, to embedded mentors that advise HN government personnel in the field. In some forms, direct support may remain low-profile and small footprint, while in others US involvement will be clearly evident and carry with it the risks and challenges more commonly associated with a large footprint approach.

(3) **Combat Operations.** The introduction of US combat forces requires a Presidential decision, and—in the context of support to an existing HN government— demands careful assessment of the benefits and tradeoffs to the COIN effort and US strategic objectives. In some cases, US forces may be engaged in combat operations while acting as embedded advisors to HN security forces. Combined action represents the next level of involvement, in which US personnel are joined with HN personnel to operate as a single combat formation, typically a platoon or a company. US forces may conduct operations in coordination with HN security forces, or constitute the main COIN force where no HN government is present. Depending on the scale of involvement, the role of US forces in relation to the insurgency and the population, and the number of US personnel deployed, participation in combat operations may fall into either the small footprint or large footprint category.

(4) **SC.** This is the broad, more encompassing approach to HN internal threats beginning with SC activities, and if required, advancing through the first two categories of a USG FID program, direct support and indirect support, respectively, for the HN COIN efforts. Although beyond the scope of SC, a calculated transition to the third category of FID (i.e., US combat operations) may be required if the threat becomes overwhelming for the HN, and if approved by the President. For a more detailed discussion of the FID aspects of SC, see Chapter V, "Planning," paragraph 3b(2), "FID."

(5) **Crisis Response Direct Intervention.** Direct intervention in a COIN operation or campaign would be the initial involvement directly by US combat operations as the result of a crisis response, not a transition through a FID program. This would be the least favored requirement for intervention. The campaigns in Iraq and Afghanistan were not standard examples of direct COIN intervention, since forces were initially deployed to bring about regime change, and there was no progressive FID program.

c. **Challenges for USG Involvement in COIN.** When analyzing the situation and considering an approach for the course of action (COA), it must be remembered that every insurgency is different and will require a carefully tailored response. The approaches outlined above should therefore be seen as broad categories and not specific models and largely based on the needs and sensitivities of the HN to foreign intervention. There is a tendency for FID and COIN assistance to creep incrementally from small scale and less intrusive forms to ever larger and more obvious assistance. This is clearly illustrated by the history of US involvement in Vietnam. The danger of this type of escalation is that the in-depth assessment and policy evaluation that occurred for the initial decision to assist may not necessarily be repeated for every increment, and the government may find itself enmeshed in a scale of effort which was not reached by logical deliberation. Because of the protracted nature of COIN operations, the possibility of escalatory involvement should be a major consideration during the formulation of the concept of operations (CONOPS). If the assessment of the situation is thorough enough and accurate, then the level of engagement chosen should be sufficient to address the problem. However, more often than not, countries significantly underestimate the scale of effort required to defeat an insurgency. If escalation of involvement is required, it should be anticipated that a full reassessment of the situation and a strategic policy decision might be required prior to a major increase of involvement.

d. The context for US involvement in COIN is based on three possible strategic objectives: assist an established HN government as part of FID; as an adjunct to US major combat operations; or US operations in a UGA. As outsiders seeking to shape the politics of a foreign society and foster legitimate and effective local governance, the US will be involved in COIN as a third party. Third-party counterinsurgents face a series of challenges in addition to those inherent to COIN. Those challenges manifest themselves in different ways and to different degrees depending on the scale of the US presence and its political and security role.

(1) **Understanding the Conflict.** Insurgencies reflect the specific social, economic, cultural, political, historical, and geographic context of the society in which they are fought. Understanding the nuances and interrelationships of these factors—how they coalesce into opportunity, motive, and means—represents a fundamental challenge for outsiders. The existence of an insurgency powerful enough that outside help is required suggests that even the HN government may not have an accurate understanding of its own society. For third-party counterinsurgents, understanding all the dimensions of the conflict, how it varies across the operational, and what constitutes a realistic politico-military strategy to foster durable stability represents a recurring challenge.

See Chapter II, "Insurgency," paragraph 2, "Nature of Insurgency," and Chapter IV, "The Operational Environment."

(2) **Willingness of HN to Reform.** Whether acting in support of an existing HN government or seeking to establish a new legitimate political authority, third-party counterinsurgents rely on local partners to assume responsibility for governance. However, the existence of an insurgency indicates that a substantial part of the population perceives the HN government providing poor governance or may even be illegitimate. While improving the capacity of the HN government to control its territory and population is key, addressing

the critical grievances is also necessary to end the insurgency. US counterinsurgents will often have to cajole or coerce HN governments and entrenched elites to recognize the legitimacy of those grievances and address them. This is especially true where reforms would involve compromising the political and financial interests of those elites. As a result, US counterinsurgents have to put as much effort into understanding and shaping the behavior of their HN partners as they do into countering the insurgents. This typically requires a critical assessment of the motivations and interests of factions and individuals within the HN government, and their connections to elements of the broader HN society. See Chapter IV, "The Operational Environment," for more detail.

(3) **Assistance as a Source of Corruption.** HN government corruption is often a root cause of the opportunity, motive, and means that lead to insurgency. In many cases that corruption is linked to the reliance of the HN government on revenue from external sources, such as the export of high-value natural resources or the rent of military bases. The reliance on external sources of revenue undermines the relationship between the government and the population, and turns the state into a source of private profit for those in power. This pattern typically results in poor governance, gross income inequality, and abusive security forces. Additional assistance provided by US counterinsurgents can unintentionally exacerbate this pattern by reinforcing the dependency of the HN government on outsiders in order to maintain control. Spending by external counterinsurgents seeking to foster stability can actually insulate the HN government from pressure to reform, or even encourage further corruption and abuses by creating perverse incentives. Reliance on international contractors can have the unintended effect of creating a contract economy, which almost by its nature invites corruption, of retarding HN government capacity building because the HN government never gets to do anything on its own, and of creating exorbitant inflation in the local market. US counterinsurgents must carefully calibrate civil and military assistance programs to ensure they are having the desired political impact, and focus assistance programs on only the critical issues driving the insurgency. Long-term development challenges are best addressed once the conflict is resolved.

(4) **Legitimacy of Outside Interveners.** Beyond relations with the HN government, US counterinsurgents also have to consider their legitimacy among the HN population. The initial legitimacy of US counterinsurgents varies depending on the nature of the conflict, but outsiders are always vulnerable to allegations of exploitation, oppression, profiteering, or neo-colonialism. If the population perceives the US as illegitimate, this perception may taint the HN government by association. Conversely, support for an abusive HN government can damage the legitimacy of the US, undermining its ability to sustain support to the COIN. Low legitimacy also constrains the political freedom of action of US counterinsurgents, making them more dependent on the HN government and less able to apply pressure for necessary reforms. These risks can be mitigated through the scale and form of engagement, but US counterinsurgents should consider how to maintain and build their legitimacy among the HN population as a challenge distinct from, but interrelated with, building the legitimacy of the HN government.

(5) **Responsibility for HN Government Actions.** A fundamental dilemma of US counterinsurgents is being held responsible for the conduct of HN partners that the US counterinsurgent does not control. HN governments face insurgencies because state

institutions are ineffective at meeting the population's needs or are outright abusive. In many cases, that behavior reflects deeply rooted problems with the nature of the HN government. It takes time to address those problems even with the support of third-party counterinsurgents, and military and civil assistance can be used in ways that third-party counterinsurgents did not intend. However, the HN population, the media, the international community, and the US population will hold the USG responsible for the actions of the HN partners that the US supports. This creates a risk that should be carefully accounted for during planning, and mitigation strategies should be developed to prevent and respond to incidents of abuse by HN partners. Such strategies should include both remedial action and clear messaging, especially to the local population. HN populations may interpret a lack of public reaction by US counterinsurgents to misbehavior by HN partners as an endorsement of such abuses.

e. **Challenges of Small Footprint Approach**

(1) **Limited Access to HN Population.** Small footprint approaches also have drawbacks. Chief among them can be the dependence on the HN government for access to the population. HN governments will often seek to portray insurgents as extremists and grievances as fabrications in order to secure assistance and insulate themselves from pressure to reform from third-party counterinsurgents. In some instances, HN governments may seek to restrict US access to credible voices of popular dissent by actively or passively limiting the mobility of US personnel on the ground. Moreover, the population may not trust HN security forces with a history of human rights abuses or perceived sectarian bias to protect them, making it difficult to counter insurgent intimidation and shadow governance.

(2) **Limited Knowledge, Oversight, and Mentoring.** HN government reporting often presents a distorted picture of the situation. While small footprint approaches have advantages, the limited number of US personnel in the operational area can make it difficult to gather sufficient information for an independent assessment. Understanding HN government decision making and monitoring its conduct—especially when employing third-party assistance—can prove a challenge with limited personnel. Moreover, embedded mentors are often critical to ensure that HNSF behave professionally and adhere to US-provided training in COIN while conducting operations. When planning for small footprint approaches to third-party COIN, JFCs should consider how many personnel will be required to ensure an accurate assessment of the situation and that US assistance is having the intended politico-military effects.

(3) **Limited Combat Capability and Influence over Security Forces.** In many COIN operations, HNSF are more of a threat to the civilian population than the insurgent forces. Their limited combat capability allows insurgents to seize and retain the initiative, while abuses against the civilian population validate the insurgent narrative and widen its support. While putting HNSF in the lead for combat operations avoids creating a dependency, doing so prematurely has undermined training and reform efforts in some cases. Where local forces are in the lead, experience has shown that embedded mentors are often critical to ensure that HNSF adhere to US-provided training in COIN while conducting operations. In extreme cases, the perceived or real drawbacks of HNSF in the eyes of the population may make them an impediment rather than asset to COIN efforts in some parts of

the operational area. In those circumstances, JFCs employing a small footprint approach will have to develop alternative/interim approaches to securing communities against insurgent violence.

   f. **Challenges of Large Footprint Approach.** Joint forces may conduct COIN with a large ground presence in situations where there is no HN government, such as in a UGA, or in conjunction with an occupation as part of a larger regime change operation authorized by the United Nations (UN) Security Council, if resistance arises, or at the invitation of an HN government.

      (1) In the case of an occupation, the law of war (see Appendix B, "Authorities in Counterinsurgency Operations") requires the occupying force to provide military governance to the local population. International law is clear in regard to the responsibilities of the occupying power—it must provide security to the local population, it must ensure access to essential services, and it must enforce local laws, unless those laws are contrary to internationally recognized human rights principles. Although some segments of the local population may view the regime change as a liberation, certain other segments of the population, often defined by their religious, ethno-sectarian, or regional identity, may view the operation as a hostile invasion. From the external counterinsurgent's perspective, whether the local population views the operation as a liberation or not, the law of war responsibilities of an occupying power still apply.

      (2) **Usurpation of Sovereignty.** The larger the foreign presence in the midst of an armed conflict, the greater the opportunity for collateral damage and the greater the risk for the second- and third-order effects of lethal operations to take their toll on the patience and welcome of the local population. If a large foreign presence overstays its welcome, the HN government will rarely be seen by the population as truly sovereign, no matter how much time, effort, and resources the JFC and civilian authorities put into reinforcing the legitimacy of the HN government. Rather, it will be perceived as a puppet government, and the commander of the foreign forces will be perceived as the true sovereign power.

      (3) **Enhancement of Insurgent Narrative.** The extended presence of large numbers of foreign forces can feed the insurgent narrative of an illegitimate occupation, create suspicions of neo-colonialism, and lead to all manner of conspiracy theories as to the true intentions of the foreign forces.

      (4) **Distortive Effect on HNSF.** A large foreign ground force can inhibit the development of HNSF by assuming too many responsibilities, by attempting to train local forces to standards that are unattainable in the local context, by using weapons and equipment that are too sophisticated for the local context, and by providing salaries and resources to local forces that are unsustainable over the long term.

   g. **Strategy and Operational Art in COIN.** During the planning process, JFCs should carefully assess the OE, the nature of the challenge, and the strategic context for US involvement. This will typically involve a more detailed analysis of the situation at the operational and tactical levels than those undertaken at strategic and policy levels. In considering how ends, ways, and means can be aligned to attain US strategic goals, JFCs should assess whether US strategic assumptions accurately reflect the situation at the operational and tactical level. Where a disconnect is evident, JFCs should engage with strategic and policy leaders to share their assessment of the challenge and request clarification or reconsideration of strategic guidance. All COIN is ultimately local; JFCs should ensure that strategic and policy leaders understand the limits of any operational approach to generate lasting stability if the political strategy does not account for the realities of politics in the operational area.

5. Operational Approaches

The operational approach is a commander's description of the broad actions the force must take to achieve the desired military end state. Framed by the strategy of a comprehensive approach to COIN, the JFC's operational approach is largely based on the JFC's understanding of the OE and the specific insurgency. Successful development of the operational approach requires continuous analysis, learning, assessment, dialogue, and collaboration between commander and staff, as well as other subject matter experts including other interagency and multinational partners in unified action. The following should influence the development of the JFC's operational approach to COIN.

a. **FID.** There must be both a legal basis and Presidential approval for US forces to conduct COIN combat operations in conjunction with or in place of HN forces. The third category of FID combat operations may be required if the first two categories of FID were insufficient for the HN to disrupt or defeat the insurgency and the HN is on the brink of being overwhelmed. The USG would either initiate or continue indirect and direct support (i.e., a FID program) of HN forces so they could at some time assume the primary and then full role in combat operations against the insurgency. This would be part of SC and direct intervention levels of USG COIN involvement. The JFC, in conjunction with the COM, must coordinate procedures for an orderly transition of a number of different security and stability activities that fall into one or more of those efforts, and those activities may be part of a range of possible activities in the operational approach to COIN. Commanders adjust their approach as circumstances change, especially the security situation. Increasing the training for HN capacity, including their ability for training themselves, in conjunction with US combat operations is normally an imperative to the USG COIN end state of transitioning total control back to the HN.

See JP 3-22, Foreign Internal Defense, *for full discussion of the three categories of FID.*

b. **Isolate the Insurgents.** While it may be required to kill or capture a number of insurgents out of operational necessity, it is still necessary to isolate the insurgency from the population and its resources, especially any external support. The ability to continue to isolate the insurgency puts it more on the defensive and disrupts its ability to conduct violence that may require confrontational police or military action, which risks generating popular resentment, creating martyrs that motivate new recruits, and producing cycles of revenge. Isolation of the insurgency should be both psychological and physical. As the HN government increases its legitimacy, the populace begins to assist it more actively. Eventually, the people marginalize and stigmatize insurgents to the point that the insurgency's claim to legitimacy is destroyed. Isolation is not an end in and of itself, but a means to reestablish legitimate government functions and regain popular support, rendering the insurgent narrative obsolete.

(1) **Deny Anonymity.** One of the greatest weapons an insurgent network has is the ability to blend in and disappear within the local population. The ability to rout an insurgency depends heavily on our ability to identify and neutralize the relevant actors within the population who are executing its activities. Counterinsurgents must actively seek to establish the identity of insurgent actors and use that information to track, target, and attack the networks they operate within. Identity intelligence (I2) operations should be executed as continuously as possible across all phases of a COIN operation.

(2) **Deprive the Insurgency.** Counterinsurgents must cut off the flow of arms and ammunition into the area and eliminate their sources of all forms of logistics. An effective weapon in denying logistics to an insurgency is populace and resource control. These two controls are distinct, yet linked, and normally a responsibility of indigenous civilian governments. They are defined and enforced during times of civil or military emergency.

(a) Populace control provides security for the populace, mobilizes HN human resources, denies personnel to the enemy, and detects and reduces the effectiveness of enemy agents. Populace control measures include curfews, registration in a biometric database, establishing persistent surveillance systems, movement restrictions, travel permits, registration cards, and relocation of the population. However, such controls on a large scale should be assessed to ensure their effectiveness against the insurgents, measured against the undesired effects created on the population that could be counterproductive and viewed as part of a "police state."

(b) Resource control regulates the movement or consumption of materiel resources, mobilizes materiel resources, and denies materiel to the enemy. Resources control measures include licensing, regulations or guidelines, checkpoints (for example, roadblocks), ration controls, amnesty programs, and inspection of facilities. Intelligence that pinpoints insurgency-related resources, safe houses, weapons caches, or other assets help focus the resource control.

(3) **CTF.** COIN operations need to determine and the exploit insurgent funding and financial weaknesses. CTF is an LOE within COIN. An insurgency is dependent upon the stability and security of their financial networks to sustain operations. CTF is used to deny, disrupt, defeat, or degrade an insurgent's local and global ability to generate, safeguard, and disperse revenue. A full understanding of the insurgency network includes an understanding of the internal and external insurgent financial network. CTF activities may occur at the tactical, operational, and strategic level. The JFC may need to rapidly expand the scope of CTF activities by establishing a TFC at the operational level. The TFC, consisting of military and USG personnel, identifies and synchronizes CTF efforts of the HN, US interagency, intelligence community, and the international community. The TFC will enhance collection, analysis, and dissemination of intelligence to map the financial network, and develop DA and indirect action to disrupt the insurgency without adversely affecting the population. Working closely with the COM and HN, the CTF identifies and targets threat finance sources and enhances collection, analysis, and dissemination of

intelligence to support and strengthen US, multination, and HN efforts to disrupt and eliminate key insurgent financial network nodes. The JFC CTF activities are dependent upon the authorities approved by the Secretary of Defense (SecDef)/President and the support and use of inherent authorities and activities of the Department of State (DOS), the Department of Justice (DOJ), and the Department of the Treasury. Effective law enforcement can be detrimental to an insurgency that uses criminal means for funding (e.g., bank robberies and kidnappings). Department of the Treasury designations and other diplomatic tools outside the scope of DOD are key to CTF. The JFC should have to work closely with the COM and the CTF lead to identify and target threat finance sources, and may even consider the creation of interagency and TFC to enhance the collection, analysis, and dissemination of intelligence to support and strengthen all efforts to disrupt and eliminate key insurgent financial network nodes. CTF activities are normally part of attack the network (AtN) operations.

For more information on CTF, see Chapter VII, "Supporting Operations for Counterinsurgency," paragraph 10, "Counter Threat Finance."

(4) **Promote Local Reintegration.** Together with HN partners, identify and separate the "reconcilables" from the "irreconcilables." Identify and report obstacles to reintegration. Help the HN address grievances and strive to make the reconcilables part of the local solution. See Chapter VIII, "Building Governance to Support Counterinsurgency," paragraph 6, "Disarmament, Demobilization, and Reintegration," for more discussion.

(5) **Insurgency Leaders.** Accurately determining whether an insurgency leader can be dissuaded from insurgency and won over to the HN side is sometimes crucial. However, attempts to win over traditional leaders can backfire if those leaders choose to oppose the HN. Insurgency leaders who refuse to accept HN overtures can strengthen their standing as they gain power and influence among insurgents, especially if this refusal is well exploited through subsequent propaganda. Insurgent authority figures need to be neutralized through changing allegiance or by bringing discredit/distrust to the leader or position. While eliminating an insurgent leader may harm or disrupt the insurgency, it may have unwanted results such as creating a martyr for the insurgents or causing popular backlash. Exploitation of known insurgent leaders should also be considered.

c. **Disaggregation.** Some insurgencies, especially those affected by transnational terrorists, may ultimately aspire to larger regional and even global ends, but they must first succeed in their own country. Whether or not such an affiliation is made, an insurgency is almost always a collection of groups, sometimes disparate groups, and typically is not one monolithic organization. Smaller groups can be subordinate parts of one unified insurgency or just willing participants who share similar goals. Associations can range from a temporary affiliation to achieve a shared objective to actually beginning the process of organizationally becoming one group of subordinate parts. From a COIN perspective, disaggregation is used to divide and conquer the groups fomenting insurgency, including any element of transnational terrorists, and cutting any external support. The first step in disaggregation is cognitive: identify fissures (i.e., vulnerabilities) in the insurgency, the easiest being identification of separate groups. This requires a deep understanding of the OE and, more specifically, an understanding of all the adversaries (i.e., insurgents, anarchists, local terrorists, transnational terrorists, organized criminal elements, and external supporters); and knowing that different groups may not be affected by the same COIN LOEs or lines of operation (LOOs). Subsequently, a strategy of disaggregation includes the following activities: containment, isolation, disruption, neutralization in detail, and perhaps resolution of core grievances. Containment, isolation, and disruption should be implemented concurrently, as soon as possible. While the previous three aspects require political consensus, the choice of what insurgency to neutralize in detail is a shared strategic policy decision among all nations involved. The cost of disaggregation is that it makes a negotiated settlement more difficult since there is no one leader or small group of leaders who exercise control over the various components of the insurgency network. Hence low-level terrorist attacks and other types of violence are likely to persist.

d. **Addressing Root Causes.** To defeat some insurgencies, counterinsurgents may have to address the root causes including popular grievances fueling the insurgency. While this might entail political and civil action of the HN government, the joint force should understand the root causes and be prepared to support the comprehensive approach to address them. Effectively addressing root causes can facilitate isolating the insurgent from the population. It is important to understand addressing root causes is not the same as solving all of the root causes. Some root causes may be HN institutional inadequacies (e.g., internal security or economic development) and some may be political, economic, or sociological grievances of segments of the indigenous population. It is also important to understand those particular grievances that insurgents exploit in their narrative.

e. **Neutralizing in Detail.** Defeating an insurgency and/or the influence of a transnational terrorist organization is an immense task. In COIN operations, the aspects of disaggregation listed in paragraph 5c, "Disaggregation," should all occur simultaneously to deal with all the groups involved with insurgency. However, countering an insurgency across a large geographic area may preclude being able to bring enough assets to bear simultaneously, even through distributed operations. Thus, political and military decision makers must choose exactly where to focus their efforts. When more assets are available or the first area is secured, a subsequent area on which to focus can be identified. Thus, where to "neutralize the insurgency in detail" is fundamentally an issue of how to allocate scarce means and where to accept risk. Neutralizing in detail is also used for CT operations in the global campaign against transnational extremist organizations.

f. **Transnational Violent Extremists.** The influence of transnational violent extremist organizations (transnational terrorists), such as al Qaeda and its associates, on certain insurgencies has added to the complexity and therefore the challenge of conducting COIN. The HN and USG COIN effort in a given country must analyze the potential for transnational terrorist activities, and whether or not they are an acknowledged part of the insurgency network(s) in the affected HN. The challenge posed by transnational extremists has been documented globally, and in some regions, it crosses area of responsibility (AOR) boundaries. US policy and strategy have designated transnational terrorists as such, and not as insurgents, even if one of their primary objectives is the overthrow of the sitting governments in the affected countries in a region. The US global campaign against transnational terrorists, and the role of Commander, US Special Operations Command as the DOD global synchronizer for CT planning, should provide seamless capabilities that are employed globally in coordination with the GCCs and integrated with their theaters' counterterrorist assets. Although the influence of the transnational terrorists may be felt across a region and globally, an insurgency is nation-centric as is a COIN effort. The COIN effort is supported, as necessary, by dedicated counterterrorist capabilities under a DOD global campaign plan which in turn is supported by appropriate theater concept/operation plans.

6. Employment Considerations

a. **Mission Command.** As joint land operations tend to become decentralized, mission command becomes the preferred method of command and control (C2). Successful mission command demands that subordinate leaders at all echelons exercise disciplined initiative, acting aggressively and independently to accomplish the mission. Essential to mission command is the thorough knowledge and understanding of the commander's intent at every level of command. Under mission command, commanders issue mission type orders, use implicit communications, and delegate most decisions to subordinates wherever possible. Mission command is especially suited to distributed operations by land forces in a COIN operation.

(1) **Decentralized Execution.** COIN requires empowering the lowest levels for decentralized execution (and in some cases decentralized planning) based upon mission command, centralized planning and direction, and mission command. The strategy and operational approach should be tailored to the local conditions. This is not just applicable between the operational and tactical levels, but within the tactical level. Distributed operations require decentralized execution in conjunction with the intelligence-operations fusion at the lowest possible level. The joint force must position joint bases and combat outposts as close as feasible to the population that it is seeking to secure, relying on local intelligence and security assessments. Commanders must provide subordinates with a mission, commander's intent, CONOPS, and resources adequate to accomplish the mission. They leave details of execution to their subordinates and expect them to use initiative and judgment to accomplish the mission.

(a) **Initiative.** Successful decentralized execution results from exercise, by subordinate leaders at all echelons, of disciplined initiative within the commander's intent to accomplish missions. It requires an environment of trust and mutual understanding and is the preferred method for commanding and controlling COIN forces.

(b) **Mosaic Nature.** The mosaic nature of COIN is ideally suited to decentralized execution. On-scene commanders often have the best grasp of their tactical situations. Counterinsurgents that win this kind of mosaic war are those able to respond to all forms of insurgent operations, often simultaneously; thus, commanders must allow them access or control of the resources needed to produce timely intelligence, conduct effective tactical operations, and manage IO.

(2) **Distributed Operations.** COIN operations often require units, sometimes widely distributed and beyond mutually supporting range of each other, to conduct nonlinear activities/operations often in small noncontiguous operational areas within the joint

operations area. These distributed operations allow counterinsurgents to respond to all forms of insurgent activities, often simultaneously, and across a large area. The JFC should consider options whereby joint capabilities can be pushed to lower levels and placed under the control or in support of units that can use them effectively. Thus, commanders must allow subordinates access to, and control of, the resources needed to produce timely intelligence, conduct effective tactical operations, and information-related capabilities within their operational area.

(3) **Distribute Resources Across Echelons.** Commanders are often faced with combat situations where they may have little experience or resources and little time to prepare. In such cases, additional assets/capabilities may be assigned or attached to a unit to allow it to perform its mission more effectively. Whether a commander has several months or only a few days to plan, prepare for, and train/rehearse for a mission, shortfalls in required assets/capabilities may become evident that require a commander and staff to seek additional assistance from outside sources. A commander may find that a changing phase of an operation requires additional or different skill sets to accomplish the mission. In these instances higher headquarters must be prepared, proactive, and expeditious in augmenting their subordinates with the expertise they require to enable effective COIN operations. Key enablers that consist of low density personnel and equipment must be adequately identified and planned for across the joint force. A thorough analysis of the COIN operation should allocate resources such as intelligence, aviation, route clearance, logistics, interpreters, translators, cultural advisors, and ordnance, among others, to allow for the requisite skill or equipment to support the joint force LOE at the correct echelon. Recent COIN experiences have shown, particularly in functions such as intelligence, that higher echelons may have to push or redistribute essential analysts to a lower level (company or platoon) where they can be employed most effectively.

b. **Task-Organizing for COIN**

(1) **Adapt to Local Conditions.** The nature of insurgency requires that the commander's operational approach be flexible enough to adapt specific tactical activities to local conditions.

(2) **Unit Mix.** Units engaged at the local level need the right mix of military personnel (e.g., low-density enablers) ideally partnered with any civilians engaged in COIN.

(3) **Intelligence Assets.** Intelligence collection and analysis assets need to be pushed to the lowest levels to enable rapid learning and adaptation (e.g., operations-intelligence fusion). Tactical units need to adapt to a decision cycle, such as the observe, orient, decide, act (OODA) loop that is as fast or faster than that of insurgents.

(4) **COIN Narrative.** The force should be organized to balance coordination and consistency between levels while fostering adaptation and innovation at local levels in line with the COIN narrative.

c. Predeployment Training Requirements

(1) **COIN Environment.** In a COIN environment, tasks will often need to be carried out in ways generally requiring specialized training and sometimes requiring development of new TTP. The targeted application of diplomatic, informational, military, and economic capabilities in a conflict situation is fraught with the risk of unintended consequences and requires a sophisticated understanding of the local situation. COIN often involves a wider range of tasks and capabilities than are required in traditional warfare.

(2) **Sociocultural and Political-Military Context.** To implement a COIN strategy successfully, US forces and the DOD civilians that support them must be prepared for the operational, geographic, and sociocultural complexities of the OE. A force's training, personnel processes, and programs must be aligned to provide deploying units, leaders, and staffs with language, cultural, tactical, interagency, and advisory skills required to conduct COIN operations successfully in support of an HN government. The deploying force must understand that military operations and TTP support the political strategy. As a guide, DOD Inspector General vetted training requirements prior to COIN deployments are shown in Figure III-2.

See Appendix C, "Example Counterinsurgency Qualification Standards Outline," for an example that expands on these requirements.

(3) **Leadership and Ethics.** One of the most difficult aspects of preparing for COIN operations is the need to prepare Service members and units to take aggressive action against the enemy while also training them to identify noncombatants from combatants and to avoid abusive behavior and use of excessive force during extremely stressful combat situations. Training must prepare Service members and units for the debilitating effects of fear and combat stress. Ensuring legal conduct during COIN operations is particularly difficult because the COIN environment is often characterized by violence, immorality, distrust, and deceit. Preserving innocent lives and maintaining human dignity are central to COIN mission accomplishment. The COIN environment often presents complex emotional and ethical dilemmas. Service members must remain faithful to basic American and military standards of behavior and respect for the sanctity of life.

Notional Predeployment Counterinsurgency
Training Requirements

1. Country orientation brief

2. Antiterrorism training

3. Rules of engagement

4. Rules for the use of force

5. Media awareness

6. Weapons qualification

7. Chemical, biological, radiological, and nuclear personnel
   protective measures

8. First aid

9. Unexploded ordnance and improvised explosive device

10. Land navigation

11. Combat lifesaver

12. Combat and operational stress and suicide prevention

13. Regulatory briefings

14. Compliance with law of war and Geneva and Hague Conventions

Figure III-2. Notional Predeployment Counterinsurgency Training Requirements

Intentionally Blank

CHAPTER IV
THE OPERATIONAL ENVIRONMENT

> *"War is not a chess game, but a vast social phenomenon with an infinitely greater and ever expanding number of variables, some of which elude analysis."*
>
> **Lieutenant Colonel David Galula (French Army),**
> ***Counterinsurgency Warfare* (1964)**

1. Introduction

a. **Understanding the OE.** An understanding of the OE enables the development of a COIN approach that includes realistic, achievable objectives, and properly aligns ends, ways, and means. Understanding of the OE is accomplished through tailoring the joint intelligence preparation of the operational environment (JIPOE) and assessment requirements for a COIN environment. Through enhanced understanding of the OE, the JFC can improve the ability to:

(1) Decipher the true nature of the problem the joint operation is meant to resolve.

(2) Develop realistic military end states and objectives.

(3) Develop an operational approach that is relevant to the nature of the conflict, appropriate for the operational area, and feasible based on available resources.

(4) Consider relevant aspects of the OE during the planning and execution of activities and operations that require lethal and nonlethal fires.

b. The OE is the composite of the conditions, circumstances, and influences that affect how the JFC uses available capabilities and makes decisions. The OE typically encompasses the relevant actors and the physical areas and factors of the physical domains and the information environment. Within COIN, understanding the OE requires a holistic view of PMESII systems. The decision making of relevant actors and the public opinion of the local population are major considerations in a COIN operation. Thus, understanding the OE requires an understanding of the factors that shape the decision making and associated behavior of significant actors. A holistic understanding of all relevant components within the OE helps the JFC to understand how the OE can be shaped, how the OE affects capabilities, and how friendly, adversary, and neutral actors' actions affect or shape the conflict. Of greatest significance, understanding relevant aspects of the OE enables the JFC to leverage aspects of the OE to achieve COIN objectives.

c. Understanding the OE in COIN informs planning, execution, and assessment of various aspects of the operation.

(1) **Planning.** During planning, understanding the OE is a critical aspect of the mission analysis process. It helps identify the true nature of the problem, the mission, and the factors within the OE that must be targeted through lethal and nonlethal means to achieve the desired political end state of the COIN operation. Understanding the OE enables the

design of missions and activities that make sense for the nature of the conflict and that are appropriate in the context of the operational area. It also enables JFC planners to improve planning by better understanding potential second- and third-order effects.

(2) **Execution.** Once a mission or activity in support of the operation is planned, understanding of relevant factors within the OE enables operators to better execute their missions in a manner that furthers progress toward the objectives of the COIN operation. Much of the information to support operations is gathered at the tactical level, and the process by which the operational level seeks to understand key aspects of the OE may involve tasking operators at the tactical level to collect certain information. However, operational-level planners also have the ability to pull from an assortment of national-level resources to provide operators the information they need to have the best chance of success.

(3) **Assessment.** Operational assessment in COIN links the theoretical (prediction of relevant actors' COAs) with the actual (how are the actors behaving?). It helps answer the question: what is the current status of the OE in relation to the established objectives of the operation? By developing a clear understanding of the current state of these relevant factors, a determination can be made about progress (or lack thereof) toward the desired end state of the COIN operation. The joint process for assessment is detailed in JP 3-0, *Joint Operations,* and is also explained in JP 5-0, *Joint Operation Planning.*

See Chapter VI, "Assessing Counterinsurgency Operations," for detail on assessment in COIN operations.

2. **Operational Environment in Counterinsurgency**

a. **Components.** The various components of the OE provide a lens through which a COIN force may gain an understanding of the decision making and associated behavior of the relevant actors. The COIN OE encompasses the relevant actors and the physical areas and factors within the physical domains and the information environment.

b. **Relevant Actors.** The most important component of the OE is the relevant actors. These include the population, the COIN force, the HN government, and the insurgents. Other relevant actors may include supporting state actors and non-state actors (e.g., transnational terrorist or criminal organizations) and/or the NGO community. By first understanding who the relevant actors are and learning as much as possible about them, the JFC develops an approach that may influence the actors decision making and behavior (active or passive) in a way that is consistent with the desired end state of the operation. In a COIN environment, individuals may fit into more than one category of actor (e.g., a tribal leader may also work as a district governor, while also working behind the scenes to provide financial and material support to the insurgency).

c. **Physical Factors.** In COIN operations, the physical factors of the operational area typically and predominantly concern the land domain. It includes the terrain (including urban settings), infrastructure (including the location of bases and ports), topography, hydrology, and environmental conditions in the operational area, as well as the distances associated with deployment to the operational area and the employment of forces and other joint capabilities. Collectively, many of these factors influence the operational design and sustainment of joint operations. In COIN, the important aspects of the physical factors are those that either provide insight into, or impact, the decisions and behavior of the various relevant actors within the operational area. Appreciation of these aspects of the OE facilitates planning and execution of the COIN operation.

d. **Information Environment.** The information environment refers to the aggregate of individuals, organizations, and systems that collect, process, disseminate, or act on information. It includes many different physical and nonphysical aspects of the OE. Depending on the specific OE, relevant aspects of the information environment may include media outlets such as radio and television; Internet communications such as e-mail and social networking sites; cellular telephone and radio communication; and channels of information flow via word of mouth. The information environment also includes the infrastructure and technology that supports the various types of communication. Understanding relevant aspects of the information environment enhances the JFC's ability to predict, respond to, and/or influence the behavior of actors within the OE.

For more detail on the holistic view of the OE, see JP 2-01.3, Joint Intelligence Preparation of the Operational Environment.

3. **Tools and Methods for Understanding the Operational Environment**

Many tools and methodologies have been developed that are worthy of consideration by the JFC for understanding the OE for a COIN operation.

a. **Traditional Intelligence Approaches.** Tailoring traditional intelligence methodologies to a focus on relevant actors improves prediction of their decision making and associated behavior and informs appropriate COAs. All of the intelligence disciplines are relevant to understanding the OE in COIN.

b. **Intelligence, Surveillance, and Reconnaissance.** Intelligence assets, especially unmanned aircraft systems, have emerged as reliable and highly beneficial to a more holistic understanding of the OE. For instance, satellite imagery can be used to show the frequented locations of various actors in operational areas, while other intelligence assets have enabled the JFC to develop a more robust understanding of broader opportunity, motive, and means of insurgents, in addition to fulfilling more traditional roles of monitoring adversary military capabilities, often in real time. Because intelligence assets are also essential to support security and lethal fires, land forces may have to compete for scarce intelligence resources and utilize intelligence assets in nontraditional ways to support COIN.

c. **Sociocultural Analysis.** Sociocultural analysis is the analysis of adversaries and other relevant actors that integrates concepts, knowledge, and understanding of societies, populations, and other groups of people, including their activities, relationships, and perspectives across time and space at varying scales. In the JIPOE process, sociocultural analysis is an application of methodologies to help discern drivers of behavior for groups and individuals. An enhanced ability to analyze the sociocultural factors provides the potential to predict, respond to, and/or influence decision making and associated behavior by the relevant actors. Several subsets of sociocultural analysis relevant to COIN that have been used in the past include:

(1) **Mapping of the Sociocultural Factors.** Sociocultural mapping integrates georeferenced social, cultural, political, economic, and infrastructure data and elements of the information environment into all-source and multi-intelligence analyses concerning the operational area. The JFC may realize significant sociocultural differences among groups/individuals associated with an insurgency in the operational area.

(2) **Human Geography.** Geography is the study of places and the relationships between people and their environments. Human geography focuses on the relationships between people and places, emphasizing spatial-temporal patterns of people, particularly their traits and activities, in the context of their geographic environment.

(3) **Sociocultural Dynamics Analysis.** This is the analysis of the social, cultural, and behavioral, factors that characterize the relationships of the population and individuals of interest in a specific region or operational area. It includes population support and stability; population and environmental characteristics; populations supporting active insurgencies; human factors; cultural factors within foreign military and security forces; foreign media analyses; and population support to covert military operations.

(4) **Human Factors Analysis.** This involves the psychological, cultural, behavioral and other human attributes that influence decision making, and information interpretation by individuals or groups at any level in any state or organization.

d. **Analytical frameworks** can be useful in understanding the OE in COIN because they encourage a more holistic analysis. However, considering the various focus areas within the analytical frameworks alone does not guarantee an operationally relevant understanding of the OE.

(1) Joint doctrine provides many analytical frameworks for analyzing the OE. The following analytical frameworks point toward a very broad set of considerations that the JFC makes in all operations:

(a) Mission, enemy, terrain and weather, troops and support available-time available, and, when appropriate, civilian considerations. For examples of civilian considerations, see Figure IV-1.

(b) Areas, structures, capabilities, organizations, people, and events (ASCOPE). See subparagraph 7a for further details regarding ASCOPE.

(c) PMESII

(2) On a cautionary note, the JFC can produce endless streams of information under each category of a framework, but operational relevance is the key to making each of these analytic processes useful. This is done through analyzing the components of the frameworks and assessing whether they support the strategy of the COIN operation or campaign and

Potential Analytical Frameworks

	P Political	M Military	E Economic	S Social	I Information	I Infrastructure
A Areas	District boundary, provincial boundary, party affiliation areas	MNF, HNSF bases, historical ambush/IED sites	Bazaar areas, farming areas, livestock dealers, repair shops	Traditional picnic areas, bazaars, outdoor meeting sites	Radio/TV/paper coverage areas, graffiti, posters, word of mouth gathering points	Irrigation networks, water tables, areas with medical services
S Structures	Provincial/district centers, meeting halls, polling sites	Provincial/district police HQ, INS leaders houses/ businesses	Bazaars, grain storage, businesses, banks	Religious sites, worship centers, popular gathering sites, restaurants	Cellular, radio, TV towers, print shops, newspapers	Roads, bridges, rail lines, gas lines, electrical lines, dams
C Capabilities	Dispute resolution, local leadership, judges, INS ability to affect	HNSF providing 24/7 security/ QRF present/ INS strength/ weapons recruiting	Access to banks, ability to withstand drought, development, black market	Strength of tribal, family, or village traditional structures, religious leaders, justice means	Literacy rates, availability of electronic media, phone service	Ability to build or maintain roads/bridges/ dams/irrigation systems
O Organizations	Political parties, INS networks affiliations, government, IGO, and NGO	Multinational and HNSF presence, INS network(s) presence	Banks, large landholders, cooperatives, economic development NGO	Tribes, clans, families, sports groups, youth groups or organizations	News organizations, influential religious centers, INS IO groups	Government ministries, construction companies
P People	Mayors, governors, councils, elders, judges, religious leaders	Multinational, HNSF, INS military leaders	Bankers, landholders, merchants, money lenders, criminals	Religious/civic leaders, elders, council members, influential families	Media owners, religious/civic leaders, elders, heads of families, merchants	Builders, engineers, contractors, local development councils
E Events	Elections, campaigns, council meetings, speeches, trials	Tactical engagements, loss of leadership, operations, unit RIP	Drought, harvest, business openings, loss of business, good/ bad harvests	Worship days, religious/civic holidays, weddings, funerals, births, market days	Worship days, political campaigns, project openings, festivals, CIVCAS incidents	Road/bridge construction, well digging, civic center/school construction

Legend

CIVCAS	civilian casualty		MNF	multinational force
HNSF	host-nation security forces		NGO	nongovernmental organization
HQ	headquarters		QRF	quick reaction force
IED	improvised explosive device		RIP	relief in place
IGO	intergovernmental organization		TV	television
INS	insurgent			
IO	information operations			

Figure IV-1. Potential Analytical Frameworks

whether they inform the decision making and associated behavior of the relevant actors within the OE.

For more information on a holistic view of the OE, see JP 2-01.3, Joint Intelligence Preparation of the Operational Environment.

e. **Network Analysis**

(1) Social network analysis can be a useful tool to determine the various connections, nodes, and influences on particular organizations and individuals. When employing social network analysis to understand the overall OE and identify COGs and critical capability (CC)/critical requirement (CR)/critical vulnerability (CV) factors, commanders and planners take care to ensure that this process remains relevant at the operational level, resisting the temptation to break the overall OE picture into small, discrete systems and individuals. The latter may be appropriate at the tactical/targeting level, but when attempting to understand the OE and its players, commanders strive for the larger, more holistic picture. Commanders and planners are mindful that COIN is mostly a population-centric, rather than enemy-centric, effort. As such, their understanding of the OE includes the influences on, and behavior of, all relevant actors, not just the behavior of the adversary.

(2) That picture includes the extended network linkages for each node. No individual or organization is simply part of one network, and very few are either entirely supportive of US goals or entirely hostile. Understanding not just the linkages to the insurgent network and the population, but the social, political, and economic linkages outside of the insurgent network allows commanders to make more informed decisions on COAs. When evaluating the OE using a social network analysis tool, commanders and planners consider the adversary, the various elements of the population, the HN government/legitimate authority that the COIN operation is supporting, and the outside influences on these actors. There is a danger in isolating one part of the OE from the others in that it may produce an oversimplified picture of the OE, leading to operational decisions that have deleterious second- and third-order effects.

f. **Social Science.** Social science is the study of people in society and how they relate to one another and to the group to which they belong. Therefore, social science offers many tools for better understanding the OE through an actor-centric approach. Some of the primary social sciences include anthropology, archaeology, criminology, economics, education, history, linguistics, communication studies, political science, international relations, sociology, human geography, and psychology.

g. **Information Management and Information Technology.** Various classified and unclassified systems, databases, and software packages have been created to assist with enhanced understanding of the OE in COIN. However, barriers to classification, connectivity challenges, and a lack of understanding of the multitude of available systems can lead to stove-piping and/or loss of information. In a COIN operation, the JFC constructs an information management architecture that makes sense for the operation, while also accounting for the factors of each entity's structures that cannot be changed. US Cyber Command and Service components can assist with the identification of portions of the DOD information networks that need to be protected from attack by insurgent or proxy forces. In an interagency, multinational operation, there are competing requirements to meet the needs of information management and information sharing for the chain of command of each entity. Thus, the JFC makes information management a planning factor as early as possible in the operation so as to minimize obstacles to information sharing and storage caused by poorly developed infrastructures in the field.

h. **I2.** The ability to accurately identify or verify an individual is a critical component in COIN operations. In traditional conflicts the identity of individual combatants typically did not matter as their uniforms easily identified them as the enemy. However, in COIN conflicts where combatants, noncombatants, insurgents, and civilians may dress the same and live and work together, the positive identification of individual combatants assumes much greater importance. I2 is not an intelligence process, but an intelligence product that results from the fusion of specific identifying attributes (biological, biographical, behavioral, and reputational information related to an individual) and other information and intelligence associated with those attributes collected across all intelligence disciplines. I2 utilizes enabling activities, like biometrics, forensics, and document and media exploitation (DOMEX), to discover the existence of unknown potential threat actors by connecting individuals to other persons, places, events, or materials, analyzing patterns of life, and characterizing their level of potential threats to US interests.

(1) **Biometrics.** Biometrics is an enabling technology that cross-cuts many activities and operations, and is a key enabler of I2. Biometrics enhances force protection and targeting by helping to positively identify persons of interest, insurgents, terrorists, criminals, and others who would do harm to US and friendly forces and facilities. Regardless of disguises, aliases, or falsified documents, an individual's biometrics will positively identify the person. Intelligence-related functions that biometrics can support or enhance include intelligence analysis, interrogation and detention tasks, high-value target confirmation, and source vetting. Other COIN-related missions biometrics can support include:

(a) Raids and cordon operations.

(b) Base access, checkpoints, and protection of critical sites.

(c) Area security operations.

(d) Border control and ports of entry.

(e) Population census or mapping the human environment.

(f) Tracking financial transactions.

(2) **Forensics.** Forensics is the application of multidisciplinary scientific processes to establish facts that can be used by a JFC to support military operations. Forensic capabilities can be used to support intelligence functions, operational activities, force protection, HN legal support, and other related efforts. Forensic capabilities aid operations by adding depth and scope to the comprehensive operational picture. Exploited materials allow the linking of specific persons to places, materials, or events. The resulting information can provide usable intelligence to target, apprehend and detain, or prosecute criminals, terrorists, and enemy combatants. Other COIN related missions forensics can support include:

(a) Force protection and population security.

(b) Support to HN rule of law.

(c) SC.

(d) Material sourcing.

(e) AtN activities.

(f) Site exploitation.

(3) **DOMEX.** DOMEX is the processing, translation, analysis, and dissemination of collected hard-copy documents and electronic media that are under USG physical control and are not publicly available. DOMEX supports many intelligence processes. Examples include human intelligence, signals intelligence, and I2. DOMEX includes two sources of information: content of the material and (for digital media) the technical setting of the data. Content is collected in one of the 8,000 languages spoken around the world, and can include a rich supply of biometric information. The content, through letters and photos, can provide significant biographical information about individuals, their interrelationships with other members of the target group, and potentially provide clues about a group's intentions. The technical setting of the data can provide firm connections between individuals and other groups. DOMEX provides support to COIN in many areas to include:

(a) Force protection and population security.

(b) Support to HN rule of law.

(c) SC.

(d) Material sourcing.

(e) AtN activities.

For more information on I2, see JP 2-0, Joint Intelligence.

4. Establish an Evolving Common Operational Picture

a. One of the ways the JFC maintains situational awareness of the OE is through a common operational picture (COP). A COP is a single identical display of relevant information shared by more than one command that facilitates collaborative planning and assists all echelons to achieve situational awareness. The COP is not a real-time common presentation, but is developed on parameters approved by the JFC for understanding relevant aspects of the OE by joint, and if possible, interagency and multinational partners. It provides a common awareness of the OE from which to diagnose the nature of the operational problem(s) that counterinsurgents are trying to resolve, and it helps counterinsurgents plan solutions in a synchronized manner over time and space. To be successful, a COP should include significant interagency partners and—to the extent

COMMON OPERATIONAL PICTURE (COP) CONSIDERATIONS FOR COUNTERINSURGENCY OPERATIONS

The processes and procedures for establishing a COP will differ for each operation or campaign. The following considerations may be applicable to a COP:

1. **Collaborative.** A COP is developed among all relevant members of the counterinsurgency force. This means a COP is civil-military, joint, interagency, and multinational based on the participants—assuming all are present and relevant. To the extent possible, include elements of the host-nation government and the nongovernmental organization community.

2. **Comprehensive.** A COP incorporates information from all relevant available sources to include entities from within and outside of the intelligence community. This information is fused together through a system that makes sense for the size and construct of the counterinsurgency force. To the extent possible, the process for development of a COP includes a strategy for overcoming cultural, classification, and information technology-related barriers to sharing information.

3. **Continuity.** A COP includes systems for maintaining continuity across deployments as personnel are moved into new roles. This is particularly essential as personnel redeploy out of theater and new personnel arrive.

4. **Evolving.** A COP includes systems for adding new information, updating information that already exists, and correcting/modifying aspects of the COP that are no longer accurate.

5. **Process for Understanding.** A COP includes systems and processes to ensure the right people develop the understanding they need from which to plan and execute. In the development of a COP, collection, collation, and analysis are only as good as the strategy for dissemination and information management.

6. **Focused and Tailored.** A COP accounts for the limits of personnel to absorb large amounts of data. The concept of a COP does not require every actor to know everything about the operational environment. Instead, at the operational level, a COP requires a collaborative understanding of the minimum information required to inform the operation.

Various Sources

possible—multinational partners, key elements of the HN, and NGOs. However, dependent upon the sensitivity of some operating information and intelligence/information, and the JFC's and COM's information-sharing procedures, a comprehensive, overarching COP may be a challenge. The COP evolves as the operation or campaign progresses. This requires agreed upon processes for incorporating new information, updating the information that has already been accounted for, and eliminating information that is old and/or no longer accurate.

b. **Importance of a COP.** A COP supports decision making and unity of effort, a core principle of COIN. Without a shared situational awareness of relevant aspects of the OE by members of the joint force, civilian agencies, and multinational partners, separate entities within the COIN force will likely analyze problems differently, leading to uncoordinated attempts at solutions that may undermine if not conflict with one another. This diminishes unity of effort, which dilutes the richness of the COIN narrative, as projected by the COIN force's actions and messaging, and leads to the inefficient or even counterproductive use of resources. While the COP is normally maintained by the JFC, subordinate commanders and leaders may also maintain their common tactical pictures (CTPs). A CTP is an accurate and complete display of relevant tactical data that integrates tactical information from the multi-tactical data link network, ground network, intelligence network, and sensor networks. At the tactical level, the CTP is a source of situational awareness. CTP data may be used to feed the JFC's COP.

5. Joint Intelligence Preparation of the Operational Environment Process Considerations for Counterinsurgency

JIPOE is the process by which the JFC understands the OE in COIN. The JIPOE process informs the JFC's ability to predict, appropriately respond to, and/or influence the decision making and associated behavior of relevant actors within the OE. Through JIPOE, information about the OE is made useful to those charged with planning and executing the COIN operation. The standard JIPOE process is outlined in JP 2-01.3, *Joint Intelligence Preparation of the Operational Environment.* This section is not meant to replace existing doctrine for JIPOE. Instead, this section discusses special considerations for the JIPOE process with respect to a COIN environment.

a. In many operations, the defeat of the enemy's military capabilities is the main focus, which means JIPOE typically supports attaining this end state. The four steps of the doctrinal JIPOE process are:

(1) Define the OE.

(2) Describe the impact of the OE.

(3) Evaluate the adversary(ies) and other relevant actors.

(4) Determine potential COAs of the adversary(ies) and relevant actors.

b. COIN is focused on both the adversary force (insurgent force) and the elimination of conditions that are driving the continued presence of insurgency. As explained in Chapter III, "Fundamentals of Counterinsurgency," COIN success requires creation of sustainable conditions that drive decision making by relevant actors that is consistent with the desired end state of the COIN force. This requires the joint force to understand and navigate the decision cycles of the various relevant actors. This decision cycle is commonly referred to as the OODA loop (see Figure IV-2).

c. Although military defeat of some aspects of the insurgent force is important in COIN, it is usually only one component of a more comprehensive approach to affect the decision

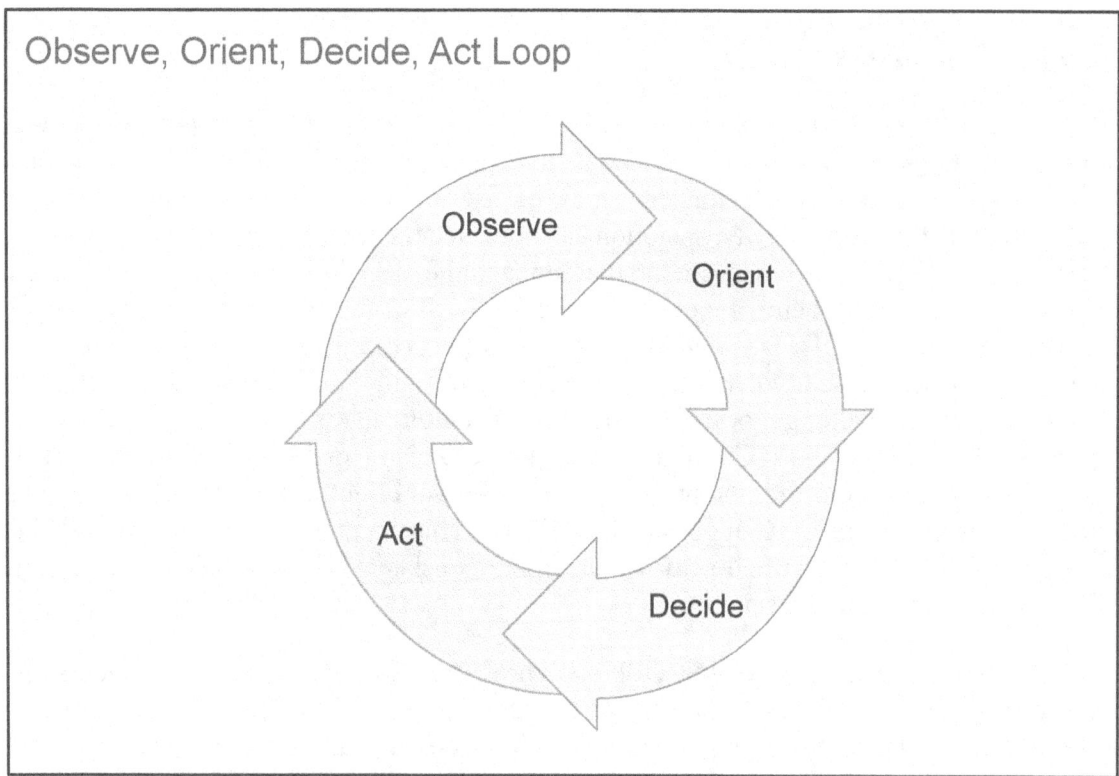

Figure IV-2. Observe, Orient, Decide, Act Loop

making and associated behavior among relevant actors that is in line with (or at least not counter to) the joint force's desired end state. Thus, JIPOE for COIN uses the same four steps of the doctrinal JIPOE process with a focus on the COIN environment.

6. Step 1: Define the Operational Environment

a. The first step of the JIPOE process in COIN is to define the OE. In order to define the OE, the JFC staff first clearly understands the purpose of the operation and the JFC's intent. Once this is established, a definition of the OE can be made, which includes:

(1) A detailed explanation of the operational area.

(2) An overview of the actors within the operational area.

(3) An overview of the physical aspects of the OE within the operational area.

(4) An overview of the information aspects of the OE within the operational area.

b. There is typically great nuance within the OE at individual locations across the broad operational area. Therefore, the JIPOE process for COIN benefits from incorporation of intelligence preparation of the battlespace and other intelligence activities occurring at the tactical, operational, and strategic levels.

7. Step 2: Describe the Impact of the Operational Environment on Adversary and Friendly Capabilities

Understanding the impact of the OE means understanding its dynamics and includes understanding factors that are driving people to engage in conflict, factors that impact how the conflict plays out, and factors that may be useful for consideration during conflict resolution. JIPOE for a COIN operation is about understanding aspects of the physical factors and information environment that impact the decision making and associated behavior of all relevant actors involved, to include the JFC. Ultimately, understanding the impact of the OE in COIN is about understanding aspects of the OE that are relevant to the decision cycles of those involved, to include USG, HN, and multinational personnel. This poses a particular challenge for the JFC, as it is difficult to analyze one's own actions with the same objectivity as the JFC is able to apply to the decision making of others. Similarly, the JFC must be conscious of the problem of the observer effect, where the act of engaging the population itself makes changes in the OE itself. This understanding enables the JFC to better shape the behavior of all actors in a manner consistent with the JFC's intermediate objectives and desired end state.

a. **Physical Factors.** The ASCOPE analytical framework is often used to understand the key physical factors within the COIN OE. In COIN, the relevance of the physical and information aspects of the OE is potentially much greater than in traditional warfare. To the extent they are relevant, understanding those aspects of the physical factors within each ASCOPE category is critical in COIN. Aspects of each component of ASCOPE are understood in an operationally relevant way by understanding them with regard to the political strategy and especially their impact on the decisions of relevant actors.

(1) **Areas.** Areas are localities or physical terrains that have direct impact on all actors. Examples include tribal regions, police districts, political boundaries, religious boundaries, territorial boundaries, military boundaries, polling stations, and government centers. Area factors may impact choices among relevant actors such as the routes various relevant actors choose to travel, the places where relevant actors choose to settle, and the people with whom relevant actors choose to interact for various reasons. Area factors also impact the JFC's decisions during the planning and execution of operations.

(2) **Structures.** Structures are existing infrastructure. Examples include hospitals, bridges, communications towers, power plants, dams, jails, warehouses, schools, television stations, radio stations, and print plants. For COIN, some cultural structures may be even more vital, such as churches, mosques, national libraries, and museums. Analysis of the relevant structures includes determining why they are important with respect to their location, functions, capabilities, and application. However, more important to understand is which structures matter, what their significance is to the political strategy, and how they impact the decision making and associated behavior of relevant actors.

(3) **Capabilities.** Capabilities are key functions and services within societies. Relevant capabilities may include, but are not limited to, administration, safety, emergency services, food distribution, agricultural systems, public works and utilities, health, public transportation, electricity, economics, and commerce. Sewage, water, electrical, academic,

trash, medical, and security infrastructure are some of the essential services that may be relevant. Capabilities often impact the security and quality of life of relevant aspects of the population and can sometimes impact decisions among the populace about whether to behave in a manner that assists a government or insurgency.

(4) **Organizations.** Organizations can be religious, fraternal, criminal, media, patriotic or service, and community watch groups. They include media, IGOs, NGOs, merchants, squatters, and other groups. Insurgents, counterinsurgents, and the population are not the only relevant actors within the OE and the JFC works to understand the impact on the OE of those organizations that are important.

(5) **People.** Analysts consider historical, cultural, ethnic, political, economic, and humanitarian factors when examining the people within the OE. Understanding who is where within the OE will almost always be a relevant factor in the decision cycles of each actor. For example, areas where people and insurgents may transit, retreat, evade, or hide may have relevance. Knowing where squatters, the homeless, refugees, displaced persons, and outcast groups are and why they are there may also be relevant.

(6) **Events.** Events are routine, cyclical, planned, or spontaneous activities that affect the OE. Some examples are planting and harvest seasons, elections, changes in government, key leader succession, economic reforms, political reforms, holidays, observances, anniversaries of key historical events, riots, and trials. Events may spur an increase or decrease in insurgent attacks. For example, insurgents may escalate violence to prevent an election, or insurgent activity may decrease during a harvest season as they assist the population. Combat operations, including indirect fires and deployments and redeployments, also affect the OE. JIPOE helps determine which events are relevant and how events help shape the behavior of relevant actors. Some factors to consider may be the political, economic, psychological, environmental, and/or legal implications of each event.

b. **Information Environment**

(1) Understanding the information environment is paramount in COIN as it is the medium through which decision making is made and disseminated. The information environment is the aggregate of individuals, organizations, and systems that collect, process, disseminate, or act on information. All actors in the OE affect the information environment and are impacted by it. The most important attribute of the information environment is that it is where the actions and the messaging of all actors combine to form the narratives that impact the mental disposition of relevant actors. The JFC works to understand the information environment in order to treat a narrative using all appropriate channels of information flow. An understanding of this environment is also important for activities such as intercepting communications of various actors to inform operations and deterring and/or exploiting nefarious communication.

(2) Those who collect information about the OE from relevant actors should be cognizant of how their collection efforts will impact actor perceptions. Due to the evolution in communications technology in recent decades, disproportionately small actors, to include insurgents, counterinsurgents, and elements of populations both inside and outside of the

WHO IS WINNING? A BATTLE OF MINDS AND PERCEPTIONS

V. Who is Winning?

1. A Battle of Minds and Perceptions

a. Not a game with points on a scoreboard

The answer to this question depends on who you ask. This is not like a football game with points on a scoreboard; it is more like a political debate, after which both sides announce that they won. That matters because we are not the scorekeepers: not NATO [North Atlantic Treaty Organization] ISAF [International Security Assistance Force], not our governments, and not even our press. The perception of all of these entities will matter and they will affect the situation, but ultimately this is going to be decided in the minds and perceptions of the Afghan people, of the Afghan government, and of the insurgents, whether they can win or are winning, and, most important, the perception of the villager who casts his lot with the winner.

b. Villagers make rational and practical decisions

Villagers are supremely rational and practical people: they make the decision on who they will support, based upon who can protect them and provide for them what they need. If a villager lives in a remote area where the government or security forces cannot protect them from coercion or harm from insurgents, he will not support the government—it would be illogical. Similarly, if the government cannot provide him with rule of law, the basic ability to adjudicate requirements legally, or just enough services to allow him to pursue a livelihood, it is difficult for him to make a rational decision to support the government. The Taliban is not popular. It does not have a compelling context. What it has is proximity to the people and the ability to provide coercion and, in some cases, things like basic rule of law, based upon the fact that they are there and can put themselves in that position. The perception of the villager matters in terms of which side he should support, so winning the battle of perception is key.

c. Allowing the facts to speak for themselves

I also think that winning the battle of perception, as it applies everywhere but particularly to us, is about credibility. As I told you, the situation is absolutely not deteriorating by every indicator, but I will not stand up and say that we are winning until I am told by indicators that we are winning. For me to stand up and claim good things that are not supported by data in order to motivate us and make us feel good very rapidly undermines our credibility. Our own forces are smart enough to do that, so I intend to tell people the best assessment that we can, as accurately as possible, and allow the facts to speak for themselves.

ISAF Commander General Stanley McChrystal, October 1, 2009, speech at the International Institute for Strategic Studies in London

operational area, can gain asymmetric advantage in the information environment. Internet communication and exploitation of the media have proven particularly useful to insurgents hoping to shape the narrative within the operational area to their favor, recruit manpower from sympathetic individuals and other already established groups with related interests, and gain other types of resource and political assistance for their cause from outside the operational area.

(3) The information environment consists of three interrelated dimensions which continuously interact with individuals, organizations, and systems. These dimensions are the physical, informational, and cognitive. Due to the political nature of COIN explained in Chapter III, "Fundamentals of Counterinsurgency," the cognitive dimension is most important and it extends to US and international public opinion. Because COIN operations and campaigns are political armed struggles that are ultimately decided in the minds of the relevant actors, they are ultimately won and lost in the cognitive dimension.

8. Step 3: Evaluate the Adversary(ies) and Other Relevant Actors

In defining the OE during COIN, an effort is made to identify the relevant actors both outside and within the operational area. The relevant actors in COIN always include the insurgents, the indigenous population, HNSF, and the HN government. However, other relevant actors may also exist. These actors might include additional insurgent or terrorist actors with regional or global ambitions, criminal elements, unofficial leaders and power brokers within the indigenous power structures, indigenous unofficial security forces (local militias), state and non-state actors in other countries, and NGOs. Globalization has led to an increase in the potential relevance of actors that reside outside of the operational area. Improvements in transport technology; the proliferation of information and communications; the deregulation of the international economy and markets; and increased migration have accelerated this phenomenon. The relevant actors and the degree to which each actor is important to COIN are different for each operation. Actors are also dynamic, and therefore certain actors may fall under multiple categories at the same time or move from one category to another over time. As operational realities, local political dynamics, and local expectations change in response to external developments, some actors may shift their allegiances based on their own perceived interests. The impending withdrawal of third-party counterinsurgent forces can be one of the most potent triggers for realignment.

a. Understanding the Insurgency

(1) Insurgencies are products of the time, place, and society in which they develop. Understanding the insurgency in its context is necessary to develop a politico-military strategy to defeat it. The opportunity/motive/means framework outlined in Chapter II, "Insurgency," provides a starting point for understanding that context. The opportunity, motive, and means factors explain how particular aspects of the OE led to the emergence of the insurgency and shaped its strategy, organization, and narrative. Analysts can extend that analysis by examining key characteristics of the insurgent group(s) in the operational area, including its:

(a) Origins and evolution over time.

(b) Objectives, narrative, and strategy.

(c) Organization and internal decision-making structures.

(d) Approach to co-opting local disputes.

(e) Extent of factionalization and internally competing entities.

(f) Relations with the population and civil society (such as informal governance structures, trade and professional organizations, ethnic or religious institutions, and sports clubs).

(g) Distinction between the insurgency military wing/component and other wings (political, social services, etc.).

(h) Relations with key local or transnational business interests/economic sectors.

(i) Recruiting and resource/logistics base.

(j) Relations with various HN government and nongovernmental institutions.

(k) Relations with other states in the region.

(l) Relations with other local and transnational non-state actors (such as criminal groups, diaspora communities, terrorist networks, and global religious authorities).

(m) Perceptions of the US and other members of the joint, interagency, intergovernmental, and multinational community.

(n) Variation in these characteristics across different factions and/or regions.

(o) Propensity and capability to capture or take US or allied military or civilian personnel hostage.

(2) Gaining an understanding of these aspects of the insurgency and how they interrelate will help analysts and planners progress from a broad understanding of the OE to an accurate COG/CC/CR/CV analysis during JIPOE, and subsequent network analysis to support COA development.

See JP 5-0, Joint Operation Planning, *for more information on operational design.*

b. **Understanding the Population**

(1) Understanding the population is critical for counterinsurgents. The population will typically be a COG for counterinsurgents seeking to gain consent of the governed in order to establish legitimacy. As described in earlier chapters, some level of civilian

"Intelligence services of intervening forces in counterinsurgency operations tend to exhibit several pathologies... A fourth pathology is the tendency to judge success based on progress in creating top-down, state based institutions, while reposing less value and significance in bottom-up societal indicators. This pathology may not be confined to intelligence services. Rather, it seems to reflect wider Eurocentric attitudes to the process of state formation. Recent research suggests that the international community, including the vast international aid and development bureaucracy and the 'peace industry' associated with international organizations such as the United Nations and the International Monetary Fund, tends to have a strong preference for top-down state formation ('nation building') based on the creation of national-level, 'modern,' Western-style institutions of the central state. Intervening forces in counterinsurgency environments seem to absorb this broader tendency, with analysts tending to give greater weight to events at the national level, or to elite-level political maneuvering, than to events at the grassroots, civil society level. Thus, while military intelligence agencies tend to focus on threat intelligence, civilian agencies tend to focus on elite-level political intelligence—whereas what most affects the mission may often be grassroots political intelligence, an oft-neglected focus of analysis. This can tend to skew assessment."

David Kilcullen (2010), "Intelligence," in *Understanding COIN, Doctrine, Operations and Challenges,* ed. Thomas Rid and Thomas Keany, (Routledge, New York)

cooperation is almost always required to locate insurgents and influence their behavior. How counterinsurgents pursue that goal will always have repercussions for the civilian population, with the potential to either reduce or increase support for the insurgency and the costs of control for the HN and its allies.

(2) Although the key characteristics of the population can vary enormously from one HN to another, or even within a given operational area, two constants apply more generally and guide efforts to understand the decision making of populations caught up in an insurgency:

(a) Whatever their political preferences at the outset of the conflict, civilians tend to cooperate with whichever side is able to establish effective control. For civilians, control means creating conditions that are predictable and tolerable—a clear set of rules that are consistently enforced under which they feel they can reasonably survive. For civilians, this encompasses both immediate physical security and access to other essentials of survival (such as food and shelter), and their prospects for security over the longer term. It also encompasses the full range of potential threats, including insurgents, criminals, paramilitary groups, and the HNSF, to include multinational and counterinsurgent forces. In situations where neither insurgents nor counterinsurgents can establish effective control, civilians will often try to remain neutral in order to survive.

(b) To understand the civilian population, the counterinsurgent works to understand the perspective of the local population, even when it is completely at odds with HN government, US, or IGO assessments. This means understanding how locals interpret the actions of insurgents, the HN government, and all other parties influencing the conflict, including the USG and other external counterinsurgents, as well as NGOs and private sector corporations. Developing that perspective requires understanding that:

    1. US actions may not always be interpreted in the same way as US actors intended.

    2. The US will be seen as endorsing any harmful actions taken by its HN partners that the US does not specifically disavow and take visible actions to address.

    3. Any action the US takes that affects the civilian population will be interpreted in the wider context of threats, opportunities, incentives, and dangers associated with the conflict that civilians are attempting to navigate.

(3) Culture and identity complicate the challenge of understanding the perspective of the civilian population. Faced with the profound uncertainty and insecurity associated with civil conflict, civilians pursue their interests rationally: their decisions are consistent with their assessment of the current local environment and how it is most likely to evolve. That assessment is heavily shaped by a range of contextual factors that include both individual and communal characteristics such as past experiences, dominant historical narratives, normative beliefs, access to information, socioeconomic factors, and the degree to which individuals are dependent on membership in their communities for survival. Often these are bundled together under the category of "culture."

(4) Many of these factors are derived from the identity that individuals and communities have adopted. As described above, identity can shape how those individuals and communities define their interests, and what they consider the best or most plausible ways to pursue them. Therefore, counterinsurgents seeking to shape the decisions and behavior of civilians work to understand the group identities and their role in local power dynamics.

(5) However, identities are rarely stable or immutable. They often evolve or are deliberately manipulated in the course of civil conflict. As described in Chapter II, "Insurgency," identities are employed strategically by individuals, communities, and insurgents to justify the actions they take to pursue their interests, even as those interests are shaped by identity. Interests and identity shape each other. As a result, counterinsurgents consider identities as both a target to be influenced and as a tool to shape the perceptions of the population. In working to reshape the political dynamics driving the insurgency, counterinsurgents consider whether their actions will bolster, undermine, or alter identities, and how that in turn will affect the support of the civilian population.

(6) To understand the population, counterinsurgents seek to understand the range of factors that shape its perceptions and behavior, including the relationships between those factors (i.e., the interdependence between geographic, demographic, social, cultural, political, economic, and institutional aspects of the population). The characteristics of the population that analysts and planners may consider include:

(a) Demographics, social divisions, and physical environment.

(b) Politically relevant identities and communities that may be based on:

1. Ethnicity.

2. Class.

3. Caste.

4. Tribe/clan.

5. Belief system.

6. Geographic region.

7. Education.

8. Ideology.

9. Profession.

(c) Exchanges and economic activity, sources of income (informal and formal), and employment.

(d) The identity and selection criteria for political and social elites at local, provincial, and national levels.

(e) Relations with the HN government, including:

1. Variations in social contract/expectations of government across different regions/sectors of society.

2. Variations across different HN government institutions (e.g., the judiciary, police, military, internal security services, municipal/district governments, and parliament).

3. Level of access/participation in government at various levels.

4. Relations between informal or civil society leaders and formal government.

5. Historical and current grievances and attempts to resolve them.

(f) Connections with diaspora communities.

(g) Civilian perceptions of the US and other members of the joint, interagency, intergovernmental, and multinational community.

WITH FRIENDS LIKE THESE: UNDERSTANDING OUR LOCAL ALLIES IN COUNTERINSURGENCY (COIN)

The US is on the horns of a dilemma when working with allies to fight insurgents. Allies experience insurgencies because of the weakness of the state, as well as other factors such as discrimination and corruption. These problems create tremendous difficulties when the US expects allied militaries to fight on its behalf—the structural problems that cause the insurgencies also shape how well allies fight them.

The implications of these weaknesses go beyond the ability (or lack thereof) of local forces to fight the insurgents and shape the relationship between the regime and the US. The US must recognize that its allies, including those in allied militaries, are often ineffective at fighting insurgents and at times can make the problem worse. US COIN doctrine, no matter how well thought out, cannot succeed without the appropriate political and other reforms from the host nation, but these regimes are likely to subvert the reforms that threaten the existing power structure. The influence of the US is often limited, as the allies recognize that its vital interests are likely to outweigh any temporary disgust or anger of an ally's brutality or failure to institute reforms.

To help overcome these problems, the US should try to increase its intelligence on allied security forces so that it can better understand the true nature of their activities. To reduce its vulnerability to manipulation, the US should also try to diversify its intelligence sources to ensure that it does not rely exclusively on the local ally for information. At times, Washington should try to act more like a third party to a conflict rather than an open and strong ally of government forces. In doing so, it can better exert leverage over the government to make useful reforms and other concessions that might help solve fundamental problems.

Edited from Daniel S. Byman, Friends Like These: Counterinsurgency and the War on Terrorism, *International Security,* Vol. 31, No. 2, (Fall 2006)

(h) Relations with/perceptions of the insurgency, especially as it relates to the interests of specific communities.

(i) Relations with/perceptions of other regional state and non-state actors.

c. **Understanding the HN Government**

(1) In most cases, US involvement in COIN has been in support of the HN government. A key lesson from those cases is the importance of understanding the strengths and shortcomings of the HN government and accounting for them in developing the strategy planning the operation or campaign. Insurgencies emerge in response to inability or unwillingness of governments to control their territory and population in a way that minimally meets the expectations of their citizens. Often this reflects deeply rooted problems that HN elites have proven unwilling to recognize or address because doing so

would threaten their political or economic interests. Moreover, HN government leaders and factions typically seek to co-opt US assistance and combat power to promote their own political and personal interests. Such manipulation has the potential not only to undermine COIN efforts in the immediate conflict, but to damage US credibility more broadly with domestic and international populations.

(2) Ideally, the US could avoid supporting HN governments that are not willing to undertake the necessary reforms. However, strategic interests may dictate otherwise, and HN governments are not monolithic: even where some parts of the HN government are cooperative, other parts may resist. Thus, a core challenge for the US is to foster the willingness within the HN government to reform institutions and governance—including but not limited to security forces—in order to address the root causes of the insurgency. This will often require a deliberate approach to empowering moderates and reformers while marginalizing hardliners within the HN government.

(3) To structure US engagement, advisory efforts, and assistance in ways that will encourage HN government reform and empower competent leaders, planners attempt to understand both the formal aspects of the HN government, such as its institutional structure, and the informal aspects, such as the competing political networks within the government, or the links between government figures and business interests. Assessments of the HN government describe the different political factions within the HN government and the distribution of power among them; how the state acquires and manages resources; how government policy is made and implemented; and the relationship between the HN government and private interests, ethno-sectarian leaders, criminal groups, and insurgents. It enables planners to determine how best to engage individuals, networks, and institutions within the HN government in order to promote the reforms necessary for effective COIN.

(4) Some considerations for analysis of the HN government include:

(a) Nature of government (such as authoritarian, democratic, confessional, theocratic, monarchy, or oligarchy).

(b) Sources of power and support.

(c) Economic base and systems for revenue collection and distribution.

(d) Structure, roles, and political interests of different institutions and levels of government.

(e) Selection process/criteria for leadership.

(f) Formal processes for making, enforcing, and reforming laws and policies.

(g) Relationship between political, security, and judicial institutions.

(h) Factions/divisions among the political elite.

(i) Factions/divisions within civil service/institutions.

(j) Origins, ideologies, and aspirations of political parties.

(k) Roles, capacity, and politics of the justice system.

(l) Structure and culture of the security forces (military, police, paramilitaries, prisons).

(m) Civil-military relations.

(n) Relations with different components of the HN society (such as ethno-cultural groups and interest groups).

(o) Mechanisms for popular consultation (including elections, shuras, town halls, and audiences with local officials).

(p) Relations with multinational organizations such as corporations and diaspora networks.

d. **Understanding the Role of Third Parties in the Conflict.** While the main protagonists in any insurgency are generally the insurgents, the HN government, and the population, globalization has multiplied and intensified their links with the rest of the world. During the Cold War that pitted East versus West in numerous insurgencies around the globe, world powers typically picked sides and supported a protagonist that best suited their national interests. The additional threat posed by transnational terrorists as a third party in nearly any conflict was highlighted by the attacks of September 11, 2001, and ensuing US efforts to counter violent extremism across a broad range of theaters. These are among the clearest examples of far-reaching globalization connectivity and its complex

---

UNDERSTANDING THE INSTITUTIONAL POLITICS OF HOST-NATION SECURITY FORCES: THE IMPACT OF THE TANDA SYSTEM ON COUNTERINSURGENCY IN EL SALVADOR

The El Salvadoran Armed Forces (ESAF) tradition of "tanda" complicated military-to-military advisory relations. Among ESAF officers, personalities and political orientation were more important than military competence. Each graduating class, or "tanda," from the Military Academy was bound to lifelong loyalty to one another. In this system, each tanda moves up through the ranks together. Officers cover for one another when they step out of line. RAND analyst Benjamin Schwarz wrote: "Adding to the pernicious effects of the tanda system is the Salvadoran military's practice of operating not through a clear chain of command but through a complex system of consensus within and between tandas. The final consequence of the tanda system is that officers are not held accountable for their actions, no matter how egregious they may be; human rights abuses therefore go unpunished, military incompetence is tolerated, and corruption runs rampant."

Excerpted from Major Scott W. Moore, US Air Force, Gold, Not Purple: Lessons from USAIDUSMILGP Cooperation in El Salvador, 1980-1992, Naval Postgraduate School, December 1997

---

interdependence. Contemporary technology and commerce have increased the importance of third parties. This section considers six categories of outsiders that may impact the dynamics of insurgencies as third parties: transnational and other non-state actors, neighboring nations, IGOs, NGOs, local civil society groups, and the US and other nation-states. For each of the first three categories, analysts need to map their interests in the region and the operational area, relations with the HN government and HN population, current and historical involvement with the insurgency; and relationship with and likely reaction to US involvement.

(1) **Transnational Non-State Armed Groups.** The presence of transnational terrorists or international organized crime groups that threaten the interests of the US is a significant consideration. Approaches that conflate the transnational threat with national insurgencies and local communities can drive them together, broadening the conflict and often providing extremists from outside the affected country a foothold to exploit. Where transnational terrorists are present, analysts carefully assess the groups' relationship to the insurgency and local communities, and how to disaggregate the terrorists from the insurgents. Transnational organized criminal organizations may also seek to profit from the conflict, by forming mutually beneficial financial or even political ties to the insurgency. In some cases, insurgencies rely on links with transnational criminal organizations to fund operations and access illicit weapons. Thus, a detailed understanding of the nature and scope of the relationship between transnational terrorist or international criminal groups and the local insurgents is critical to developing an effective operational approach.

(2) **Other Transnational and International Non-State Actors.** A range of nonviolent categories of transnational and international non-state actors can also be important to the conflict dynamics. While these actors may not be intentionally shaping the conflict, their economic role may make them politically significant. A complete analysis should consider the role of such actors, including:

(a) Diaspora networks, who may back the insurgents or be potential partners for counterinsurgents.

(b) International corporations, whose activities may be a source of stability or instability, depending on the context and the perceptions of the population and HN government.

(c) Transnational financial institutions, ranging from modern banks to hawala networks can play a key role in interdicting material support for insurgent groups. Hawala are informal Islamic value transfer networks that operate in many parts of the Middle East, North Africa, the Horn of Africa, and South Asia outside of formal banking and financial systems.

(3) **Neighboring Nations.** These participants can be pivotal to the dynamics and outcomes of insurgencies. If supporting the insurgents, they can provide critical access to sanctuary areas and resupply, including resources typically unavailable to self-proclaimed foreign fighters and others without formal state support. As partners for counterinsurgents, they can be equally invaluable, coordinating to control borders, cut insurgent logistic

networks, interdict illicit activities, and counter the exploitation of border areas as sanctuaries. In some cases, US forces and other third-party counterinsurgents may require the support of neighboring states to establish secure aerial ports of debarkation and ground lines of communications, and permission for overflight in order to project airpower from platforms and bases located outside the operational area.

(4) **IGOs.** IGOs are organizations created by a formal agreement between two or more governments on a global, regional, or functional basis to protect and promote national interests shared by member states. Most IGOs are regionally focused, and as such when IGO member states could be adversely affected by an insurgency in their region, the organization may act collectively to deny legitimacy, sanctuary, and support to insurgents. IGOs can act as important facilitators for cooperation among states, pressure the HN government to make difficult but necessary political reforms, impose sanctions on insurgents and their supporters, and in some cases muster and deploy multilateral expeditionary civilian and military capacities to support stabilization efforts. IGOs can also play an important role in HA and development.

(5) **NGOs.** NGOs typically fall into three broad categories: humanitarian relief, development, and United States Agency for International Development (USAID) implementing partners. Inter Action, the alliance or umbrella organization of US based NGOs, can serve a useful liaison function. The UN Office for the Coordination for Humanitarian Affairs can play a useful liaison role. NGOs adhere to the humanitarian principles of humanity, impartiality, neutrality, and independence. JFC planners respect their adherence to these principles. Some humanitarian NGOs may coordinate with military relief activities and should be conducted in accordance with the *Guidelines for Relations Between US Armed Forces and Non-Governmental Humanitarian Organizations in Hostile and Potentially Hostile Environments.* NGOs may provide the JFC with insight, assessments, and analysis with respect to the OE and the conflict. However, any information provided by the NGOs to the JFC must not compromise their independence and their goal to be perceived as independent by the population.

(a) Local and international NGOs engaged in development work are inherently political, but are still protected as civilians from direct attack under the law of war. Such NGOs may not draw on the law of war as the legal framework for their activities and do not necessarily operate based on the same principles. However, they often attempt to remain neutral in the midst of the conflict, or even engage in grassroots peace building. As a result, they can have important impacts on the civilian population and the politico-economic dynamics of the conflict. Because of their typically long-term presence in operational areas, they often have detailed knowledge of the local population. Some multi-mandated NGOs do recognize the practical benefits of independence and impartiality in their role when operating in complex political environments.

(b) USAID can serve as a bridge between the military and its implementing partners, which can be contractors, grantees, or cooperative agreement partners depending on the type of agreement USAID signs with the signing organization. USAID implementing partners may include NGOs as well as for-profit organizations, which can determine the type of relationship the JFC is able to have with the implementing partner. Since these organizations are recipients of USAID funding, they may be targeted by the opposition based on the perception they are aligned with US, multinational, or HN government interests. These organizations also face the possibility of extortion by malign actors for profit.

(6) **Local Civil Society Groups.** These include religious institutions, cultural groups, and local aid societies that could even be considered small HN NGOs. Each can face retaliation if seen to be assisting COIN forces. JFCs in coordination with the COM and HN government determine the best way to work with these groups, if required, especially to mitigate the risks of retaliation as they coordinate with them, understanding their role in the HN society and potential for not supporting the insurgency is a plus even if they do not partner with the HN government COIN effort. Also, such groups can be a critical source of information about local sociopolitical dynamics, so for example, an overt hands-off approach coupled with some discreet relationships may be necessary. However, as with other HN entities, JFCs do not accept the information from local groups without pause, because they may have self-serving or particular perspectives or agendas that do not represent all components of the population.

(7) **US and Other Multinational COIN Partners.** The commitment of the USG to support a COIN effort by an HN government comes with strategic direction and planning guidance. The JFC's CONOPS provides guidance and intent to facilitate actions that implement that strategic guidance. USAID is the lead US development agency. A USAID senior development officer is assigned to US Special Operations Command and the geographic combatant commands to familiarize the JFC with development plans, programs, and resources as well as the policy and strategic guidance. Planners are provided to guide their efforts, but they also are aware of and susceptible to the geopolitical and domestic US political context that may influence public opinion regarding many of the effects created by their operations. Other third-party partner nations in the COIN effort also should be expected to face that same type of situation.

(a) The political nature of COIN and the global media environment significantly complicate the relationship between policy, strategy, and the operational level. Insurgents are often cunning, adaptive, and media-savvy adversaries that will seek to provoke, exhaust, and discredit US efforts in the same way as they do those of the HN government. To develop an operational approach for US and other third-party COIN efforts that will prove resilient in the face of such adversity, operational planners need to clearly understand the JFC's guidance and intent. When operating in a multinational COIN operation, US planners understand the strategic context for their partners' involvement and incorporate those considerations into the JFC's planning process. This will provide an operational approach developed in the appropriate strategic political context by the commander and staff that accounts for the political aspects of the insurgency in the operational area and areas of interest (AOIs) and properly frames US interagency and multinational partners involvement.

(b) The inner workings of other interagency and multinational partners are also important to understand. A unified chain of command is unlikely in whole-of-government and/or multinational operations. Thus, development of an operational approach that drives unified action must account for the strengths and limitations of all civil-military entities within the multinational force. For example, the JFC must understand whether or not a development agency is capable of and/or willing to conform to the operational approach being developed by the JFC. If not, then planning must account for this through interagency coordination. Only through a firm baseline understanding of the capabilities, processes, and procedures of each entity within the multinational force can the JFC develop an achievable operational approach resulting in unity of effort.

e. **COG Analysis**

(1) A thorough understanding of the OE is essential to COG analysis. Because there are various significant actors involved, their opportunities, motives, and means should be understood, so the JFC planners can more accurately determine appropriate points of influence. The degree to which they understand the OE will determine the level of fidelity of any COG analysis, network analysis, or other tools for developing COAs. COGs consist of certain critical factors (CCs, CRs, and CVs) that help commanders identify and analyze COGs, and formulate the decisive points, LOOs, and LOEs to affect them.

(2) The COG analysis for COIN includes understanding critical factors for friendly (US, multinational, HN, and other local) supporters relevant populations, insurgents, other protagonists (e.g., transnational terrorists), and any external supporters for either side. In COIN, it is not enough to attack the enemy's COGs and protect your own; in a population-centric conflict, supporting the population's COGs also takes a central role. Influencing the behavior of outside actors also requires an understanding of their COGs, CVs, CRs, and CCs.

(3) One danger in reliance on a COG analysis is the possibility of losing the holistic picture of the OE and those within it. Planners cannot be tempted to reduce the analysis to a simple systems perspective. Networks, groups, and influences are not viewed in isolation. Part of the operational art associated with a COG analysis in a COIN operation is the ability to understand the effect of an action relating to a particular COG on the entire OE. While determining COGs, CVs, CRs, and CCs will certainly allow planners to focus on each particular group, it should not result in a narrow fixation with a loss of the collective perspective.

9. Step 4: Determine Potential Courses of Action of the Adversary(ies) and Other Relevant Actors

Based on the holistic understanding of the OE developed during the first three steps of JIPOE in COIN, enhanced insight into the decision making of relevant actors is achieved. Decision making helps drive behavior. Thus, improved understanding of decision making enables the JFC to better determine likely COAs of the relevant actors within the OE. The fourth step of the JIPOE process builds upon this holistic view to develop a detailed understanding of probable COAs of the relevant actors as they relate to the desired end state of the JFC. Step 4 of JIPOE for COIN asks the following questions based on the enhanced understanding gained in steps 1-3 of relevant aspects of the OE:

a. What are each relevant actor's desired end state and intermediate objectives?

b. What tasks will each actor try to complete to attain their desired end state and intermediate objectives?

c. How will each actor attempt to complete these tasks?

d. What is the likely outcome of each actor's likely actions?

e. How will each actor's desired end state and intermediate objectives change (if at all) based on these likely outcomes?

f. What are likely follow-on COAs? (As discussed in Chapter II, "Insurgency," insurgent strategies can change as the situation changes, combining various strategies or moving to entirely new approaches. A dynamic analysis of possible COAs is essential to staying within the opposition's decision cycles.)

COUNTERINSURGENCY IN NORTHERN IRELAND: DISAGGREGATION AND UNDERSTANDING THE OPERATIONAL ENVIRONMENT

As a fairly young officer, I was in Belfast, responsible for a patch of West Belfast. A bus route came to my area, at the end of its route from Belfast city center. There was a roundabout, and the bus would sit there for twenty minutes and then turn round and go back down into Belfast. Most Friday nights, somewhere around 9 o'clock, this bloody bus would get burned. There would be a riot, and people would throw stones at the fire brigade when it came, and then we'd all turn out and fire batten rounds and things at the hooligans throwing the stones, and then someone would shoot at us and we'd shoot back. A good time was had by all. The BBC [British Broadcasting Corporation] and everyone were all in there. A burning bus can really get everyone going.

This was going on rather more than I was prepared to put up with. But I couldn't stop it. I just wasn't able to defeat this. Until we came up with a cunning wheeze, which involved me persuading two soldiers that it was in their interest to hide in a hidden box on the top of this bus, and when the hooligans appeared with the buckets of petrol and the box of matches, they would leap out before they lit the petrol and capture the hooligans with the petrol, and we would all rush in and help them. These two soldiers agreed that this was a wizard wheeze and hid in the box. We drove the Trojan Horse in. And, sure enough, we got them. A quiet conversation took place between the regimental sergeant major and these two little hooligans.

It turned out that this thing that we had been treating as IRA [Irish Republican Army] terrorism, disrupting the streets, a come-on operation so that we would be pulled in so that then we could be sniped at—that was our complete logic and understanding of it—was wholly and totally wrong. This had nothing to do with terrorism at all. It was the black taxis, and they were paying these hooligans to burn the buses so they got more trade. We hadn't been fighting anybody. But as one clawed away at it, I learned a lot. Yes, the IRA were benefiting from this. They were able to show us as being part of the problem, because we went onto the housing estate, invaded their space, et cetera, et cetera, et cetera. They were now defending and were given legitimacy because they were the defender. They were taking 10 percent off the taxi drivers, because they knew what was going on, so they got money as well.

So we then started to develop an operation, which went on for a long time—this is timeless, remember. About eight years later, I am back there, at a rather more senior level, and we knock off the whole of the financial structure of that part of the IRA. It starts with that event. As you went through the file, the opening entry was the black taxi man who was handing over the 10 percent. We found out who he was, and you've got the beginning of a piece of string. But it took eight years.

The other bit of information was that in the wallets of one of these little hooligans was a check for £10 from the BBC. And down we went to the BBC and said, "What the bloody hell are you doing?" It turned out that this little hooligan would ring up. Having been paid by taxi drivers 50 quid to burn a bus, he then rang up the BBC and said, "There's going to be an incident at such and such." So the cameras were already there. War amongst the people, the theater. Nobody is in control in the sense that we think there is a master plan. So your operation must be a learning operation.

The currency of war amongst the people is not fire power. That's the currency of industrial war. The currency of war amongst the people is information—not just intelligence, information—what you put out, what you get in. That's what is going on on that confrontational seesaw.

General (ret) Sir Rupert Smith, UK Army, former Deputy Supreme Allied Commander, North Atlantic Treaty Organization (NATO); author of *The Utility of Force: The Art of War in the Modern World*. Quoted from a speech at the Carnegie Council on Ethics in International Affairs, 24 January 2007

CHAPTER V
PLANNING

1. General

a. **Joint Operation Planning.** Operational art, operational design, and joint operation planning process (JOPP) are complementary elements within the Adaptive Planning and Execution system. The JFC, supported by the staff, gains an understanding of the environment, defines the problem, and develops an operational approach for the joint operation/campaign through the application of operational art and operational design during the initiation step of JOPP. Commanders transmit their operational approach to their staff, subordinate and supporting commanders, agencies, and multinational/nongovernmental entities as required in their initial planning guidance so that their approach can be translated into executable plans. As JOPP is conducted, commanders refine their initial operational approach so the staff understands the basis for COAs and an eventual CONOPS. Operational design supports commanders and staff in their application of operational art with tools and a methodology to conceive and construct operations and campaigns. Operational design helps the commander develop the operational approach, which broadly describes the actions the joint force needs to take to reach the political and military end state. Finally, JOPP is an orderly, analytical process through which the JFC and staff translate the operational approach into detailed plans and orders. COIN plans and orders should integrate and synchronize operations, forces, and capabilities in a manner that addresses the root causes of insurgency (i.e., the opportunity, motive, and means discussed in Chapter II, "Insurgency") and neutralizes insurgents. This includes combining forces and actions to achieve concentration throughout the OE, culminating in achieving the objectives. Synergy in COIN consists of physical and psychological aspects. In the complex COIN environment, it is impossible to accurately view the contributions of any individual organization, capability, or the area in which they operate in isolation from all others. Each may be critical to success, and each has certain capabilities that cannot be duplicated. Commanders and staff must work with the COM and country team to develop mechanisms to synchronize the operation or campaign plan and achieve civil-military synergy in operations.

For a detailed discussion on operational art and operational design in JOPP, see JP 5-0, Joint Operation Planning.

b. **Operational art** provides the vision that links tactical actions to strategic objectives. More specifically, the interaction of operational art and operational design provides a bridge between strategy and tactics, linking national political aims to tactical combat and noncombat operations that must be executed to accomplish these aims. Likewise, **operational art promotes unified action** by helping JFCs and staffs understand how to facilitate the integration of other civilian agencies and multinational partners toward achieving strategic and operational objectives.

c. **Operational design** supports operational art with a general methodology and *elements of operational design.* This methodology helps the JFC and staff reduce the uncertainty of a complex OE, understand the nature of the problem or challenge facing them, and construct an operational approach to create effects, achieve objectives, and attain the desired end state. The elements of operational design are individual tools, such as COG and LOO, which help the JFC and staff visualize and describe the broad operational approach.

(1) Operational design extends operational art's vision with a creative process that helps commanders and planners answer the ends–ways–means–risk questions. **The commander is the central figure in operational design.** The elements of operational design are individual tools that help the JFC and staff visualize and describe the broad operational approach. Operational art, operational design, and JOPP blend in complementary fashion as part of the overall process that produces the eventual plan or order that drives the joint operation.

(2) Operational design requires the commander to encourage discourse and leverage dialogue and collaboration to identify and solve complex, ill-defined problems. To that end, the commander must empower organizational learning and develop methods to determine if modifying the operational approach is necessary during the course of an operation. This requires continuous assessment, evaluation, and reflection that challenge understanding of the existing problem and the relevance of actions addressing that problem.

(3) **Operational design** employs various **elements** to develop and refine the commander's operational approach. These conceptual tools help commanders and their staffs think through the challenges of understanding the OE, defining the problem, and developing this approach, which guides planning and shapes the CONOPS elements of operational design. Operational design for COIN should reflect a comprehensive approach applicable to the phase or stage of the operation or campaign. Operational design should incorporate all actors, with particular attention placed on interagency partners and HN participants, if there is a legitimate HN present. During execution, commanders and planners continue to consider operational design elements. Reframing may become necessary due to friendly, enemy, or other effects changing the OE significantly. This may be to adjust both current operations and future plans to capitalize on tactical and operational successes as the joint operation unfolds.

2. Elements of Operational Design

a. **Termination.** If the joint force is supporting an HN's COIN efforts, termination will depend on diplomatic discourse between the HN, the US, and other partner nations. This discourse is normally based on the projected security environment and the opportunity, motive, and means that underlie the insurgency. Insurgencies in which ideology and/or identities are perceived as critical factors may be especially difficult to negotiate. Some insurgencies or groups of insurgencies will be both value and interest-based. The drivers of conflict also impact the conditions necessary for termination.

b. **Military End State and Objectives.** The military end state normally will represent a point in time or circumstance beyond which the President does not require the military instrument of national power to achieve remaining objectives of the national strategic end state. **The combined political and military nature of COIN, however, makes the overall military end state very close or even the same as the national end state.** Aside from its obvious role in accomplishing strategic objectives, clearly defining the conditions of the end states promotes unified action, facilitates synchronization, and helps clarify (and may reduce) the risk associated with the joint campaign or operation. In COIN, commanders should include both the national end state and the military end state in their planning guidance and commander's intent statement.

c. **Effects.** Identifying desired and undesired effects within the OE connects military strategic and operational objectives to tactical tasks. Combined with a systems perspective of the COIN environment, the identification of desired and undesired effects informs a holistic view of the OE. Counterinsurgents plan joint COIN operations by developing strategic and operational objectives supported by measurable strategic and operational effects and assessment indicators. **Effects are useful in planning COIN; however, effects can be difficult to accurately predict given their highly sociocultural and political nature. The difficulty in predicting these effects reinforces the need for wide participation and lengthy discourse when planning COIN.** Nonlethal effects may enable the JFC to neutralize or incapacitate targets immediately in the OE. Nonlethal effects are created by the use of weapons, devices, and munitions that are explicitly designed and primarily employed to minimize collateral damage. The integration of nonlethal effects in support of COIN operations has the potential to mitigate the occurrence of undesired outcomes.

(1) **Adapting to the Local Environment.** The sociocultural factors encountered in the OE need to be considered when developing actions to create the desired effect. Understanding friendly and enemy forces is not enough; other factors, such as those described in Chapter IV, "The Operational Environment," paragraph 8b, "Understanding the Population," can be equally important.

(2) **Direct and Indirect.** A direct effect is the first order consequence of an action, and an indirect effect is a delayed consequence associated with an action. **Indirect effects are often more important in COIN, which is one of the factors that tend to make COIN both protracted and difficult.** These effects establish conditions, and counterinsurgents should determine the best sequence of actions to create these effects. **Discourse should develop and refine the necessary conditions for success in COIN.**

d. **COGs.** COGs are inherently complex and dynamic in that they change depending on each belligerent's objectives and the OE. Changes to COGs must be carefully planned for and analyzed. Changes to COGs often indicate a change in the nature of operations. JFCs consider not only the insurgents' COGs, but also identify and protect their own COGs. Counterinsurgents must similarly determine the friendly strategic and friendly operational COGs. Critical factors analysis provides commanders with a detailed, systemic understanding of friendly and adversary COGs, and the knowledge to balance resources accordingly to protect them as the situation requires.

See paragraph 8e, "COG Analysis," of Chapter IV, "The Operational Environment," for more information on COG and critical factors analysis.

e. **Decisive Points.** Decisive points are a logical extension of COGs critical factors. Counterinsurgents should identify decisive points to leverage friendly capabilities to exploit insurgent vulnerabilities. **A decisive point is a node, system, or key event that allows a**

marked advantage over an insurgent and greatly influences the outcome of COIN. Decisive points are not COGs; they are keys to attacking or protecting COG CRs. **In COIN, this can be influential individuals in the population, and leader engagement and providing them security may provide the counterinsurgents an advantage over the insurgents.** When it is not feasible to attack a COG directly, commanders focus operations to weaken or neutralize the CRs—therefore CVs—upon which it depends. These CVs are decisive points, providing the indirect means to weaken or collapse the COG. Decisive points at the operational level provide the greatest leverage on COGs, where tactical decisive points are directly tied to task and mission accomplishment.

(1) **Prioritization.** COIN typically presents more decisive points than the joint force can control, destroy, or neutralize with available resources. Through critical factors analysis, commanders identify the decisive points that offer the greatest leverage on COGs. They designate the most important decisive points as objectives and allocate enough resources to create the desired results on them. Decisive points that enable commanders to seize, retain, or exploit the initiative are crucial. Controlling these decisive points during operations helps commanders gain freedom of action, maintain momentum, and dictate tempo. If the adversary maintains control of a decisive point, it may exhaust friendly momentum, force early culmination, or facilitate an adversarial counterattack.

(2) **Stability Decisive Points.** Decisive points assume a different character during stability operations. These decisive points may be less tangible and more closely associated with critical events and conditions. For example, they may include repairing a vital water treatment facility, establishing a training academy for HNSF security forces, securing a major election site, or quantifiably reducing crime. While most of these decisive points are physical, all are vital to establishing the conditions for defeating an insurgency, addressing root causes, and building HN capabilities, capacity, and ultimately legitimacy.

f. **LOOs and LOEs.** An LOO defines the interior or exterior orientation of the force in relation to the enemy or connects actions on nodes and/or decisive points related in time and space to an objective(s). An LOE links multiple tasks and missions using the logic of purpose—cause and effect—to focus efforts toward establishing operational and strategic conditions. LOEs are a key tool for counterinsurgents to visualize the operational design as positional reference to insurgent forces may have little operational relevance. **Each LOO and LOE represents a conceptual category along which the counterinsurgents (HN government, JFC, or civilian agencies) intend to attack the insurgent strategy and build HN government legitimacy. COIN requires the synchronization of activities along multiple and complementary LOOs and LOEs in order to work through a series of tactical and operational objectives to attain the military end state.** In operations like COIN that involve many nonmilitary factors, LOEs may be the only way to link tasks, effects, conditions, and the desired end state. LOEs are often essential to helping commanders visualize how military capabilities can support the other instruments of national power, and are a particularly valuable tool when used to achieve unity of effort in operations involving multinational forces and civilian organizations, where unity of command is elusive, if not impractical. Commanders may use both LOOs and LOEs to connect objectives, decisive points, and COGs, but LOEs allow commanders to consider the less tangible aspects of the OE where other instruments of national power or irregular military activities may dominate.

(1) **Main Effort.** Commanders may specify an LOE as the main effort. In this case the other LOOs and LOEs shape the OE for the main effort. **This prioritization may change as COIN creates or exploits insurgent vulnerabilities, insurgents react or adjust their activities, or the environment changes.** In this sense, commanders adapt their operations not only to the state of the insurgency, but also to the OE.

(2) **Interdependence.** Success in one LOE reinforces successes in the others. **Progress along each LOO and LOE contributes to attaining a stable and secure environment for the HN.** Stability is reinforced by popular recognition of the HN government's legitimacy, improved governance, and progressive, substantive reduction of the core grievances of the insurgency. **There is no list of LOEs that applies in all COIN or all phases of COIN.** LOEs should be based on the holistic understanding of the OE and what must be done to attain the end state. Military objectives in COIN will be intertwined with diplomatic, informational, and economic efforts from the national to the local level. In particular, information-related capabilities are continuously ongoing and are associated with all military and HN efforts to some extent. The starting conditions for insurgencies often arise due to dissatisfaction by a certain segment of the population with the HN government. The goals of multinational and HN diplomatic, informational, military, and economic efforts are to reduce support for the insurgents and increase support for the HN government. This is achieved by a coordinated and comprehensive COIN operation along the LOOs and LOEs until the government is viewed as effective, legitimate, or at least benign by a majority of the population and insurgent support is marginalized.

g. **Direct and Indirect Approaches.** The approach is the manner in which a commander contends with a COG. Direct attacks against enemy COGs resulting in their neutralization or destruction is the most direct path to victory. **It is often difficult or impossible to attack an insurgency's strategic COG or operational COG; thus, COIN often requires an indirect approach.** As a result, the insurgent's CVs can offer indirect pathways to gain leverage over the insurgent's COGs. In this way, JFCs employ a synchronized combination of operations to weaken insurgent COGs indirectly and over time by attacking CRs that are sufficiently vulnerable.

h. **Anticipation.** Anticipation is essential to effective planning and execution for COIN. Counterinsurgents must use intelligence to ascertain the insurgents' approach and campaign plan, which will assist in anticipating insurgent activities. A shared, common holistic view of the OE aids counterinsurgents in anticipating opportunities and challenges. **Knowledge of the population, friendly capabilities, insurgent and other adversarial capabilities, intentions, and likely COAs allows COIN to focus efforts on where they can best impact the situation.** However, anticipation is not without risk, especially if insurgent deception is effective.

i. **Operational Reach.** Operational reach is the distance and duration over which a joint force can successfully employ military capabilities. Operational reach may be a factor in COIN if there are limitations set on the number, type, or general footprint of forces that can support an HN's COIN efforts. Operational reach can also be a factor if the joint force faces insurgency when there is no HN government.

j. **Culmination.** Culmination has both an offensive and a defensive application and can occur at any level of war. Culmination may, during COIN or stability operations, form the erosion of national will, or the decline of popular support (at home or abroad), pose questions concerning legitimacy or restraint, or create lapses in protection leading to excessive casualties. A well-developed assessment methodology is crucial to supporting the commander's determination of culmination, both for insurgent and friendly actions.

k. **Arranging Operations.** Counterinsurgents must determine the best arrangement of COIN operations to accomplish the assigned tasks and joint force mission. This arrangement often will be a combination of simultaneous and sequential operations to achieve objectives for the end state conditions with the least cost in personnel and other resources. **A variety of factors must be considered when determining this arrangement for COIN operations, including the population's current view of counterinsurgent credibility, HN legitimacy, and the insurgents in general.** The arrangement of COIN operations impacts the tempo of activities in time, space, and purpose.

(1) **Phases. Reaching the end state for COIN requires the conduct of a wide array of operations over a protracted period.** Consequently, the planning of COIN operations normally provides for related phases implemented over time. **Phasing helps commanders visualize and think through the entire COIN operations and to define requirements in terms of forces, resources, time, space, and purpose.** The primary benefit of phasing is that it assists in systematically achieving objectives that cannot be attained all at once by arranging smaller, related operations in a logical sequence. Each phase should represent a natural subdivision of the campaign or operation's intermediate objectives. **Transitions between phases are designed to be distinct shifts in focus by the counterinsurgent force, often accompanied by changes in command relationships.** The need to move into another phase normally is identified by assessing that a set of objectives is achieved or that the insurgent has acted in a manner that requires a major change in focus for the joint force and is therefore usually event driven, not time driven. Changing the focus of the operation takes time and may require changing priorities, command relationships, or force allocation. While the phasing construct is a helpful planning tool, phases are not linear and do not represent a clear-cut distinction in reality. Conditions in the operating environment may force returning or regressing to earlier phases, and various geographic areas within the theater may be in different phases at any given time, even within a single city. JFCs and joint forces must be agile in recognizing how conditions affect phasing. Similarly, they must be prepared to shift from military to civilian control based on the operating environment.

(2) **Branches and Sequels. Many COIN operation plans require flexibility by having branches and sequels.** Both branches and sequels are plans associated with the base plan, all of which are created using the initial problem frame. When transitioning to a branch or a sequel, counterinsurgents should examine if reframing the problem is required by the current conditions.

(a) **Branches.** Branches are options built into the basic plan. Branches may include shifting priorities, changing unit organization and command relationships, or changing the very nature of COIN itself. Branches add flexibility to plans by anticipating situations that could alter the basic plan. Such situations could be a result of insurgent action, availability of friendly capabilities or resources, or many other potential situations. It is vital to prioritize COIN branch planning efforts with respect to the most likely and most dangerous branch plans.

(b) **Sequels.** Sequels are subsequent operations based on the possible outcomes of the current operation—victory, defeat, or stalemate. **In COIN, sequels can focus on different phases or shifting the overall approach.** For example, unanticipated success might allow for a more indirect US approach, or defeat might require a more direct US approach to shore up HNSF.

(3) **Simultaneity and Depth.** Simultaneity refers to the simultaneous application of military and nonmilitary power against the adversary's key capabilities and sources of strength. **Simultaneity in COIN contributes directly to an insurgency's erosion and ultimate collapse by addressing root causes and placing more demands on insurgent military forces and functions than can be handled.** Simultaneity also refers to the concurrent conduct of operations at the tactical, operational, and strategic levels. **For COIN, depth applies to time as well as to space.** This reflects that most insurgencies protract the conflict by design. **Because of the inherent tight interrelationships between the levels of war in COIN, commanders cannot be concerned only with events at their respective echelon, but must understand how their actions contribute to the military end state and the strategic end state.**

(4) **Timing and Tempo.** The joint force should conduct operations at a tempo and point in time that best exploits friendly capabilities and inhibits the enemy. **However, the intelligence operations dynamic ultimately determines the tempo that the counterinsurgents can maintain. Good intelligence will allow for successful operations that may in turn result in more usable intelligence.** Provided accurate, predictable, and timely intelligence, counterinsurgents can dominate the action, remain unpredictable, and operate ahead of the insurgency's ability to react.

l. **Forces and Functions. Commanders and planners can plan campaigns and operations that focus on defeating adversary forces, functions, or a combination of both.** In conventional planning, the JFCs structure operations to attack both adversary forces and functions concurrently to create the greatest possible friction between friendly and adversary forces and capabilities. These types of operations are especially appropriate when friendly forces enjoy technological and/or numerical superiority over an opponent. However, in COIN operations, the adversary is difficult to target and a greater amount of apportionment of forces should be applied to the appropriate COG. Addressing the root causes of concern of an adversary's support base can accomplish the intended disruption of the adversary's balance, thereby creating vulnerabilities to be exploited and may contribute directly to the collapse of adversary capability and will. COIN should focus on addressing the root causes and drivers of conflict in addition to defeating the insurgency as a military force.

See JP 3-0, Joint Operations, *and JP 5-0,* Joint Operation Planning, *for more detail on the elements of operational design.*

3. Military Operational Considerations for Counterinsurgency

Within the context of operating in a given HN, there are several operations, programs, and activities that may be conducted as a part of or simultaneously with COIN, including negotiation and diplomacy, SC (FID, SFA, and SA), unconventional warfare (UW), CT, counterguerrilla operations, stability operations, and PO. Each may be conducted simultaneously with or independently of the others but each would likely require overlapping operational areas within the HN. Additionally, each may have different root causes and objectives, but would become part of the overarching COIN operation/campaign. Other key operations related to COIN are CMO, IO, MISO, maritime security operations (MSO), and counterdrug operations.

a. **Negotiation and Diplomacy.** Negotiation and diplomacy is a way to influence an insurgency. The counterinsurgent must convince the HN government and subordinate elements, such as the ministry of defense or ministry of the interior to remove the root causes of the instability; some of these root causes may be caused by or aggravated by ministerial policies themselves. At the strategic and operational levels it could be working with the HN senior military leadership to assist them in evaluating the root causes of the insurgency. In other situations, the ministerial level official or general officer (being advised) may be able to influence other governmental organizations that could be a root cause of the insurgency. At the tactical level this could be a key leader engagement. These engagements can be used to shape and influence foreign leaders at the strategic, operational, and tactical levels, and may also be directed toward specific groups such as religious leaders, academic leaders, and tribal leaders (e.g., to solidify trust and confidence in US forces). Military leaders at all levels are being asked to work with their foreign partners, usually to foster a safer society. In utilizing qualified military leaders and advisors in negotiation and diplomacy, it may prevent an insurgency, and garner change in a peaceful manner.

b. **SC. SC involves all DOD interactions with foreign defense establishments to build defense relationships** that promote specific US security interests, develop allied and friendly military capabilities for self-defense and multinational operations, and provide US forces with peacetime and contingency access to an HN. These activities help the US and HN gain credibility and help the HN build legitimacy. These efforts can help minimize the effects of or prevent insurgencies and thwart their regeneration. The key subsets of SC in support of COIN are:

(1) **SA** is a group of SC programs funded by DOS to be administered by DOD/Defense Security Cooperation Agency. SA encompasses efforts of civilian agencies as well as those of the military. **SA is the provision of defense articles, military training, and other defense-related services by grant, loan, credit, or cash sales in furtherance of US national policies and objectives.**

(2) **FID** is the participation by civilian and military agencies of a government in any of the action programs taken by another government or other designated organization to

free and protect its society from subversion, lawlessness, insurgency, terrorism, and other threats to its security. The FID strategy focuses on building viable political, economic, military, security infrastructure, and social institutions for the needs of the local population. The focus of all US FID efforts is to support the HN's IDAD program. FID can only occur when there is an HN that has asked for assistance. The US will generally employ a mix of diplomatic, economic, informational, and military instruments of national power in support of these objectives (see Figure V-1). FID conducted by conventional forces and special operations forces (SOF) can assist the HN in reducing these contributing factors to insurgency and terrorism. FID operations involve military training and building infrastructure (e.g., schools, roads, and wells) in conjunction with foreign aid programs administered by DOS. FID operations can be indirect support or direct support (noncombat or combat).

(a) **Indirect Support.** These are FID operations that emphasize the principle of HN self-sufficiency. Indirect support focuses on building strong national infrastructures through economic and military capabilities that contribute to self-sufficiency.

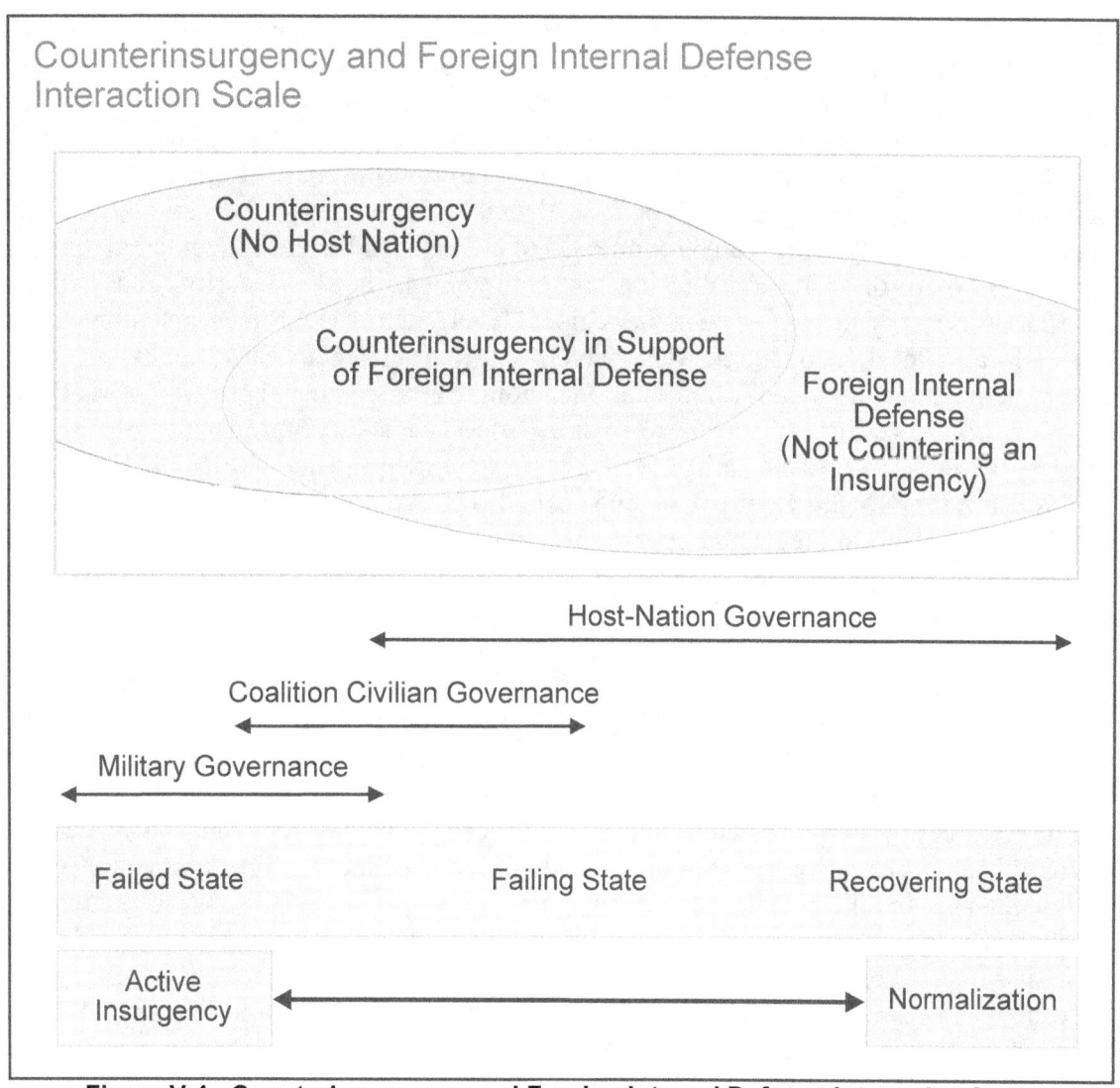

Figure V-1. Counterinsurgency and Foreign Internal Defense Interaction Scale

(b) **Direct Support (Not Involving Combat Operations).** These operations involve the use of US forces providing direct assistance to the HN civilian populace or military. They differ from SA in that they are joint or Service funded, do not usually involve the transfer of arms and equipment, and do not usually, but may, include training local military forces. Direct support operations are normally conducted when the HN has not attained self-sufficiency and is faced with social, economic, or military threats beyond its capability to handle. DOD support could include activities such as providing intelligence, mobility support, or logistics support.

(c) **US Combat Operations.** The introduction of US combat forces into FID operations requires a Presidential decision and serves only as a temporary solution until HN forces are able to stabilize the situation and provide security for the populace. If combat is authorized, normally this will include major operations.

For further information, see JP 3-22, Foreign Internal Defense.

(3) **SFA** consists of the DOD and whole-of-government activities that contribute to unified action by the USG to support the development of the capacity and capability of foreign security forces and their supporting institutions. **SFA encompasses joint force activities conducted within unified action to train, advise, assist, and equip foreign security forces in support of a partner nation's efforts to generate, employ, and sustain local, HN, or regional security forces and their supporting institutions.** This includes activities from ministry-level to tactical-level units of action, and the national security support base. Security forces can be comprised of civilians, SOF, and conventional military forces. They are often responsible for law enforcement, border security, and stability operations. Security forces can be at the regional level, such as UN forces, and all levels of the HN from local to national. Many actors can participate in SFA, including joint, intergovernmental, interagency, multinational, nongovernmental, and others. These efforts focus on the HN's efforts to increase its security forces' capability and capacity. **JFCs must ensure trainers and advisors are well prepared and qualified for their particular mission for the HN engagement to be successful.** Developing HN tactical capabilities alone is inadequate; strategic and operational capabilities must be developed as well. HN organizations and units should reflect their own unique requirements, interests, and capabilities—they should not simply mirror existing external institutions. SFA includes organizing institutions and units, which can range from standing up a ministry to improving the organization of the smallest maneuver unit. Building capability and capacity in this area includes personnel, logistics, and intelligence and their support infrastructure. In time, the HNSF must establish the capacity to generate its own forces through recruiting, vetting, and induction of enlistees as well as officer candidates; initial entry training for all personnel, to include basic warrior or police skills and advanced technical, tactical, and leadership training; and processes for promotion, noncommissioned officer training, and senior leader training. This should include the establishment of proper oversight and accountability mechanisms, law of war training for the enlistees and for those overseeing them. The HNSF must also develop processes for acquisition and life-cycle management of major end items, as well as processes for procurement of all classes of supply, and contracting of other services or capabilities. Further, at the executive direction levels, the HNSF must establish policies and a system of orders and directives that supports the HN statutory framework, and

drives standardization of policies and procedures through top-down flow of information and a robust command inspection program. In sum, US or coalition mentors, advisors, and trainers charged with conducting SFA activities in a COIN environment must look beyond the immediate tactical conditions on the ground, and collaborate with multiple agencies to develop the supporting infrastructure required for the HNSF to sustain and regenerate itself over the long term.

c. **UW.** UW consists of whole-of-government activities conducted to enable a resistance movement or insurgency to coerce, disrupt, or overthrow a government or occupying power by operating through or with an underground, auxiliary, and guerrilla force in a denied area. UW can support COIN operations by giving the JFC and/or the GCC an additional option for curtailing support to an ongoing insurgency. For example, if a neighboring state to the one in which a COIN operation is being waged has proven to be a major source of insurgent resources, personnel, and support, the JFC may recommend UW operations inside that insurgent-supporting state in order to modify that nation's counterproductive behavior or even remove its government altogether. While SOF play a major role in the execution of UW operations and posses specific tactical UW competencies, the JFC must ensure operational and strategic synchronization of COIN and UW activities. The JFC must ensure sufficient resources are provided to, and are mutually supporting of, both COIN and UW operations. UW is politically sensitive, with both strategic and long-term national and international implications. The JFC must secure appropriate authorities, conduct precise and detailed planning, and exploit innovative designs such as unique C2 relationships or organizations for successful UW execution.

For further details on UW, see JP 3-05, Special Operations.

d. **CT.** CT are actions taken directly against terrorist networks and indirectly to influence and render global and regional environments inhospitable to terrorist networks.

e. **Counterguerrilla Operations.** Counterguerrilla operations are operations and activities conducted by armed forces, paramilitary forces, or nonmilitary agencies against guerrillas. Counterguerrilla operations are essential supporting efforts, or a subset of COIN operations focused on the insurgents' military forces.

f. **Stability Operations.** Stability operations refer to various military missions, tasks, and activities conducted outside the US in coordination with other instruments of national power to maintain or reestablish a safe and secure environment and provide essential governmental services, emergency infrastructure reconstruction, and humanitarian relief. **Stability operations are consequently fundamental to COIN. Stability operations address the root causes of insurgency as well as drivers of conflict and are therefore essential to long-term success.** US military forces should be prepared to lead the activities necessary to accomplish these tasks when indigenous civil, other USG departments and agencies, multinational, or international capacity does not exist or is not yet capable of assuming responsibility. Once a legitimate civil authority is prepared to conduct such tasks, US military forces may support such activities as required with an emphasis on transition to HN or legitimate civil authority. Integrated civilian and military efforts are essential to success and military forces need to work competently in this environment while properly supporting the agency in charge. Effectively planning and executing stability operations require a variety of perspectives and expertise. DOS is charged with responsibility for a whole-of-government approach to stability operations that includes USG departments and agencies (including DOD), the HN, alliance or coalition partners, NGOs, IGOs, and other actors. Military forces should be prepared to work in informal or formal integrated civil-military teams that could include, and in some cases be led by, representatives from other USG departments and agencies, foreign governments and security forces, IGOs, NGOs, and members of the private sector with relevant skills and expertise.

For further details on stability operations, refer to JP 3-0, Joint Operations, *JP 3-07,* Stability Operations, *and Department of Defense Instruction (DODI) 3000.05,* Stability Operations.

g. **PO.** For the Armed Forces of the United States, PO are **crisis response and limited contingency operations** involving all instruments of national power and international efforts and military missions to contain conflict, restore the peace, and shape the environment to support reconciliation and rebuilding and to facilitate the transition to legitimate governance. PO include peacekeeping operations, peace enforcement operations (PEO), peace building post-conflict actions, peacemaking processes, and conflict prevention. PO may be conducted under the sponsorship of the UN, another IGO, within a multinational force, or unilaterally.

See further details in JP 3-07.3, Peace Operations.

h. **Related Operations.** The complex nature of COIN often requires many types of operations to effectively shape the OE and set the conditions to reach the desired end state. For example, all or part of unsuccessful PEO can transition to COIN as the situation devolves and becomes more unstable. COIN and PEO can also occur simultaneously if some parties have agreed to peace while one or more use insurgency to reach their goals. More important, successful COIN can become long-term PEO as part of a larger FID framework. Other key operations related to COIN are CMO, IO, MISO, MSO, counterdrug operations, cyberspace operations, etc.

4. Additional Operational Options for Counterinsurgency

There are several options to consider when conducting COIN operations: generational engagement; limited support/light footprint; identify, separate, isolate, influence, and reintegrate (ISI2R); AtN operations; partnering; and shape, clear, hold, build, and transition (SCHBT). Each option offers a different but complementary avenue and must be weighed against the OE and the actors involved and may be used individually or in conjunction with each other.

a. **Generational engagement** seeks to get the HN to educate and empower relevant population groups to participate in legal methods of political discourse and dissent. It also empowers youth to protest in nonviolent manners and participate in development and decision making in their communities and robs the insurgency of a disillusioned population. If it is assumed that most insurgencies last for years, then it becomes important not only to engage the present day leaders, but form and mold (done by HN) the next generation of leaders to become successful participants in the existing form of government. A note of caution comes with generational engagement; the population or youth groups may demonstrate and protest the very government the counterinsurgent hoped they would support. However, this is might not be a failure, but rather a success. As is expected in functional societies, mass mobilizations and protests are preferred reactions to government failures instead of violent resistance or coup attempts. In order to ensure that active, engaged youth don't become future insurgent fighters, it is important to create channels for youth leaders to engage with their elders and power brokers in their own communities.

b. **Limited support/light footprint** is an option that leverages special operations, indigenous ground forces, robust intelligence, as well as air support, to counter an insurgency. This avoids a large footprint of US or multinational forces in an area which, if present, may serve to alienate the population, succeed less, and cost more. With this option an insurgency can be countered by using advisors and providing indigenous forces with assets and resources (intelligence, communications, aerial support, etc.).

c. **ISI2R** is an option that combines several activities that seek to affect relevant population groups to separate them from the insurgency. It is also proactive in addressing root causes of instability thereby deflating the purpose of the insurgency. ISI2R places a heavy emphasis on disarming and reintegrating former insurgents and creating the conditions that insurgents would prefer over surrender and continued fighting. Its premise is to identify and separate the insurgents from the population. This has traditionally been a cornerstone requirement for forces conducting COIN. Identifying who is an insurgent and who is not and then applying resources to separate them from the population helps commanders and planners to more effectively focus their efforts on making the insurgency feel alone and their causes for conflict not supported by the population. Once the insurgent leaders and members feel isolated from the population in supporting their cause, peaceful efforts can be made to influence insurgents to surrender and return and be reintegrated into being a peaceful member of society. The importance of influencing members of an insurgency to surrender cannot be overstated. The importance of how the former insurgent is reintegrated into a peaceful society is also critical since the way in which the war is won will decide how long the peace will last. Another manner in which this can manifest is when the insurgents and the government have extreme distrust between one another and need a third party to intervene in some aspect of the peace process.

d. **AtN** operations involve lethal and nonlethal actions and activities that identify, determine relevance, and seek to generate effects on appropriate hostile and relevant actors' networks. These operations may occur continuously and simultaneously at multiple levels (tactical, operational, and strategic). In COIN operations, AtN seeks to destroy the insurgent forces physical infrastructure including aspects that can be used to support the insurgent cause. AtN would proactively target the physical and societal mechanisms that support and fuel the insurgency. AtN is neither a process nor sequential, but rather a framework that integrates existing processes and methods, and focuses them on considering, identifying, and engaging relevant networks. Commanders and staffs must first understand the OE in network terms. An important feature of any network is its adaptability to a changing environment; one change to a node or link may substantially affect the entire network. Because of this dynamic nature of complex adaptive systems, a second imperative for effective AtN operations is to closely link operations and intelligence. The third essential element for an effective strategy is to rapidly assess the effects created by operations and feed the assessment into the intelligence process. AtN operations conducted at the tactical level and in Service doctrine are referred to as targeted threat infrastructure. For more information on targeted threat infrastructure, see Field Manual (FM) 3-24/Marine Corps Warfighting Publication (MCWP) 3-33.5, *Counterinsurgency.*

e. **Partnering** is an arrangement between US and HN forces in which they operate together to achieve mission success while building capability and capacity. Partnering should be a union of the organizations involved. It cannot be done on occasion, when convenient, or as time permits. Nor should it be limited to periodic or occasional combat operations. Real partnering is muddled and potentially complex—a continuous, collective, and collaborative effort on both large and small tasks toward a common goal. It requires mutual respect despite differences in size, skill, training, capability, or culture. In every partnership, each participant has relative strengths. Effective partnering will exploit all these relative strengths and overcome respective weaknesses. It requires flexible and innovative leaders capable of forging strong personal relationships—which are a key to successful COIN efforts. Successful COIN partnerships are designed to end as HN forces gain the capability and capacity to stand alone. Nontraditional threats, such as the insider threat, can undermine partnering and SFA activities as well as the cohesion of US and HN forces during the conduct of COIN operations. Strategically, they can threaten not only the US's objectives, but also undermine the overall efforts of the international community. Tactically, the breakdown of trust, communication, and cooperation between HN and US forces can affect military capability. Eliminating and/or minimizing the insider threat, especially by proper preparation and training of forces, is critical to mission success. However, more stringent force protection controls and measures that are overtly heavy-handed must be well balanced yet culturally sensitive enough to not send the wrong message to the very people and organizations the US is trying to assist. Adversaries may view attacks against US forces as a particularly effective tactic, especially when using co-opted HN forces to conduct these attacks. While these types of "insider" or "green on blue" attacks have been context-specific to a particular theater, JFCs should nevertheless ensure that their force protections plans take into account the potential for these types of attacks and plan appropriate countermeasures as the situation dictates. To reduce the potential for insider attacks, the JFC should establish vetting procedures to identify individuals whose motivations toward the HN and USG are in question. It is imperative to remove all unvetted personnel from training. The insider threat can be further mitigated via counterintelligence screenings (with periodic rescreening) and biometric enrollments of potential military recruits and applicants for base employment. Local records checks should be part of command standard operating procedures. In certain cultures, recruits and applicants for employment can be required to submit statements from recognized and trusted elders addressing the candidate's trustworthiness. Combined action and community stability operations are two types of effective partnering techniques and described in the following paragraphs.

(1) **Combined Action.** Combined action is a technique that involves joining US and HN troops in a single organization, usually a platoon or company, and in some cases at the battalion level, to conduct COIN operations. This technique is appropriate in environments where large insurgent forces do not exist or where insurgents lack resources

and freedom of maneuver. Combined action normally involves joining a US rifle squad or platoon with an HN platoon or company, respectively. Commanders use this approach to hold and build while providing a persistent counterinsurgent presence among the populace. This approach attempts to first achieve security and stability in a local area, followed by offensive operations against insurgent forces now denied access or support.

(a) Combined action can work only in areas with limited insurgent activity. The technique should not be used to isolate or expel a well-established and supported insurgent force. Combined action is most effective after an area has been cleared of armed insurgents.

(b) The following geographic and demographic factors can also influence the likelihood of success:

1. Towns relatively isolated from other population centers are simpler to secure continuously.

2. Towns and villages with a limited number of roads passing through them are easier to secure than those with many routes in and out. All approaches must be guarded.

3. Existing avenues of approach into a town should be observable from the town. Keeping these areas under observation facilitates interdiction of insurgents and control of population movements.

4. The local populace should be small and constant. People should know one another and be able to easily identify outsiders. In towns or small cities where this is not the case, a census conducted using biometrics is the most effective tool to establish initial accountability for everyone.

5. Combined action or local defense forces must establish mutual support with forces operating in nearby towns. Larger reaction or reserve forces as well as close air support, attack aviation, and air assault support should be quickly available. Engineer and explosive ordnance disposal assets should also be available.

(c) Thoroughly integrating US and HN combined action personnel supports the effective teamwork critical to the success of each team and the overall program. US members should be drawn from some of the parent unit's best personnel. Designating potential members before deployment facilitates the training and team building needed for combined action unit success in theater.

(2) **Community Stability Operations.** Community stability operations are local-level stability operations designed to augment wider COIN operations. Community stability operations are a bottom-up COIN strategy that establishes expanding security and stability bubbles around rural communities. As the security bubble expands outward, more and more "white space" is created that is inhospitable to the insurgents and allows for the establishment and solidification of legitimate local governance. As these security bubbles expand and connect, they simultaneously force the insurgents out and connect local informal

governance structures to the HN government. The central actor in community stability operations is the platform. The platform could be multinational forces living among the people in rural areas (surrounded by the insurgents and the populace), building relationships and assisting the populace to stand up against insurgents, while re-empowering their traditional local governance structures within the community.

f. **SCHBT** combines multinational (including the US) and HN forces and agencies, especially military, law enforcement, local leaders, and local government. The combined efforts combat insurgents, protect the population, and address the root causes, neighborhood by neighborhood, town by town, city by city.

(1) Each phase of SCHBT will have aspects of offense, defense, and stability; however, the proportions of these operations will depend on the current phase. In general, security forces conduct offensive operations to eliminate guerrillas, transition to securing and defending the area, and finally focusing on stability operations to facilitate the comprehensive approach to address the prerequisites of insurgency and core grievances. SCHBT operations expand outward from secured areas into contested and insurgent dominated areas. Strike operations are used in conjunction with SCHBT operations in order to keep insurgents off balance, thus supporting SCHBT efforts by preventing or degrading insurgent interference.

(2) Key points of an effective clear, hold, build approach:

(a) Physically and psychologically separates the insurgents from the population.

(b) Provides the conditions for economic, political, and social reforms.

(c) Safeguards the population and infrastructure.

(d) Provides training and opportunities for HNSF to improve and take the lead in operations, especially taking and maintaining control.

(e) Provides opportunity for the HN police and other institutions and agencies to gain and maintain rule of law.

(f) Provides essential services and addresses the root causes of the insurgency.

(g) Repatriates and resettles internally displaced persons and refugees to their homes.

(h) Trains local workers and materials to rebuild and provide a sustainable economic and social system.

(i) Denies the enemy active and passive support.

(j) Gains the support of the populace.

5. Termination (End State), Transnational Military Authorities, Reconciliation, Reintegration, and Political Reform

a. **Termination.** A COIN operation will eventually reach a conclusion, as an insurgent victory, a negotiated settlement, or an HN government victory. The termination of US combat operations can also precede any of those events. Effective COIN planning cannot occur without a clear understanding of the military end state and the conditions that must exist to end military operations. Knowing when to terminate US combat operations and how to preserve achieved advantages for success of the HN is key to attaining the US national strategic end state. To plan effectively for termination, the supported JFC must have a shared understanding with the COM, and they must understand how the President and SecDef intend to terminate the joint operation and ensure that its outcomes endure. **The more difficult aspect of military termination is probably the transition** of tasks and activities from military to civilian authorities (either interagency or multinational partners or the HN). This could also be described as the transitions from phase III (dominate) to phase IV (stabilize), and then to phase V (enable civil authorities), and finally a return to phase 0 (shape).

b. **Transitional Military Authorities.** In some cases a transitional military authority may be required in UGAs, occupied territory, or an allied or neutral territory liberated from enemy forces, including insurgent or resistance movement. A transitional military authority is a temporary military government exercising the functions of civil administration in the absence of a legitimate civil authority. It exercises temporary executive, legislative, and judicial authority in a foreign territory. The authority to establish military governance resides with the President. US forces will only assume control prescribed in directives to the JFC. If established, the transitional military authority will eventually relinquish control of the OE, with activities assumed by the HN or another authority. It is important to plan transition from the start of the operation. (For example, it will be easier to transition US detention operations to the HN if such detention operations from the start take into account HN legal framework and HN ability and resources to sustain detention facilities that might be constructed by US forces.) Transitional military government is different than a strictly military government, which is the supreme authority the military exercises by force or agreement over the lands, property, and indigenous populations and institutions (IPI) of domestic, allied, or enemy territory, therefore substituting sovereign authority under rule of law for the previously established government.

(1) Transition is a sequence of actions required to shift responsibility from one organization to another. Transitions require an allocated period of time that allows for the myriad of tasks to be completed. Thinking of it as a general series of actions expands the scope of transitions thinking and more accurately reflects what must occur.

(2) Effective transitions are critically important when conducting COIN operations. Whether the transition is between military units or from a military unit to a civilian agency, all involved must clearly understand the tasks and responsibilities being passed and the time expected for completion. Enabling coordination between units, agencies, organizations, etc., helps reduce the friction normally associated with transitions. Early identification of a

collaborative transition planning team can help build the foundation for an effective transition physically, functionally, and contextually, as well as reduce its duration.

c. **Reconciliation and Reintegration.** DODI 3000.05, *Stability Operations,* directs the Services to include stability operations (which includes transition) to their military task list and give it the same training priority as conventional combat operations. The elements of operational design and art are useful tools for helping to analyze, identify, and describe transitions but may limit the insight into transitions associated with IW. Transitions in COIN require more refinement to assist planners and commanders in executing operations in depth with regard to time. Reconciliation and reintegration of insurgent forces can be achieved through the stabilization framework provided in DODI 3000.05, *Stability Operations,* and associated Service documents.

d. **Political Reform.** Once the insurgent political infrastructure is destroyed and local leaders begin to establish themselves, necessary political reforms can be implemented. These aspects of COIN should ideally be led by civilian agencies, IGOs, or NGOs, with the military in a supporting role. The JFC should coordinate actions in these areas with the COM and the country team. Other tasks are to:

(1) Establish HN government agencies to perform routine administrative functions and begin improvement programs.

(2) Provide HN government support to those willing to participate in reconstruction. Participation should be based on need and ability to help.

(3) Develop regional and national consciousness and rapport between the population and its government. Efforts may include participating in local elections, making community improvements, forming youth clubs, and executing other projects.

(4) Provide systems for safely reporting adversary or friendly acts of intimidation, violence, crime, and corruption.

6. Assessment

Assessment is the continuous monitoring and evaluation (M&E) of the current situation and progress of a joint operation toward mission accomplishment. It involves deliberately comparing forecasted outcomes to actual events to determine the overall effectiveness of force employment. In general, assessments should answer two questions: Is the JFC doing things right? Is the JFC doing the right things? More specifically, assessment helps JFCs determine progress toward achieving objectives and whether the current tasks and objectives are relevant to reaching the end state. It helps identify opportunities, counter threats, and any needs for course correction, thus resulting in modifications to plans and orders. This process of continuous assessment occurs throughout the joint planning process.

For more discussion on assessment, see Chapter VI, "Assessing Counterinsurgency Operations," and JP 5-0, Joint Operation Planning.

CHAPTER VI
ASSESSING COUNTERINSURGENCY OPERATIONS

> *"Assessment and learning enable incremental improvements to the commander's operational approach and the campaign or contingency plan."*
>
> **Joint Publication 5-0,** *Joint Operation Planning*

1. General

a. **Introduction to Operation Assessment.** Operation assessment offers perspective and insight, and provides the opportunity for self-correction, adaptation, and thoughtful results-oriented learning. COIN operation assessment requires an integrated approach to support commander and policy maker decisions regarding the implementation and resourcing of operations to accomplish strategic objectives. From engagements in Iraq, Afghanistan, the Philippines, and the Horn of Africa, principles of operation assessment have emerged to support operation planning and execution across multiple echelons. The COIN operation assessment process detailed in this chapter provides these basic principles to integrate staff and intelligence perspectives through the planning and execution cycle of operations (see Figure VI-1). Effective assessment is necessary for counterinsurgents to recognize changing conditions and determine their significance to the progress of the COIN operation. It is crucial to the JFC's ability to identify anticipated and unanticipated effects and successfully adapt to the changing situation. A continuous discourse among counterinsurgents at all echelons provides the feedback the senior leadership needs to appropriately adapt operations to the current situation.

b. **Learning and Adjusting.** Commanders must be attuned to a change in the OE (particularly in the political realm) that may cause the initial plan of the operation to be in question. Often times, these changes will occur independently and will not necessarily be linked in any way to the actions of the joint force and multinational partners. In an ideal world, the commander of military forces engaged in COIN operations would enjoy clear and well-defined operation or campaign end states from the beginning to end. The reality is that with the political volatility inherent in COIN operations many goals emerge only as the operation or campaign develops. Environmental conditions may develop that did not exist during planning of the COIN operation or campaign that require changing previous frames of reference and operational objectives. Consequently, operational assessment in COIN requires balancing disciplined process with analytical flexibility to facilitate operational adaptation.

c. **The Purpose of Operation Assessment in COIN**

(1) Assessment of a COIN operation is a key component of the commander's decision-making cycle. It helps the JFC determine changes within the OE, as well as the results of tactical, operational, and strategic actions, in the context of overall mission objectives. During the planning process, operation assessments inform the commander's decisions to employ limited resources to attain defined military end states. The decision to adapt plans or shift resources is based upon the integration of the intelligence assessment of

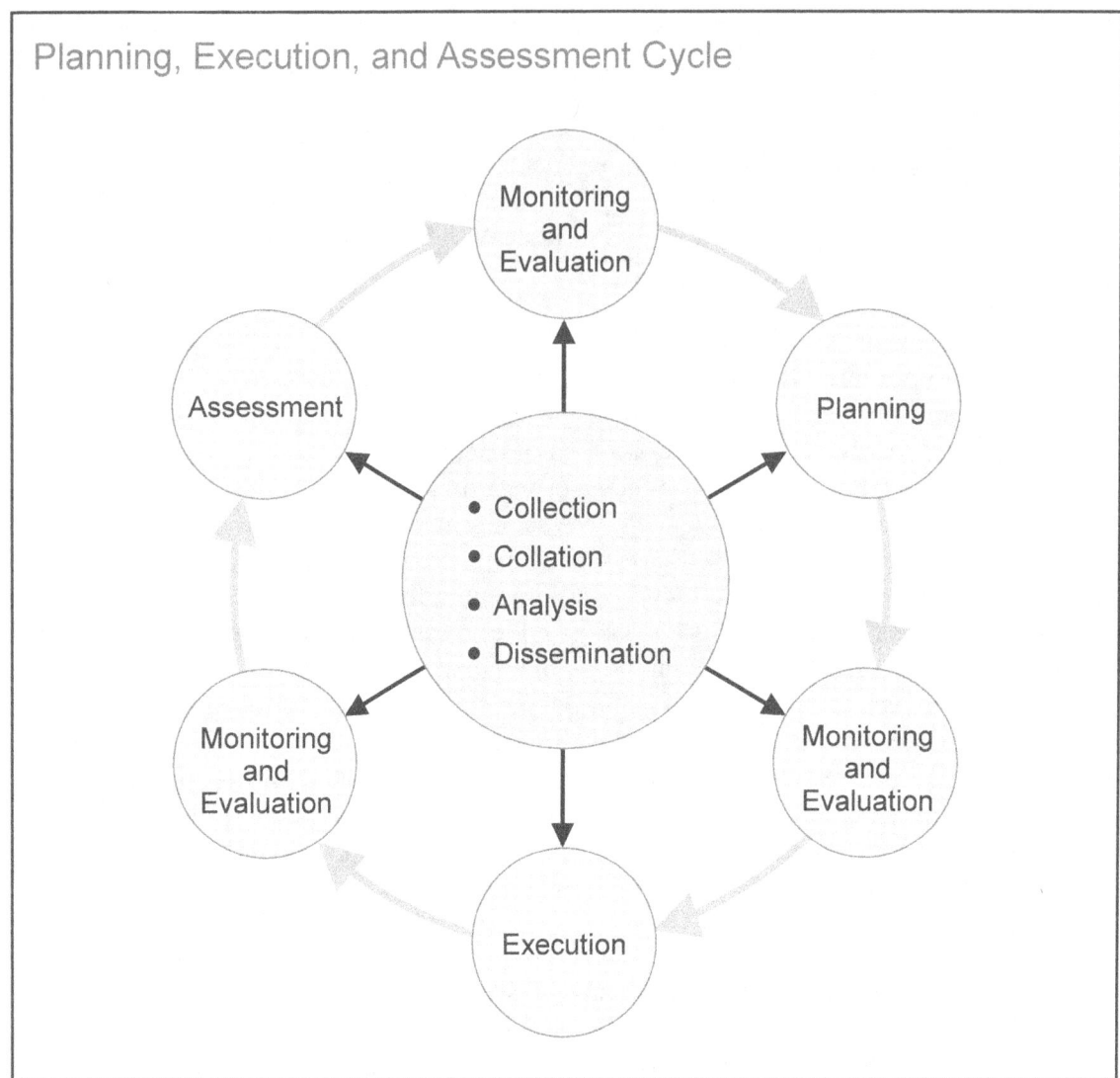

Figure VI-1. Planning, Execution, and Assessment Cycle

the OE and staff estimates of the joint force's ability to conduct operations in pursuit of the end state. However, the complex, dynamic, and uncertain nature of COIN operations mean that some end state conditions may be ill-defined or change while the operation progresses.

(2) During planning, the commander and staff describe the current conditions of the OE, the desired conditions at the end state of an operation, and identify the barriers that prevent the establishment of the desired conditions. The commander and staff develop an assessment plan to focus and integrate information from various sources to reduce the uncertainty of their observations and conclusions about the OE. This information may be derived from interagency partners, multinational partners, the HN government, subordinate commands, NGOs, and various intelligence sources.

(3) In COIN operations, it is difficult to isolate the effects of specific actions. The commander and staff focus information requirements to answer specific questions about the operation plan, and they develop the assessment plan using the same structure as the

operation plan. The integration of operation planning and assessment links joint force actions to changes in observed conditions within the OE in order to support the commander's decision cycle and adapt future plans.

(4) The outputs of an assessment communicate the effectiveness of the operation plan toward desired end states; describe risks involved in the accomplishment of the plan; and recommend necessary changes to the plan in order to attain a desired end state. Additionally, assessments help the commander to report observations and conclusions about the impacts of the operation plan and make recommendations to senior commanders or policy makers.

d. **Use of Operation Assessment.** Effective operation assessments link the employment of forces and resources to intelligence assessments of the OE. Properly executed assessments allow the commander to do the following:

(1) Compare observed OE conditions to desired end state conditions.

(2) Determine whether key planning assumptions are still valid.

(3) Determine whether the desired effects have been created and the objectives have been achieved.

(4) Determine the effectiveness of resources allocated against objectives.

(5) Determine whether a decision point has been reached.

(6) Identify the risks and barriers to mission accomplishment.

(7) Identify opportunities to accelerate mission accomplishment.

(8) Develop recommendations for branches and sequels.

(9) Communicate the evaluation of the plan to the higher headquarters, staff, subordinate units, policy makers, interagency partners, and others as necessary.

e. **Assessment Complexities in COIN**

(1) In traditional operations, operation assessment tends to involve a calculation of the current state of the OE, measures of performance (MOPs), and measures of effectiveness (MOEs) with regard to primarily military objectives and the military operational end state. This is not the case in COIN, because military objectives, while important, are just one key aspect of the broader HN's political objectives of a COIN operation.

(2) Operation assessments in COIN differ from assessments of many traditional operations because success of the operation often relies on nonmilitary factors and factors outside of the joint force's direct control. This increases the focus on diplomatic, informational, and economic objectives. As with traditional operations, the operation assessments will link the performance of the joint force to the conditions of the current OE.

This helps the joint force estimate the impacts of its actions on the environment. As explained in Chapter III, "Fundamentals of Counterinsurgency," the military aspect of a COIN operation is important because it helps to create the conditions for achievement of diplomatic, informational, and economic objectives and end states. Because the LOEs and LOOs within COIN are interdependent, the impact of military actions can be difficult to isolate in the OE. Often, this requires that the joint force determine progress toward these objectives to understand the relationships that exist between nonmilitary and military objectives.

(3) COIN operations often involve complex political and societal issues that may not lend themselves to quantifiable MOEs; therefore, assessment staffs in COIN require skill sets in operationally relevant qualitative research analysis. This includes a degree of area knowledge specific to social science skill sets and an understanding of COIN and/or operational relevance in COIN analysis.

(4) The JFC and staff must establish which assessment factors within the OE are important and ascertain the status of these factors with regard to the COIN operation's intermediate objectives and end state. The complexity of COIN operations usually does not allow for uniform or quantifiable MOEs. Because no two COIN operations and no two locations within an operational area are the same, all COIN operations must be assessed on their own merits. The JFC and staff must continually develop and enhance their understanding of the OE to identify the key factors particular to their operation.

f. **Tenets for Operation Assessment in COIN.** There is no single approach to operation assessments that can address the diversity of COIN operations and the OE in which they will be conducted. However, all operation assessments must be linked to the operation plan being executed. The commander uses operation assessments to visualize and describe the desired outcomes of the operation, and direct forces and resources toward accomplishing the mission. Operation assessments at the strategic, operational, and tactical level will differ in terms of the amount of time and staff required to execute them. However, the principles of assessments are the same at all levels. For every assessment, there is a cut-off for information inputs, and the assessment team ultimately develops the best assessment possible within the time constraints of the assessment deadline. Operational assessments are conducted with a degree of regularity that is appropriate for the nature of the specific operation and the capabilities of the joint force. The following tenets should guide the commander and the joint force staff in developing an operation assessment plan:

(1) **Commander-Centric.** The commander's involvement in operation assessment is essential. The commander's level of interest and specific requirements for decision making drive the operation assessment plan. The assessment plan must focus on the information and intelligence that directly support the commander's decision-making requirements.

(2) **Subordinate Commander Involvement.** Assessments are more effective when used to support conversations between commanders at different echelons. Operation assessments link echelons of command by identifying the activities and impacts critical to success and sharing the assessment methods used to shape operational decisions. A common

understanding of operational priorities allows subordinate commanders across regions to directly communicate their most relevant information.

(3) **Staff Product.** Staff integration is crucial to planning and executing effective assessments. The development of an operation assessment plan is the responsibility of commanders, planners, and operators at every level and not the sole work of an individual advisor, committee, or assessment entity. The development of an operation assessment plan is a process nested within the planning process, and the assessment integrates roles across the joint force staff. The chief of staff is generally best suited to direct the integration of assessments across staff elements. Properly structured, operation assessments enable the staff to examine and understand how actions in one LOE/LOO will impact others. By integrating perspectives from across the staff, the assessment will avoid errors which arise from limited focus, such as duplication of effort, incorrect identification of causes, or insufficient information to prioritize issues by level of impact.

(4) **Integrated into the Planning Process and Battle Rhythm.** To deliver decision-quality information at the right time, the assessment plan must both be timed with the commander's decision cycles and provide triggers to enable commanders to respond to critical changes in the OE. Because the assessment plan shares the same structure as the operation plan, any cyclic assessments should support the operation cycle.

(5) **Integration of External Sources of Information and Intelligence.** The operation assessment plan should allow the commander and staff to integrate information that updates the understanding of the environment in order to inform future planning efforts. To get a complete understanding of the OE, it is important to include specific feedback mechanisms to/from the HN, and interagency, multinational, and nongovernmental partners. For aspects of the operation plan for which nonmilitary influence has high impact or is not well understood, input from these sources is critical to refine understanding of the OE and reduce risk to success which is inherent in military operations in a COIN environment.

(6) **Credible and Transparent.** Assessment reports should cite all sources of information used to build the assessment. The staff should use methods that are appropriate to the environment and to the task of assessing a complex operation. As much as possible, sources and assessments should be unbiased. All methods and limitations in the collection of information, and any assumptions used to link evidence to conclusions, should be clearly described in the assessment report.

(7) **M&E Is Continuous.** While an operation assessment may be developed for a specified time, M&E is continuous in a COIN operation. Through M&E, the JFC maintains real-time understanding of developments in the OE. The information collected and analyzed during M&E can be used to inform planning, execution, and assessment of operations. MOPs and MOEs may be looked at during M&E, as JFC actions that are either helpful or harmful to the current situation within the OE may be discovered. In a COIN operation, it is possible to properly execute a given activity with the intended tactical effect, yet still not have the desired operational or strategic effect on the insurgency or the rest of the OE. However, like with broader assessment, M&E is focused on developments in the OE. Like in the main operation assessment process, M&E for COIN is conducted first at the lowest

possible level, or by those with the most accurate understanding of each location within the operational area. Based on M&E reporting at the lower levels, higher headquarters can then conduct their own M&E that feeds into the assessment process.

2. The Assessment Process and Assessment Plan

a. Relevant factors for assessments in COIN are rarely uniform across regions and operational phases. In previous COIN operations, the JFC assessment process attempted to develop operational-level metrics for the entire OE. Because the importance of relevant factors was highly localized, and in some cases, not applicable, an indicator of progress in one location did not necessarily hold true for other locations. Relevant factors for assessment of a given area may change over time due to changes in the OE that may, or may not, be related to actions by the JFC. An operation assessment process must include established standard operating procedures for dissemination of localized assessments through the various higher headquarters. Each headquarters falling under the joint operational command must produce its own assessments that incorporate the lower level assessments they receive and disseminate their own assessment, along with the original lower-level assessments higher up the chain. Only through this process can assessment at the operational level account for the nuance in local context and the varied nature of the conflict spanning the entirety of the operational area.

b. To account for the differences between various locations within a given operational area, COIN operations require decentralized command structures. This principle extends to the operation assessment planning for COIN. Operation assessment in COIN relies on those with the most in-depth knowledge of specific locations within the operational area, usually subordinate units, to identify and assess factors relevant to their localities. The joint force should structure the assessment plan to incorporate the reporting and assessments of subordinate commands without being prescriptive as to what information is collected or how it is analyzed.

c. The Operation Assessment Process

(1) The assessment process operates during the planning and execution cycle. Figure VI-2 shows the steps of the assessment process, the inputs and outputs of each step, the primary personnel involved in the step, and where in the planning and execution cycle the step occurs. This process supports the clear definition of tasks, objectives, and end states, and gives the staff a method for selecting the commander's critical information requirements (CCIRs) that best support decision making.

(2) The basic steps of the assessment process are integrated into the commander's decisions for operations.

(a) Identify information and intelligence requirements.

(b) Create assessment plan to support the operation plan.

(c) Collect and analyze information and intelligence.

The Steps of the Assessment Process

Assessment Step	Operations	Personnel	Input	Output
Identify Information and Intelligence Requirements	Plan	Commander and planners for operations, intelligence, and assessments	Clearly defined end states, objectives, and tasks	Information and intelligence requirements collection plans
Design Assessment Plan	Plan	Operations planners, assessment planners	Operation plan,CCIRs (PIRs and FFIRs) linked to decision support template	Assessment plan
Collect Information and Intelligence Requirements	Execute	Intelligence analysts, current operations, assessment team	Multi-source intelligence reporting, joint force resource and disposition information	Estimates of OE conditions, enemy disposition, friendly disposition
Conduct Event-Based and Periodic Assessments	Execute	Intelligence analysis, operations planners, assessment team	Intelligence assessments, staff assessments, and analysis methods	Estimate of joint force effects on OE
Report Results: Feedback and Recommendations	Execute	Assessment team, operations planners	Estimate of joint force effects on OE	Assessment report and decision recommendation
Adapt Plans for Operation and Assessment	Plan	Commander, planners for operations, assessments, and intelligence	Commander's guidance and feedback	Changes to operation plan and assessment plan

Legend

CCIR	commander's critical information requirement		OE	operational environment
FFIR	friendly force information requirement		PIR	priority intelligence requirement

Figure VI-2. The Steps of the Assessment Process

    (d) Conduct event-based and/or periodic assessment.

    (e) Provide feedback and recommendations.

(f) Adapt operation plan and assessment plan.

d. **Identify Information and Intelligence Requirements**

(1) The assessment process begins during mission analysis or operational design when the staff begins to identify the operational variables needed to understand what to measure and how to measure it. Each element of the operational plan directs resources against a particular action with an intended effect. Information is needed to understand whether planned actions were executed, and intelligence is needed to interpret changes to the targeted aspect of the OE.

(2) The staff selects an operational variable framework (ASCOPE, etc.) to describe its understanding of current conditions and desired conditions within the OE. Clearly understood end states are critical to measuring progress in a COIN operation or campaign. However, COIN operations and campaigns rarely have well-defined end states. Poorly defined end states can produce poorly defined plans and assessments. This creates a situation where effectiveness of the COIN operation is difficult to ascertain, and the result is an increased risk in wasting time, resources, and opportunities to successfully accomplish the mission. To address this, the staff should define specific goals in terms of the operational variable framework. This links ill-defined end states to assumptions about the observable behaviors necessary to determine progress toward those end states. These observable behaviors should be translated into information and intelligence requirements and integrated into the operation plan as CCIRs.

(3) As part of operational design or the operational framework and in order to clarify the connections between assumptions, operations, and end states, the staff should clearly articulate how they believe the operation will lead to the desired end states. Because of the uncertain nature of COIN operations, a better understanding of the OE may develop over time, providing an opportunity for better operation plans. Assessment can facilitate this by explicitly describing the critical assumptions upon which the operation was planned. These assumptions can be tested and refined in ways that will create opportunities to improve the plan and, consequently, to reach the end state.

(4) At the start of a COIN operation or campaign, the commander and staff develop a baseline assessment. The baseline provides an understanding of the initial conditions of the environment. During planning, a baseline assessment allows the commander and staff to set goals for desired rates of change within the environment and thresholds for success and failure. This focuses information and intelligence collection on answering specific questions relating to the desired outcomes of the plan.

(5) Figure VI-3 compares the perspectives, sources, uses, and results of information and intelligence. These distinctions in external versus internal focus show that intelligence is used to understand the environment, and information from staff and subordinate command reporting is used to determine if the joint force executes operations according to plan. The operations assessment provides comprehensive internal and external perspective of the joint force's impact on the OE.

Comparison and Use of Information and Intelligence

	Information	Intelligence
Perspective	Internal focus.	External focus.
Sources	Staff section and subordinate command reports, host-nation reports, NGO information.	All-source intelligence, intelligence agency reports, host-nation reports.
Use in Plans	Friendly force information requirements assumptions linking force posture to operations.	Priority intelligence requirements assumptions linking operations to effects.
Use in Assessments	Determines if plan is executed properly.	Determines if plan is creating desired conditions.
Result of Assessments	Resource efficiency of the plan.	Resource effectiveness of the plan.
Example of IIRs	Allocation of coalition trainers to train HNSF within a specific region. Readiness assessment of HNSF.	Security assessment within a particular region.
Example of Assessments	Estimation of best number of trainers for a type of HNSF unit at a specific capability rating.	Estimation of HNSF ability to sustain security within a given region.
Example of Conclusions	Helps staff to estimate if coalition trainers increase/decrease/have no impact on the HNSF ability to provide security for a given region.	
Example of Decision Requirements	Increase/decrease/do not change the level of multinational training support to HNSF within a given region.	

Legend

HNSF host-nation security forces NGO nongovernmental organization
IIR information and intelligence requirement

Figure VI-3. Comparison and Use of Information and Intelligence

(6) Nonmilitary aspects of the OE are critically important in COIN operations. Information derived from multiple agencies, warfighting functions, and subordinate commands may be focused to address specific questions about nonmilitary relationships within the OE. Answering these questions will not allow the commander or staff to determine a cause-and-effect relationship between joint force actions and observation with OE. However, it will aid in developing insights into expected behaviors and inform the understanding of the OE.

(7) Assessment questions should be directly linked to the desired operating conditions articulated during the operational design process. When possible, the staff that

develops the desired end state conditions should also design the assessment questions during the planning process, with the commander's direct participation. Examples of assessment questions in a COIN environment are:

(a) **Security Conditions.** Has sufficient security been established to sustain stability?

(b) **HNSF.** Can the HNSF (in a specified area) handle local security requirements without joint force or multinational force assistance?

(c) **HN Governance Capacity.** Is there sufficient HN government control, rule of law, and stability to prevent reemergence of an insurgent threat?

(8) The staff should develop assessment questions based upon the critical assumptions laid out during planning. This links the operation assessment to the structure of the operation plan, intended actions, and the expected outcomes. These questions allow the staff to validate or invalidate assumptions made during planning as they play out in execution.

(9) Assessment questions test the assumption that define the cause (action) and effect (result) relationship between operational activities and end states. If expected progress toward an end state does not occur, then the staff may conclude that that the intended action does not have the intended effect. The uncertainty of the OE in a COIN environment makes the use of critical assumptions particularly important, as operation planning may need to be more dynamic for elements of the OE which are initially not well understood when the plan is developed. In some cases, if an aspect of the OE is particularly uncertain, assumptions not used in the operation plan may be tested in order to trigger a change to the operation plan if those assumptions bear out. If information indicates that actions are executed as planned, but intelligence indicates that the intended end state is not being reached, then the assumptions may need to be revisited to improve the operation plan. Once the assessment can identify an incorrect assumption, steps can be taken to improve the operation plan by identifying the fault, correcting the assumption or the logical relationship, and adjusting the subsequent operations and activities.

(10) Going through this process helps the staff to determine knowledge and information gaps, and helps the staff gauge the value of the information and intelligence they collect. This process also helps eliminate redundant and obsolete reporting requirements for subordinate units. An information or intelligence requirement can either be quantitative (e.g., number of enemy-initiated attacks), or qualitative (e.g., report of progress made during a key leader engagement). In either case, the information or intelligence requirement must add value to a specific decision in the commander's decision-making cycle. Explicitly collecting information or intelligence requirements for assumptions, execution, and OE response enables better revisions to the operation plan. Here are some of the questions the staff may ask to determine the value of proposed information and intelligence requirements:

(a) **Usage.** What aspect of the operations plan does this information or intelligence requirement inform? What decision does it support?

(b) **Source.** How will the information or intelligence requirement be collected? Who is collecting the information or intelligence requirement? What is our confidence level in the reporting?

(c) **Cost.** What is the cost of collection (e.g., the risk to forces, resources, and/or mission)?

(d) **Time.** When is the information or intelligence requirement no longer valuable?

(e) **Impact.** What is the impact of knowing the information or intelligence requirement? What is the impact of not knowing the information or intelligence requirement? What is the risk if it is false?

(f) **Comparison.** Is this a primary or secondary indicator of operational actions or effects? If the information or intelligence requirement is unavailable, are there other information or intelligence requirements that can serve as proxies?

(11) As the planning process continues, the staff develops tasks and objectives, and defines the observable changes they expect to see in the collection and assessment plans. Well-defined objectives establish a single desired result or goal; link directly or indirectly to higher-level objectives or to the end state; are prescriptive, specific, and unambiguous; and do not infer ways and/or means (i.e., they are not written as tasks).

(12) Clearly defined objectives are SMART (specific and discrete, measurable, achievable, relevant and results oriented, and time-bound):

(a) **Specific and discrete.** Describes a single, clearly worded goal directed at creating specific conditions that lead to the end state.

(b) **Measurable.** Defined in terms of specific observable behavior and linked to information or intelligence requirements.

(c) **Achievable.** Sets reasonable targets or bounds and does not depend on unlikely or unpredictable events.

(d) **Relevant and Results Oriented.** Focused on outcomes that contribute progress toward the end state. Framed in terms of success, beginning with outcome-oriented verbs/phrases.

(e) **Time-Bound.** Must be completed by a certain date or event.

e. **Create the Assessment Plan**

(1) Effective assessment design allows for more concise and well-defined plans and communicates a clear understanding of the actions necessary to achieve the desired end state and the underlying assumptions linking action to end state. Assessment plans link the intelligence estimates of the current OE conditions to information about friendly force status

and actions. A well-designed assessment plan will include (at a minimum) the following planning activities:

(a) Develop the commander's assessment questions.

(b) Document the selection of operational variables during mission analysis.

(c) Document the development of information and intelligence requirements.

(d) Document the definition of the end state in terms of acceptable conditions, rates of change, thresholds of success/failure, and technical/tactical triggers.

(f) Identify tactical-level considerations; link information and intelligence requirements to commander's intent, end states, objectives, and decision points.

(g) Identify strategic and operational-level considerations; in addition to tactical-level considerations, link assessments to LOOs and the associated desired conditions.

(h) Document collection and analysis methods.

(i) Establish method to evaluate triggers to the commander's decision points.

(j) Establish methods to determine progress toward the desired end state.

(k) Establish methods to estimate risk to the mission.

(l) Coordinate development of recommendations for plan adjustments, branches, and sequels.

(m) Establish the format for reporting assessment results.

(2) When selecting the general framework for planning the assessment, the joint force staff must consider how CCIRs will be integrated into the decision-making process, how the commander prefers to view information, and the complexity of the OE. Regardless of which technique the commander and staff select, it should allow the staff to convey the nonlinear relationships between diplomatic, informational, military, and economic objectives (or whichever framework the operation plan uses); highlight risks and opportunities; summarize decision recommendations; and integrate multiple sources of qualitative and quantitative information and intelligence requirements.

(3) Part of assessment planning involves connecting specific assessment questions to critical assumptions regarding the relationship between the actions and the end state. Identifying the appropriate level of detail to use when describing assumptions can be challenging and can require iteration to get right. Too many information and intelligence requirements make the assessment plan burdensome and unmanageable. On the other hand, poor definition of critical assumptions means that the staff is not getting enough information or intelligence to understand the impacts of actions on the OE. In turn, this wastes opportunities to address problems and improve resource allocation.

f. **Collect and Analyze Information and Intelligence Requirements.** During mission execution, the joint force uses the collection plan and defined reporting procedures to gather information about the OE and the joint force's actions as part of normal C2 activities. Typically, staffs and subordinate commands provide information about plan execution on a regular cycle. Intelligence staffs provide intelligence about the OE and operational impact both periodically and responsively to decision triggers. In accordance with the assessment plan, the assessment team assists the planning and intelligence staff with determining the presence of decision point triggers and coordinates assessment activities across the staff.

g. **Conduct Event-Based and/or Periodic Assessment.** Normally, operation assessments have two components: decision point assessments and end state assessments. Decision point assessments are generally event-based assessments that occur because conditions within the OE meet the triggers specified in the decision support template. End state assessments compare the evolving OE to the desired end state. End state assessments are either periodic or event-based; they can be done as stand-alone assessments or accompany decision point assessments. These assessments should facilitate discussion between commanders, subordinate commands, civilian leadership, and policy makers. Detailed descriptions of decision point assessments and end state assessments appear in subsequent sections.

(1) **Decision Point Assessment.** Decision point assessment uses the continuous monitoring of information to determine if the triggers for a decision point exist. Once the staff determines the requisite conditions exist for a decision point, it conducts an assessment of the available COAs, and provides recommendations. In general, decision point assessments support the following types of decisions:

(a) Transition of operational phases.

(b) Execution of branches and sequels.

(c) Changes to the allocation of resources.

(d) Adjustments to operations.

(e) Adjustments to orders, objectives, and end states.

(f) Adjustments and changes to priorities of effort.

(g) Adjustments to command relationships and command structures.

(h) Changes to policy (e.g., TTP or ROE).

(i) Changes to strategic guidance.

(2) **End State Assessments.** End state assessments identify the progression of the OE against a desired end state and the amount of change from the baseline assessment. There are numerous acceptable methods for compiling information regarding the OE to generate an end state assessment. Understanding the amount of change that occurs between

assessments helps the staff to anticipate whether a decision point is imminent or helps to characterize the risk involved with a decision under consideration. Depending upon the commander's decision-making requirements, the operational tempo, or the OE conditions, end state assessments may be periodic or event-based. Periodic assessment cycles should not preclude the staff from generating end state assessments on demand.

h. **Provide Feedback and Recommendations**

(1) At some point during mission execution, the commander and/or the staff may recognize that the conditions of the operating environment do not reflect those conditions anticipated by the plans. Based upon a current assessment of the operating environment, a staff can estimate the effect of force and resource allocation, determine whether key planning assumptions are still valid, determine whether objectives are being met, or determine if a decision point has been reached. Based upon these determinations, the staff may identify the risks and barriers to mission accomplishment or identify opportunities to accelerate mission accomplishment.

(2) The assessment team develops an assessment report and develops recommendations for the commander based upon the guidelines set forth in the assessment plan. Assessment reports serve the functions of informing the commander about current and anticipated conditions within the OE and the ability of the joint force to impact the OE, and communicate progress to multiple partners in the COIN operation. When possible, the commander should use the assessment report as part of the strategic communications plan by declassifying key findings for communication with a broad audience.

i. **Adapt Operation Plan and Assessment Plan.** All of the conclusions generated by the staff evaluations regarding end state accomplishment, force employment, resource allocation, validity of planning assumptions, decision points, etc., lead to the development of recommendations for continuation, branches, sequels, or conclusion to the current order or plan. Assessments inform changes to improve the conduct of operations and effectiveness of plans by informing the following decisions:

(1) Update, change, add, or remove critical assumptions.

(2) Transition phases.

(3) Execute branches and sequels.

(4) Reallocate resources.

(5) Adjust operations.

(6) Adjust orders, objectives, and end states.

(7) Adjust priorities.

(8) Change priorities of effort.

(9) Change support commands.

(10) Adjust command relationships.

(11) Adjust decision points.

3. Operation Assessment Methods

a. **Contextual Assessments.** This method capitalizes on the decentralized nature of COIN operations to build assessment from the bottom up. Commanders at each echelon determine what is important to help them describe progress toward achieving objectives and attaining end states through a reporting period (typically a month or a quarter of a year). This obviates the need for the kind of centralized metrics that generally do not account for differences between tactical and operational AORs within the OE.

(1) This process benefits from clear and well-defined strategic end state conditions. However, it can also be effective when end state conditions are unclear or shifting. Because commanders can almost always assess progress toward local objectives, this process will always produce a baseline of contextual, relevant, and informed information to support commanders' decisions.

(2) This narrative reporting process begins at the battalion level (or equivalent), the first level at which a staff exists. Each staff and commander gather all information they consider relevant for assessment, typically relying on CCIRs and existing operations and intelligence information. At higher levels, staffs will begin to incorporate other information like interagency reporting. Subordinate units write their assessments, which are then aggregated into a single document and passed up the chain of command to the joint force staff level. At each level, the staff and commander provide an assessment summary and a commander's personal assessment, while retaining all of the quantitative and qualitative detail in the reports. This allows senior commanders to either read summaries of subordinate assessments or to immediately obtain contextual detail as needed.

(3) Contextual assessment leverages all types of information, including both qualitative information like human intelligence reports and quantitative information like the number of armored vehicles available to HN combat forces. The type of information used is less relevant than the way the information is presented: assessment narratives should place all data—qualitative and quantitative—in understandable local context.

(4) Once all reports have been aggregated, the joint force staff writes its periodic or event-driven assessment and submits it to the commander for review. This commander-driven assessment process is completed with the inclusion of the JFC's personal assessment, which is substantiated by layers of contextual reporting and assessment from the bottom up.

(5) One of the primary benefits of contextual assessment is that it is transparent. All sources should be cited with a simple reference to a primary source document or clearly identified as subjective analysis or opinion. Once aggregated, the contextual assessment will contain a wide array of transparent and cited information.

(6) Because contextual assessments are presented as narratives, they necessarily contain a good deal of subjective interpretation of inclusive data. This weakness should be sufficiently mitigated if included data are correctly cited. This process is generally less useful for events-driven assessment and more useful for periodic assessment.

b. **Stage-Based Assessment Plans.** A stage-based assessment plan uses sets of basic criteria to establish a common framework, with an emphasis on identifying key issues and potential means of addressing them, along with risk to the operation or campaign if they are not addressed. A stage-based assessment plan may use rating scales to describe the range of possible conditions that an LOO or LOE may produce.

(1) The rating scale should describe the range of possible conditions using no more than two relevant factors and must be articulated in a clear and concise manner. The stages must be developed in conjunction with the plan, and preferably, by the planners. The stages should describe high-level desired conditions rather than attempting to capture every nuance of every area of operations and be broad enough to represent change in conditions on time scales relevant to the operation or campaign.

(2) The results of the LOO/LOE end state assessment are then organized to answer the commander's questions. The stage-based approach allows the staff to focus attention on a narrowly selected list of information and intelligence requirements, and incorporate subordinate commanders' assessments into their conclusions.

(3) This allows the staff to graphically display past end state assessments, evaluation of current conditions, forecasted outcomes, desired end state conditions, risks (depicted by the gaps between the forecasted outcomes), and opportunities. These techniques are well-suited to COIN because they display progress in a nonlinear way, and they allow the staff to graphically depict the interrelated nature of COIN objectives.

(4) To execute the stage-based assessments method, the staff requires more training than other methods. Depending on the echelon, this method may not be well suited for quick-turn assessments or frequent assessments. However, it does simplify the collection of information and intelligence requirements as key indicators and allows the staff to maintain a manageable list of information and intelligence requirements.

4. **Organizing for Operation Assessments**

Assessment planning is normally the responsibility of the joint planning group/operations planning team lead planner. Once the plan is operationalized, a range of cross-functional expertise is required to analyze progress toward the desired effect, objectives, and end state. There are numerous methods for organizing a staff to conduct operation assessment in COIN. At each of the senior headquarters in Iraq and Afghanistan, commanders utilized assessment cells, teams, and working groups to develop the assessments methodology and compile relevant data from subordinate units, their staffs, and interagency and multinational partners to develop the campaign assessment. Assessments are commander-centric and require integration and feedback mechanisms within the organizational battle rhythms to inform decisions and necessary shifts in the operational plan. Combatant commands and their associated Service component headquarters are typically robust enough to conduct more detailed assessment. However, subordinate units may have a reduced capability to conduct assessments, depending on horizontal and vertical support requirements for assessment input and/or output products. Within a COIN operation, more robust assessment capabilities at the joint task force (JTF) level and below may be required. Synchronization of the collection and assessment efforts will help to minimize duplicative efforts among organizations. Devoting appropriate priority to the art and science of assessing progress (or lack of it) will help the commander know if the operation is proceeding as planned or requires modification to accomplish the desired end state and mission. At the strategic level, it is common for assessments reporting to be levied by the organization's higher headquarters. Planning for these requirements in advance will reduce the unanticipated burden to a commander's staff.

Intentionally Blank

CHAPTER VII
SUPPORTING OPERATIONS FOR COUNTERINSURGENCY

> *"Further, functional and Service components of the joint force conduct supported, subordinate, and supporting operations, not independent campaigns."*
>
> **Joint Publication 3-0,** *Joint Operations*

1. Integrating Operations to Support the Strategic Narrative

Failure to incorporate the strategic narrative into actions through the operational level down to the individual counterinsurgent will do greater harm more quickly than almost any action in COIN. If done correctly, operations nested with a strategic narrative are strengthened through sense of purpose, unity of effort, and the ability to gain and maintain initiative against insurgents. The strategic narrative is most effective when incorporated across the joint force and embedded in all that counterinsurgents say and do.

2. Cyberspace Considerations in Support of Counterinsurgency Operations

The joint force relies on cyberspace to develop a clear understanding of the OE. At the same time the increasing reliance of cyberspace technology as a means of disseminating messages by the insurgents has provided an LOE that joint forces can use to attack insurgents. Cyberspace operations provide security within the environment and help to isolate insurgents within the affected area or separate them from external support secured through cyberspace. Insurgent funding requirements may require reliance on criminal activities, cybercrime, piracy, and smuggling as the common means to secure funds. Cybercrime threatens freedom and commerce within cyberspace, undermines economic security, and contributes to the destabilization of governance and the security situation. Insurgent use of laptops and DVDs [digital video discs] in secret hideouts at local or globally positioned Internet cafes can, with sufficient quality, replicate the training, communication, and planning capabilities required to sustain attacks on joint forces. Carefully planned cyberspace operations are capable of creating the effects to deny the enemy freedom of action and maintain US and joint forces freedom of maneuver in support of COIN operations. As with the employment of any capabilities in COIN, all of the potential desired and undesired effects, including friendly fire and collateral damage, must be considered.

a. Offensive cyberspace operations should be considered if the insurgency is utilizing cyberspace to recruit or obtain funding, weapons, equipment, direct operation, or intelligence. Offensive cyberspace operations may complement actions in the physical domains.

b. Defensive cyberspace operations (DCO) detect and respond to enemy or adversary actions involving attack, exploitation, intrusion, or effects of malware on friendly networks and may trigger other events or operations to protect freedom of maneuver or HN governance, sovereignty, people, and critical infrastructure from insurgent operations. DCO also assure HN use of cyberspace in support of the free flow of commerce and sustained logistics. DCO are vital as a force multiplier to identify insurgent activities and create conditions to deny or defeat insurgent operations both in cyberspace and in the physical domains.

c. **Building HN Cyberspace Capability.** SFA may assist the HN to build or improve its cyberspace capability and capacity. The cyberspace component of security includes HN telecommunications, interagency organizations, and military C2 communications that may be loosely affiliated with the HN governance organizations.

3. **Considerations for Air Operations in Counterinsurgency**

Air forces capabilities include close air support, precision strikes, personnel recovery (PR), air interdiction, intelligence, communications, electronic warfare (EW), combat support, counterair, airspace control, and air mobility. Air forces and capabilities may provide considerable asymmetric advantages to counterinsurgents, especially by denying insurgents secrecy and unfettered access to bases of operation. If insurgents assemble a conventional force or their operating locations are identified and isolated, air assets can respond quickly with joint precision fires or to airlift ground forces to locations to accomplish a mission. Airpower enables COIN operations in rough and remote terrain, areas that insurgents traditionally have considered somewhat safe from surveillance and attack.

a. **Air C2.** The C2 relationships established for engagement operations should consider both the need for flexibility and the training level of forces to be employed. As in all military operations, air operations must be able to provide precision strikes operations due to the nature of COIN and the demand for low collateral damage and friendly fire.

(1) **C2 Architecture.** The joint force air component can integrate and deconflict the unique HN, multinational, and/or interagency partner aviation capabilities with those employed by the joint force. This integration and deconfliction facilitates the safety of all aircraft operating within the operational area and supports the efficient use of available airspace and air facilities.

See JP 3-30, Command and Control for Joint Air Operations.

(2) **Planning.** Air planners require visibility and awareness from the time planning begins and throughout each phase, of actions planned at all echelons to provide the most effective air support, so coordination should occur at all levels. Furthermore, COIN planning is often fluid and develops along short planning and execution timelines, necessitating some degree of informal coordination and integration for safety and efficiency.

b. **Air Mobility.** Air mobility aircraft provide the joint force with the ability to perform intertheater and intratheater transport of cargo, equipment, and personnel. This transport can include deployment to remote regions to deliver resources and personnel and can be used to rapidly deploy, sustain, and reinforce ground forces as part of security and counterguerrilla operations. Air mobility can be used to support political goals by extending effective governance to remote areas and delivering highly visible humanitarian aid. Sustainment tasks are enabled through air, land, airdrop, and aerial extraction of equipment, supplies, and personnel. Fixed-wing transports are best suited for carrying ground forces into forward staging areas. Vertical-lift platforms are ideal for carrying ground forces to remote sites that are unable to support fixed-wing operations. Lift capable of moving small units around the battlefield have proven very valuable in assisting COIN forces. The ability to maneuver while engaged with an adversary is extremely powerful in managing the battle and ensuring that the adversary is unable to disengage at a time and place of the adversary's choosing. Casualty evacuation is integral to any operation involving the employment of personnel in hostile-fire situations, with vertical-lift assets best suited for this task. While land forces can execute these basic missions alone, airlift bypasses weaknesses insurgents have traditionally exploited. However, airlift is more costly than surface or maritime transportation and in some circumstances may be inhibited by terrain, weather, and threats such as man-portable surface-to-air missiles and rocket-propelled grenades. Also, requesting airlift may be subject to limitations due to availability and other priority requirements. It is usually a small percentage of the overall transportation network during major operations; however, in particularly challenging situations, airlift may become the primary transportation mode for sustainment and repositioning of forces.

c. **Precision Engagement.** The joint force air component can provide close air support, air interdiction, and strategic strikes that include the use of precision-guided munitions. The use of fires, regardless of source, against insurgents must be carefully considered and targets confirmed in terms of their authenticity and value. They must also be lawful objectives under the law of war (combatants or military objectives). The use of lethal force must respect the principles of military necessity, distinction, proportionality, and humanity. Additionally, insurgents may have signature reduction methods, deception methods, and man-portable air defense systems that must be considered and addressed.

See JP 3-60, Joint Targeting, *for more information on the targeting process.*

(1) **Air Power.** In determining the appropriate capability to create the desired effect, planners should look at not only the direct but the longer term indirect effects that may be created. Collateral damage and civilian casualties can be portrayed by the insurgents as unnecessary, and if perceived as such by the local population, it does much to undermine the HN and US COIN efforts. Insurgents will inevitably exploit such incidents especially through propaganda, using international media coverage when possible.

(2) **Intelligence.** Just as in traditional warfare, attacks on key nodes usually reap greater benefits than attacks on dispersed individual targets. Effective strike operations are inextricably tied to the availability of actionable intelligence, effective intelligence collection, and detailed systems analysis that identifies and fully characterizes the potential targets of interest. Persistence is critical as it is often not known in advance how long a particular node will remain stationary.

(3) **HN Precision Engagement.** If US or multinational forces conduct the strike, there may be the perception that the HN government is dependent on foreign forces for its survival. This may have the indirect effect of delegitimizing the HN government in the public's perception. Precision engagement should be designed to employ HN airpower resources to the greatest extent possible. Properly trained and structured teams of airpower advisors, ranging from planning liaison to tactical operations personnel, offer potential for

HN unilateral and combined actions against high-value targets. Use of these options serves to enhance the legitimacy of the HN government and also achieves important security objectives. Use of assets controlled by US agencies outside DOD, but not directly affiliated with it, may also prove useful in providing precision strike capability.

d. **Interoperability Between Ground and Air Operations.** Video downlink and data link technology have revolutionized real-time air to ground employment allowing air assets to seamlessly integrate into and support the ground commander's scheme of maneuver. Armed aircraft on-call or scheduled as airborne force escorts may provide ground forces with the critical situational awareness, flexibility for maneuver, and immediate fire support necessary to succeed in the dynamic COIN environment. Airpower's ability to quickly support ground forces can reduce the risk to dispersed ground units, lower the need for mutual support between ground units and therefore decrease overall troop requirements. This allows counterinsurgents to further disperse ground forces in areas and in numbers that would not be feasible without air power—mutual support can come from the air rather than from other ground forces or indirect ground fire. Dispersion of ground forces facilitates the actual and perceived level of security. However, joint planners must carefully balance the risk of catastrophic tactical surprise of dispersed ground forces with the benefits gained from dispersion. Additionally, airpower can provide battlefield air operations capabilities which include air traffic control, assault zone assessment, establishment and control, joint terminal attack control, fire support, operational preparation of the environment, special reconnaissance (SR), C2 communications, personnel and equipment recovery, humanitarian relief, and battlefield trauma care.

e. **PR.** As previously stated, COIN encompasses operations characterized by violence, persistent conflict, and increasing state fragility. In an environment with such fluidity, PR planning must encompass the widest range of operations, from a struggling state to a failed state and everything in between. For planners at all levels, this means planning for search and rescue in permissive environments, to PR, and nonconventional assisted recovery in environments where other types of recovery are not feasible or possible. Plans must include the capabilities of interagency organizations and our multinational partners. See JP 3-50, *Personnel Recovery,* for specific PR planning guidance.

f. **Basing.** During COIN operations, the joint or multinational force (along with HN forces) will use the available air facilities provided by the HN or will construct expeditionary airfields. COIN planners must consider where to locate airfields, including those intended for use as aerial ports of debarkation and other air operations. US air forces frequently build and provide infrastructure to HN air services as part of performing COIN operations. Airpower operating from remote or dispersed airfields may present a smaller signature than large numbers of land forces, possibly lessening HN sensitivities to foreign military presence. Employment of long-range bombers for COIN operations has increased due to technological advances in the accuracy of precision munitions, the number of munitions that can be transported by each aircraft and the aircraft's endurance (due to the ability to be refueled while aloft). Often these platforms are free from the basing limitations of shorter range tactical platforms. Commanders should ensure that all logistics and maintenance requirements are properly considered for remote and austere locations. Additionally, commanders must properly protect their bases and personnel from air, ballistic missile, and guided rocket, artillery, missile, and mortar threats.

g. **Building HN Airpower Capability.** Where appropriate, US and multinational aviation SFA operations strive to enable the HN to provide its own sustainable air capability. Airpower capability can be a catalyst for government legitimacy, projecting a catalyst for government legitimacy, projecting national sovereignty, and accelerating the nation's overall internal stability as well as regional security. Rebuilding HN air capability will require long lead times. Planners, therefore, need to establish a long-term program to develop an HN airpower capability. The HN air force should be appropriate for that nation's requirements and sustainment base. For conducting effective COIN operations, an HN air force may be able to provide aerial reconnaissance and surveillance, air transport, close air support and interdiction for land forces, helicopter troop lift, medical evacuation, and counter air. Likewise, airlift supports essential services, governance, and economic development by providing movement of personnel and supplies, particularly in a COIN operation with improvised explosive devices (IEDs) and other dangers on the roads. HNSF thus should include airlift development as the HN's first component of airpower. In order to build HN air power capability, the joint force will focus on providing HN air forces with training and equipment services so that they can become capable of independent operations in compliance with the law of war. Infrastructure, to include airfields and a viable air traffic control system construction and development, is also frequently required. Development of supporting services (maintenance, logistics, and planning) often requires the most extensive timelines when working with HN air services. HN air services often include a mixture of civil and military aviation assets that provides unique challenges to air force efforts at engagement.

4. Space Capabilities

Space capabilities provide advantages needed for success. Space contributions to COIN include intelligence collection, satellite communications (SATCOM), and positioning, navigation, and timing (PNT). Space operations provide insight into the AOIs or OE including adversary actions and capabilities. Monitoring AOIs from space helps provide information on enemy location, disposition, and intent; aids in tracking, targeting, and engaging the adversary. It also provides situational awareness, warning of attack, and feedback on how well US forces are affecting the adversaries' understanding of the OE. Space forces support the COIN's ability to concentrate combat power at the proper time and place by providing SATCOM to coordinate and direct forces, and PNT to synchronize operations, navigate, and guide precision munitions. PNT provides essential, precise, and reliable information that permits joint forces to more effectively plan, train, coordinate, and execute operations. Precision timing provides the joint force the capability to synchronize operations, and enables communications capabilities such as frequency hopping and cryptological synchronization to improve communications security and effectiveness. PNT also enables precision attack from stand-off distances, thereby reducing collateral damage and allowing friendly forces to avoid threat areas.

For additional information, see JP 3-14, Space Operations; *JP 3-17,* Air Mobility Operations; *JP 3-22,* Foreign Internal Defense; *Air Force Doctrine Annex (AFDA) 3-2,* Irregular Warfare; *AFDA 2-6,* Air Mobility Operations; *AFDA 3-05,* Special Operations; *Air*

Force Doctrine Document (AFDD) 3-14, Space Operations; *AFDA 3-22,* Foreign Internal Defense, *FM 3-14,* Army Space Operations; *and FM 3-24/MCWP 3-33.5,* Counterinsurgency.

5. Maritime Considerations in Support of Counterinsurgency Operations

The expeditionary character of maritime forces may provide access when access from the other operational areas is denied or limited. Maritime forces may provide direct support to the joint force that does not include combat operations, to include logistic support, intelligence/communication sharing, humanitarian relief, and CMO in the form of maritime civil affairs (CA), and expeditionary medical aid and training.

a. **MSO.** MSO may be used to counter terrorism, insurgency, and crime, while complementing the effort to protect the HN, its sovereignty, the people, and critical infrastructure from insurgents. It also facilitates access to HN ports and free flow of commerce and sustained logistics support through the waterways. Riverine units provide security along inland waterways, which helps to isolate insurgents within the affected area or, if the river is an international border, from external support. Piracy threatens freedom and safety of maritime navigation, undermines economic security, and contributes to the destabilization of governance and the security situation. MSO can be used to provide the HN's access to sea lines of communications, while eliminating a source of funding used for sustaining insurgent operations.

b. **Deterrence and Patrols.** Naval support to COIN may consist of deterrence, escort operations, presence, patrols, and defending critical infrastructure. Maritime interception operations are used to enforce sanctions or blockades, support law enforcement operations, and provide a means to extend situational awareness in the maritime domain. The presence of maritime forces can be adjusted as conditions dictate to enable flexible approaches to escalation, de-escalation, and deterrence. A visible presence just offshore demonstrates support for a partner nation, which may send a strong message to insurgents and their sympathizers. Naval forces' ability to loiter over the horizon may reduce a large US footprint while still maintaining the ability to influence COIN operations being conducted ashore.

c. **Sustainment and Transport.** Maritime forces can provide land-based forces with key sustainment capabilities. This includes commercial vessels' provision of the majority of bulk supplies. The expeditionary nature of naval forces, however, may transport forces within the theater as well. Naval forces can also provide a forcible entry capability for insurgent-controlled areas or bases bordering waterways or in the littorals.

d. **Naval Aircraft.** Naval aircraft are multimission platforms which provide rapid response capabilities such as precision strikes, C2, EW, and combat search and rescue. Naval aircraft have the added flexibility in that aircraft carriers are self-sustaining, secure bases that can be quickly repositioned within theater. Theater-based maritime patrol aircraft further complement the flexibility with their endurance and multimission capability.

e. **Precision Strikes and Naval Fires.** Naval forces also are capable of launching precision-guided munitions from surface or subsurface platforms, while surface combatants can conduct naval surface fire support for expeditionary forces ashore.

f. **Building HN Maritime Capability.** SFA also applies to assisting the HN with building or improving its maritime capability and capacity. The maritime component of security forces includes HN navy, marine, and coast guard elements, and interagency organizations which may be loosely affiliated with the HN maritime organization. These may include fishery patrols, interior security, port authority, customs, and immigration. Further considerations to enhance the HN maritime capability may include establishment or expansion of maritime domain awareness efforts. Development of a robust automated identification system, tied into an interagency maritime operations center, will increase the HN's ability to track and identify vessels of interest that are potentially involved in illegal or illicit activities. SFA planners must develop a long-term plan to assist the HN in these areas. As with the land and air, assistance to the maritime elements of an HN must be appropriate for that nation's requirements and sustainment base.

g. **Maritime CA**. The maritime component may also contribute to the HN rebuilding effort with a dedicated maritime CA teams that have skill sets uniquely tailored to those areas most likely to influence HN rebuilding efforts in maritime and naval affairs. These are:

(1) Maritime law.

(2) Marine fisheries and resource management.

(3) Port administration and port operations.

(4) Maritime interagency coordination.

(5) Port/waterborne security.

(6) Customs and logistics.

(7) Port/intercoastal surveys.

(8) Control of maritime immigration.

6. Conventional Ground Force Considerations in Support of Counterinsurgency Operations

a. Conventional ground forces bring capabilities that play an important role in the military contribution to COIN operations. These forces and capabilities are especially critical for successful counterguerrilla, intelligence, humanitarian, and informational efforts. Army and Marine Corps aviation contributions include close air support, precision strikes, armed overwatch, PR, and air mobility. Army and Marine Corps aviation forces and capabilities provide considerable asymmetric advantages to counterinsurgents, especially by denying insurgents secrecy and uncontested access to bases of operation. Army and Marine Corps aviation enables counterinsurgents to operate in rough and remote terrain, areas that insurgents traditionally have used as safe havens. Ground forces can also provide precision fires on targets as an all-weather day or night capability. If insurgents assemble a conventional force or their operating locations are identified and isolated, aviation and ground surface-to-surface assets can respond quickly with precision fires or to airlift ground forces to locations to accomplish a mission.

b. Ground forces surface-to-surface fire support elements can also provide for precision fires. These capabilities are available to ground forces conducting lethal counterinsurgent operations during conditions when aviation assets are incapable of lending support. These capabilities are also scalable and of various ranges. Use of these capabilities, just like use of Air Force and naval precision strikes, requires precise targeting, and quality, continuous, and actionable intelligence to ensure not only the target is struck, but friendly fire and collateral damage are considered. Staffs should plan for and conduct drills for the employment of all precision fires and ensure fire support elements are fully integrated.

7. Special Operations Considerations in Support of Counterinsurgency Operations

a. **SOF and COIN Approaches.** SOF may conduct a wide array of missions with HNSF or may be integrated with US conventional forces. They are particularly important when the joint force is using an indirect approach to COIN. In a more balanced or direct approach to COIN, however, they should be used to complement rather than replace conventional forces in traditional warfare roles.

b. **SOF Core Activities and COIN.** SOF are specifically organized, trained, and equipped to accomplish the following special operations core activities: DA, SR, UW, FID, SFA, CT, civil affairs operations (CAO), MISO, hostage rescue/recovery, HA/disaster relief, and countering weapons of mass destruction (CWMD). With the exception of UW, any of these SOF core activities may be involved in COIN in the HN. SOF must adhere to the same principles of COIN as conventional forces. Even if focused on DA missions, SOF must be cognizant of the need to win and maintain popular support. The following core activities are briefly discussed, because they are not discussed elsewhere in this publication.

(1) **DA.** DA missions may be required in COIN to capture or kill key insurgent leaders or other vital insurgent targets. The specific types of DA are raids, ambushes, and direct assaults; standoff attacks; terminal attack control and terminal guidance operations; PR operations; precision strike operations; and antisurface operations.

(2) **SR.** SOF may conduct SR into insurgent strongholds or sanctuaries. Activities within SR include environmental reconnaissance, armed reconnaissance, target and threat assessment, and post strike reconnaissance.

(3) **CWMD.** If weapons of mass destruction (WMD) become available, insurgents may attempt to integrate them into their arsenal for physical destruction and, more important, psychological and political impact. Insurgents will try to use WMD as part of terrorism and will attempt to integrate their use with their propaganda. The type of WMD and available means of delivery will constrain insurgent targets. Insurgents may attack conventional forces with WMD out of necessity or by choice. Insurgent concepts for employment of WMD may

include conventional and clandestine delivery of chemical, biological, radiological, and nuclear (CBRN) weapons for the purposes of disruption, destabilization, coercion, or revenge. Broad objectives for acquisition and employment of CBRN weapons may include the capabilities to:

(a) Defeat, influence, intimidate, and deter an opponent.

(b) Disrupt HN, US, and multinational forces and operations.

(c) Forestall defeat or prolong the struggle.

(d) Punish opponents for countering insurgent efforts.

For additional information, see JP 3-26, Counterterrorism, *JP 3-05,* Special Operations, *JP 3-22,* Foreign Internal Defense, *AFDA 3-2,* Irregular Warfare, *AFDA, 3-22,* Foreign Internal Defense, *and US Special Operations Command Directive 525-89,* Unconventional Warfare. *For detailed discussion of integrating conventional forces and SOF, see US Special Operations Command Publication 3-33,* CF and SOF Multi-Service Tactics, Techniques, and Procedures for Conventional Forces and Special Operations Forces Synchronization Handbook and Checklist. *For additional information on CWMD, see JP 3-40,* Countering Weapons of Mass Destruction.

c. **Army Special Operations Forces (ARSOF) Capabilities.** ARSOF elements (special forces, rangers, and aviation) can support COIN operations by HN forces and conducting combat or other operations as required. ARSOF also has CAO and military information support elements that can support COIN.

d. **Marine Corps Special Operations Forces (MARSOF) Capabilities.** MARSOF can support COIN operations through FID assess to train, advise, and assist HN military and paramilitary forces. MARSOF will additionally conduct the portion of SFA oriented toward supporting an HN's efforts to counter threats from subversion, lawlessness, and insurgency. MARSOF can also execute DA, SR, and other special operations core activities in support of COIN as required.

e. **Navy Special Operations Forces (NAVSOF) Capabilities.** NAVSOF can support COIN operations by providing SEAL and special boat teams to train HN forces or conduct combat or other operations as required.

f. **Air Force Special Operations Forces (AFSOF) Capabilities.** AFSOF support COIN operations by working with HN aviation forces from the ministerial level to the tactical unit. When required, AFSOF provide persistent manned and unmanned intelligence, surveillance, and reconnaissance, mobility, C2, combat support, and precision strike to support COIN operations. AFSOF maintain specially trained combat aviation advisors to assess, train, advise, assist, and equip HN aviation capability thereby facilitating the availability, reliability, safety, and interoperability of these forces into COIN operations. Additionally, AFSOF special tactics teams enhance the air-to-ground interface, synchronizing conventional and special operations during COIN operations.

For additional information on SOF capabilities, see JP 3-05, Special Operations, *AFDA 3-05,* Special Operations, *and AFDA 3-22,* Foreign Internal Defense.

8. Detainee Operation Considerations in Support of Counterinsurgency Operations

a. **General.** How counterinsurgents treat captured insurgents has immense potential impact on insurgent morale, retention, and recruitment. Humane and just treatment may afford counterinsurgents many short-term opportunities as well as potentially damaging insurgent recruitment. Abuse may foster resentment and hatred, offering the enemy an opportunity for propaganda and assist potential insurgent recruitment and support. It is important that all detainees or other persons captured in any conflict, regardless of how it is characterized, shall be treated, at a minimum, in accordance with Common Article 3 of the Geneva Conventions of 1949, unless they are entitled to a more protective standard based on status.

b. **Detainees.** Counterinsurgents must carefully consider who will be detained, and the manner and methods that will be used to detain them. Detainees can be vital sources of information. Counterinsurgents detaining people who are not part of the insurgency or do not support insurgency damages the counterinsurgents' credibility and legitimacy; thus, ill-defined, poorly supervised detainee operations can prolong the war, increase resentment, and undermine any efforts to ameliorate grievances or discredit the insurgents' narrative. I2 products can provide substantial support to effective detainee operations, including decisions to detain an individual, interrogation activities, and follow-on prosecution.

c. **Detention.** The methods and infrastructure for detention of insurgents are complex and important. The exact chain of custody and responsibility is vitally important and must be carefully planned, prepared, and conducted. Detainees should be biometrically enrolled as quickly as possible following initial detention. Biometric database searches on incoming detainees can frequently reveal additional infractions, further justifying continued detention. At a minimum, it provides a tracking tool for every individual detained for whatever reason across the country. It also provides a highly effective interrogation tool. The infrastructure and sustainment effort must be able to cope with the volume of people in detention. The methods and perception of credibility and legitimacy for the release of personnel in detention is also important. **Fairness may help the counterinsurgent cause while any negative perceptions will hurt efforts in the long term.** For those in custody, reintegration efforts should begin as soon as possible. Detention should protect and empower moderate detainees.

d. **Detainee Voluntary Programs.** It is vital that detainees have voluntary access to a wide array of programs. These programs help protect and empower moderate detainees from extremist influence, prepare detainees for release, and encourage them to not rejoin the insurgency when released. While the programs must be tailored for each area and insurgency, they can include vocational, educational (especially reading and writing), and religious programs.

e. **Release Authority.** For transfer or release authority of US-captured detainees during COIN, SecDef or designee shall establish criteria for transfer or release and communicate those criteria to all commanders operating within the operational area. How to reintegrate released detainees is of vital importance and requires careful planning. Coordination is required with respect to the local governmental and security forces of the area that the detainee will be released to, especially if this was the same area where the individual was detained. Release procedures and policy must be closely coordinated with disarmament, demobilization, and reintegration (DDR).

For more information on detainee operations, see JP 3-63, Detainee Operations.

9. Counter-Improvised Explosive Device Operations

a. Insurgents have traditionally relied on IEDs as a means of delivering fires against friendly forces and civilians. IEDs have the capability, if not countered and neutralized, of not only hindering the operational momentum of a COIN effort, but also creating the effects of terrorism and insecurity that can erode legitimacy of the HN government and the will to fight the insurgents.

b. IEDs may incorporate military munitions and hardware, but are generally constructed from components that are nonmilitary in nature. IEDs are employed by threat groups across the globe to achieve their objectives. This is, in part, due to IEDs' potential to produce strategic effects beyond their tactical impact. IEDs are designed to kill opponents and influence their actions, discredit them among the populace, and degrade their ability to achieve their objectives. Insurgents employ IEDs to demonstrate their freedom of action; demoralize, distract, and discredit US, multinational, and HN security forces; create fear within the general population; gain media exposure; and negatively impact US, HN, and partner nation interests. Meeting this threat requires a national effort based on a whole-of-government approach that addresses the device, the network that designs and emplaces the device, and the social-political aspects of the OE that facilitate IED employment.

For more detailed discussion on countering IEDs, see JP 3-15.1, Counter-Improvised Explosive Device Operations.

10. Counter Threat Finance

a. **CTF.** CTF operations may be conducted to disrupt and deny finances or shut down networks. CTF operations are often planned and conducted by the cooperating members of the international community and reach from the strategic to the tactical level.

b. **The Insurgent Financial Network.** No two threat networks are the same; however, there are a number of similarities.

(1) Insurgents may generate funds through a multitude of means that range from local to international efforts both overt and covert. Funds may come from individuals, groups, businesses, criminal networks, and donor states. Activities may also involve fraud and use of front companies. Insurgents can generate funds through illicit collection of taxes, duties, counterfeiting, black marketing, narcotics and human trafficking, illicit proliferation of natural resources, and kidnapping for ransoms.

(2) Insurgents will launder and move funds locally and globally. Effective organizations are shrewd, calculating, and security minded, and they use global financial systems, front companies, and undergoverned, corrupt, or unregistered money services. States lacking secure governance of these financial institutions provided added security. Targeting these institutions can also affect the local population that utilizes these services.

c. **Roles.** The Defense Intelligence Agency Counter Threat Finance Intelligence serves as the intelligence conduit for DOD elements involved in CTF. Counter Threat Finance Intelligence aligns analysis, collection, and intelligence, and synchronizes defense and national intelligence capabilities. Each geographic combatant command has a CTF office. CTF requires a balancing of national security resources as well as a recognition of the shared responsibility for this mission that exists among law enforcement, foreign policy and legal authorities, national policy authorities, and military and intelligence.

d. **Operations.** CTF operations include squeezing profits and revenue sources and streams; driving up operational, financing, and transactions costs and risks; identifying, tracking, and interdicting commercial and financial transactions and smuggling activities; and freezing or seizing real property and other physical capital assets and financial capital assets and reserves.

e. **Uses.** CTF can be used in COIN to counter, disrupt, or interdict the flow of finances to an insurgency, thereby reducing its operational effectiveness. Additionally, CTF can be used against corruption, as well as drug and other criminal money-making activities that fund or fuel insurgencies and undermine the legitimacy of the HN government. In such cases, CTF is aimed at insurgent organizations as well as other malevolent actors in the environment.

For a broader discussion of CTF, see Department of Defense Directive (DODD) 5205.14, DOD Counter Threat Finance (CTF) Policy.

For more specific application of CTF in operations, see JP 3-15.1, Counter-Improvised Explosive Device Operations.

11. Public Affairs

a. **General.** Public affairs (PA) supports the commander's COIN objectives and helps shape the OE through the timely, truthful, and accurate informing of and interaction with internal and external audiences. The use of PA ranges from communicating guidance and direction from national authority and the commander throughout the force to countering insurgent and other adversary propaganda and disinformation to informing US and international publics.

b. **Perceptions.** Insurgents and counterinsurgents know popular perception drives support, and support is vital to success. HN and US information, the media's reporting, insurgent propaganda, and other contributors to the information environment influence how the populace perceives the combined COIN effort, the insurgency, and the HN's legitimacy. A commitment to releasing timely, truthful, and accurate information, whether good or bad, builds trust and supports the credibility of the HN and US. The power of timely, truthful, and accurate release of information, hinges, however, on the alignment of actions, words, and images. This alignment and consistency is essential to support strategic and operational approaches to COIN. If what is said or shown is not what was or is being done, credibility becomes suspect and possibly destroyed. This pushes the more favorable perceptions in the direction of the insurgents.

c. **Timeliness, Tone, and Context.** Timeliness does not always mean immediate or rapid. In many cases, however, the quick release of information through PA to the public can set the tone and the context of a situation and the reporting and public dialogue that follows. Being "first to the chalkboard" with accurate and truthful information provides an advantage that can impact narratives and support US and HN credibility. It will not always be possible to release information quickly enough to achieve this advantage and will not always counter or negate insurgent disinformation, but establishing the story in the US and HN's tone and context will almost always create an advantage.

d. **Understanding the OE.** Close coordination among PA, intelligence, IO, MISO, and other LOOs and LOEs is critical to understanding the OE. Each will likely bring unique information and confirming information to the effort. There are also overlaps in the specific types of information most applicable to them in the planning and execution of their operations. Due to the small number of personnel in some of these functions, the JFC should minimize duplication of efforts and look for efficiencies through the proactive sharing of information.

e. **Communication Planning and Execution.** Communication planning and execution requires close coordination, deconfliction, and synchronization among PA, IO, MISO, CMO, and other related functions. This improves consistency in communicating themes, messages, narratives, and other information, adapted as necessary, to key audiences. The best communication results are realized when PA, IO, MISO, CMO, and other related functions are coordinated and synchronized early in the planning process. Many PA activities and some by other LOOs will simultaneously or independently support public diplomacy or otherwise be connected with the efforts of DOS, other USG departments and agencies, HN, other nations, and NGOs.

f. **Assessment.** PA should be an integral part of operational assessment discussed in Chapter VI, "Assessing Counterinsurgency Operations." Close coordination among these LOOs and LOEs is critical to effective assessment. Significant assessment requirement overlaps exist among them. Due to the small number of personnel in some of these functions, the JFC should minimize duplication of efforts and look for efficiencies through the proactive sharing of information.

g. **CMO and Community Engagement.** PA provides specialized skills in communicating, developing relationships, and interacting with local communities while conducting operations. PA should be involved in the planning, preparation, and execution of engagements within the local/HN communities to support the CMO plan.

h. **Support to Public Diplomacy.** PA activities should be planned and coordinated with any other activities supporting public diplomacy and DOS to ensure unity of effort and maximum effect.

i. **Joint Public Affairs Support Element (JPASE).** JPASE provides ready, scalable, and rapidly deployable joint PA capability to combatant commanders (CCDRs) in order to facilitate rapid establishment of joint force headquarters, bridge joint PA requirements, and conduct PA training to meet theater information challenges. Like similar on-call forces, they are designed to respond quickly to the emergent situation until longer-term forces are deployed.

12. Identity Intelligence Operations

a. **General.** I2 operations activities assist US forces, the HN, and partner nations to positively identify, track, characterize, and disrupt threat actors conducting and facilitating insurgent activities in the OE. I2 operations enablers include a dedicated information sharing architecture with access to national-level biometrics, forensics, DOMEX, and derogatory reporting databases, expeditionary exploitation facilities, TTP for individual encounters, site exploitation, and evidentiary handling, as well as training on fielded collection devices. When employed appropriately, I2 operations can provide commanders with decision quality information on insurgent actors, their activities, possible intent, and tools of their trade.

b. **Operations.** I2 operations activities range from encounter-based and targeted collection activities like checkpoint or census operations; site exploitation activities including follow-on forensic, engineering, and captured media analysis; I2 analysis and production; and support to follow-on planning. Sociocultural factors must be taken into consideration when conducting some I2 operations activities (e.g., biometrics collection), as they may be seen as overly intrusive by the general population. However, when conducted in concert with HN forces, I2 operations can greatly increase operational precision as well as the general security of the HN population.

c. **I2 Support.** I2 support provides the analytic rigor behind the positive identification and characterization of individual actors encountered within the OE. I2 support to I2 operations assists commanders in identifying insurgents and their networks, isolating them from the target population, and making engagement and influence decisions to neutralize their effects.

d. **Building HN I2 Capabilities.** SFA may include assisting the HN with developing or improving its I2 operations capability and capacity. These improvements may include training, equipping, and partnering activities using biometrics, forensics, and DOMEX capabilities. COIN planners should develop a long-term plan to assist the HN in these areas.

CHAPTER VIII
BUILDING GOVERNANCE TO SUPPORT COUNTERINSURGENCY

"With a few exceptions, lasting insurgency endings are shaped not by military action but by social, economic, and political change. At their core, insurgencies are battles for the control of public support…The government may defeat the insurgent military cadre, but, with few exceptions, insurgencies do not end until case-specific root causes are addressed."

Ben Connable and Martin Libicki, *How Insurgencies End* (2010: RAND)

1. Principles of Governance

Supporting indigenous governance is often an important COIN tool to counter insurgent efforts to seize, nullify, or challenge governing authorities.

a. **Governance. Governance consists of the rules, processes, and behavior by which interests are articulated, resources are managed, and power is exercised in a society.** These rules and processes must be seen as predictable and tolerable in the eyes of the population to be deemed legitimate. They are manifested in three core functions: representation, security, and welfare.

(1) **Representation** includes political participation, decision-making procedures, responsiveness to the needs of the population, and accountability for decisions and their implementation. The effectiveness and legitimacy of representation depend on their appropriateness in the local context. For example, participatory governance does not necessarily equate to Western-style democratic institutions; it could consist of local shuras—informal gatherings of village or tribal leaders common in some countries in the Middle East and Central Asia.

(2) **Security** pertains to the maintenance of a monopoly (or at least superiority) over the legitimate use of force. It includes border defense, protection of the population/public security, and maintenance of law and order.

(3) **Welfare** refers to the delivery of services according to the expectations of relevant local populations. Service delivery in this context does not refer to a suite of public services derived from Western states' or international development models but rather to baseline expectations of the local population in a given operational area if they are to deem governance legitimate.

b. **Counter the Insurgent Narrative.** The challenge for counterinsurgents is to correctly identify those deficiencies in governance that serve as effective motives for the insurgency, i.e., those deficiencies that are exploited by insurgents in order to mobilize popular support for the insurgency. If an underrepresented segment of the population provides the majority of insurgent recruits and is susceptible to the insurgent narrative based on its lack of access to political participation and decision making, LOEs should primarily focus on the representation function of governance rather than security or welfare. Similarly, any COIN LOEs focused on service delivery should normally target those inadequate

SECURITY, LAND, AND CONFLICT IN ITURI

Since 1999, the Ituri district in northeastern Democratic Republic of Congo has been the site of an intense ethnic war characterized by extreme brutality against civilians. The Hema and Lendu communities had long-running disputes over land, but the insecurity, external manipulation, and collapse of state authority associated with the Second Congo War led to a major escalation that by 2003 had cost more than 50,000 lives through direct violence. Attacks against civilians by armed actors on all sides were driven by a desire to control illegal mining sites and to settle land disputes by force of arms.

In 2003, in the wake of the Ituri crisis and the temporary intervention of the French-led Interim Emergency Multinational Force, MONUC [United Nations Organization Mission in the Democratic Republic of the Congo] launched a military campaign to compel the various armed groups to enter the demobilization, disarmament, and reintegration (DDR) program. Intense military pressure applied systematically and often in conjunction with the Congolese government military led to over 15,000 combatants entering the DDR process by August 2005 and a significant reduction in the number of attacks on civilians.

However, MONUC and the Congolese government failed to capitalize on the opportunity created through military action. MONUC viewed the ethnic militias as warlord groups and the conflict as fundamentally driven by illegal exploitation of natural resources rather than land disputes. The legitimacy and administrative capacity of the Congolese government in Ituri was limited, and despite efforts by local officials, a key driver of the conflict went unaddressed. As MONUC's main effort shifted to addressing insecurity in the Kivus, analysts and local peace building actors warned that the underlying conflict dynamics had the potential to reemerge and generate new violence as military pressure eased. Thus Ituri serves as an example of the need for integrated military and nonmilitary lines of operation to fully exploit military success and build toward long-term stability.

Adapted from Thierry Vircoulon, "The Ituri paradox: When armed groups have a land policy and peacemakers do not," in Ward Anseeuw and Chris Alden (eds.), *The Struggle over Land in Africa* (Cape Town: Human Sciences Research Council Press, 2010)

services that are being exploited in the insurgent's narrative. Ideally, a small number of key activities can then be directed along the most promising LOEs to weaken the insurgency.

c. **Do Fewer Things Better.** A thorough analysis of governance structures and actors is needed to identify which ones can be leveraged to generate effects in support of COIN objectives. Ideally, the COIN operation will focus on a few high-impact nonlethal LOEs that have the most promise to weaken the insurgency—those LOEs that address grievances subsumed into the insurgent narrative—rather than pursuing wholesale state-building efforts as a default. Such an approach will generally be preferable to a wholesale governance effort based on standardized or Western notions of core governance functions, which would risk exceeding the capacities of the USG and joint force as well as the HN government, and thus be counterproductive to the COIN effort. If support to indigenous governance is either misdirected (such as by imposing Western governance functions that local populations do not want) or falls short of the population's expectations, there is a risk that the USG will be blamed, resulting in the loss of legitimacy for the USG and potentially the HN government. Even when the formal political and legal responsibility for governance lies with the HN government, the population may overestimate USG capabilities and capacities to influence outcomes and attribute any shortcomings to US incompetence or underhandedness.

d. **Integrate Lethal and Nonlethal Activities.** Many governance issues have the potential to cut across lethal and nonlethal LOEs. For example, land and water rights have featured prominently in insurgent narratives and COIN efforts, particularly in agrarian societies. Grievances connected to land and water rights require the synchronized application of civilian and military COIN activities to address the major drivers of the insurgency. Similarly, the problem of how to handle detained insurgents typically connects to other aspects of the security and justice/rule of law functions, such as the availability of humane detention centers and the capacity to prosecute individuals in a timely manner under a justice system that is perceived to be legitimate by the local population. Counterinsurgents will, therefore, likely be faced with a need to prioritize efforts while also remaining cognizant of the linkages and cross-cutting effects these efforts will have in other areas.

e. **Distinguish Governance from Government.** While governance may be predominantly provided by a formal central government, this is not always the case, and the two terms are not synonymous. Governance functions may be carried out by a variety of actors in an operational area with considerable local variation. Depending on conditions in the operational area and the USG strategic goal supported by the COIN operation, the JFC may need to deal with different governance actors and structures depending on the local context. Formal indigenous governance structures may include central, regional, and local governments. Informal structures are likely to vary considerably between HNs and within them and may be very difficult to understand for outsiders. They could include tribal and clan structures, religious and spiritual leaders, clubs and associations, as well as criminal or insurgent organizations.

(1) **Understand Indigenous Governance Structures.** Counterinsurgents need to understand both formal and informal governance structures and their respective roles in an operational area. Efforts to improve representation, security, and welfare functions in line with COIN objectives are more likely to succeed when they work with and through the existing local structures instead of trying to build capacity and institutions based on US or Western models. The overall picture is likely to be a mixed one, with some local structures potentially impeding the COIN objective and others potentially advancing the COIN objective. For example, certain informal governance actors may prey on the local population to an extent that locals consider excessive. Other informal actors may be able to promote COIN objectives if locals consider that they offer a good alternative to the insurgents' efforts to provide governance. Often pre-conflict governance structures will need to be adapted to account for changes in society. However, it is typically better to adapt than to reinvent them. COIN forces should avoid creating parallel structures and programs that displace local governance structures and render the local structures impotent or obsolete.

(2) **Reconcile Local Expectations with USG Goals.** In a COIN environment, what is and is not seen as effective and legitimate governance by the population will depend on the local context. A careful analysis is needed to determine what the local population considers appropriate and to what extent a failure to meet these expectations is contributing to the insurgency. The results will have to be reconciled with the USG's strategic goals being pursued via the COIN operation. If democratic governance is part of the broader USG strategy, COIN efforts focused on locally appropriate governance to undermine the insurgent narrative will have to be reconciled with this more long-term agenda, which may generate challenges in terms of PA, IO, and interagency coordination. Generally, counterinsurgents seek to ensure that governance arrangements are inclusive instead of reinforcing societal divisions. The USG, and at times the joint force, may be able to assist by channeling assistance in ways that force cooperation across those divisions while also countering the insurgent narrative.

f. **Unified Action and Unity of Effort.** The joint force may become involved in governance and political reform efforts in a supported or, more likely, supporting capacity. In either case, a variety of potential partners could be involved. Ideally, the efforts of HN partners, USG departments and agencies, especially DOS and USAID, IGOs, and NGOs are well coordinated. At a minimum, the joint force is well aware of who is doing what in the operational area. Joint force activities to support governance and political reform leverage and support existing efforts of interagency and interorganizational partners. Projects and programs at different institutional levels (e.g., ministries, departments, bureaus) and at different levels of governance (national, provincial, tribal) are harmonized to support the COIN objectives. Coordination efforts generally seek to prioritize HN partners and USG departments and agencies (see Appendix A, "Civil-Military Operations," for more detail on key actors and unity of effort).

g. **Interagency Challenges.** The goal of unified action may be challenged by interorganizational differences. USG civilian and military actors may encounter differences with respect to national versus local orientation, long-term versus short-term outlook, project selection, and the reliability of local partners. A common understanding of the overall mission cannot be assumed. Even where an overall USG strategy for a particular operational area has been agreed to by all USG departments and agencies involved, individuals are likely to interpret that mission through their particular agency's prism. For example, the commander's LOEs in a COIN operation may not coincide with the political or economic development efforts of civilian agencies. As a result, JFCs should communicate early and often with interagency partners and build workable coordinating mechanisms. Coordination is best addressed early in the process, ideally during the early phases of planning (mission analysis).

h. **The Joint Force as Supported and Supporting Actor in Building Indigenous Governance.** The joint force may be in a supporting or supported role in a COIN operation depending on the nature and phase of the operation as well as the specific location within the operational area.

POLITICAL GOVERNANCE AND STRATEGY IN AFGHANISTAN

There is strong evidence that a positive and sustainable change in many poor and conflict affected societies has historically come about largely through the action of institutions for governance, including security, justice, and other public goods. There is equally strong evidence that significant improvements in governance institutions take more than a decade, and usually more than a generation, to achieve. Where formal, government, or state institutions are absent or weak, informal, non-state, and hybrid (state and non-state) institutions often come into being.

These patterns are evident in Afghanistan. Government institutions have made real progress over the past decade, but much of that progress has been halting, uneven, and not convincingly irreversible. The country's politics and economy are undeniably influenced by a mix of formal, informal, and illicit actors and power brokers. Some contribute to stability; others threaten it. The government does not have a monopoly on governance—and that fact will not change substantially in our lifetimes. Afghanistan is, and always has been, a hybrid political system.

The US and the international community have tended to treat Afghanistan's hybrid system as a problem to be solved, not a resource to be employed. As a consequence, much international activity has taken place along two opposing tracks. On what could be called the governance track, official strategy has required supporting the government, combating corruption, and building state institutions, under the explicit theory that insurgents can be marginalized if development and governance programs can help build a constructive relationship between the Afghan people and their leaders. On the politics track, the reality of power politics has at times required offering payments and contracts to power brokers in exchange for intelligence, passage, or cooperation, under the implicit theory that some of them are indispensable for stabilization because they control much of what happens in their areas of Influence.

Both of these tracks have their merits, but they have tended to work at cross-purposes. Those working to improve governance are explicitly trying to build government capacity at the expense of nongovernment power brokers and patronage systems. Those working with power brokers out of necessity are implicitly undermining the effectiveness of the government and some informal systems. In addition, proponents of both tracks have been overambitious compared to the resources available, while the resources available have been excessive compared to what the country can absorb. The excess and mismanagement have limited the effectiveness of aid and distorted the country's politics and economy in counterproductive ways. In the politics track, contracts, payoffs, and military or intelligence partnerships with power brokers have not been coordinated effectively (if at all), and have too often empowered malign actors more than has been needed to get things accomplished on the ground.

> **The governance and politics tracks need to be moving in the same direction for there to be any hope that the country will not descend into civil violence and economic collapse as international attention and resources fade. Formal, informal, and hybrid actors, institutions, and networks will need to share the burden of governing and will need a modest level of international support to do so. Power brokers will need to be co-opted into this hybrid system with just enough enticements to keep them from becoming spoilers.**
>
> **Lamb, Robert D. (2012)** *Political Governance and Strategy in Afghanistan*, **A Report of the Center for Strategic and International Studies (CSIS) Program on Crisis, Conflict, and Cooperation (CSIS: Washington, DC)**

(1) **Direct Responsibility for Governance.** Historically, the US military has taken on full governing responsibilities in a number of major military operations, including COIN or in anticipation of a possible insurgency. A full-scale occupation will likely entail either a transitional military government or a transitional civilian government. While the scenario of full-scale military government may be unlikely in the future, the joint force may still be required to carry out governance activities on a transitional basis either with an explicit mandate or on an ad hoc basis, as happened in Kosovo, East Timor, Afghanistan, and Iraq. In such cases, the ideal of civilian control over governance functions has to be weighed against the need for immediate action to prevent prolonged periods of anarchy. It may then be appropriate to implement a gradual transition in which the joint force retains the ultimate authority to directly act on dangerous dynamics while most decision making is undertaken by HN actors, USG civilians, or international civilians.

(2) **Direct Support to Indigenous Governance.** In the absence of a US or other international civilian presence, the joint force may be directly supporting indigenous governance activities. This has particularly been true during early phases of COIN operations in post-combat environments when it typically takes longer for a civilian presence to deploy to the operational area.

(3) **Supporting Indigenous Governance in Support of USG and/or Other Civilian Personnel.** The most typical COIN scenario will feature an interagency USG presence and/or other international actors. Even future heavy footprint operations are likely to include a significant USG civilian presence as well as other civilian actors, such as partner nations' civilian agencies, IGOs, and NGOs. In such cases, the joint force will be supporting others in building indigenous governance. In a small footprint scenario, the joint force can typically expect civilians to be in the lead on governance activities, coordinated through the country team (see Appendix A, "Civil-Military Operations," for more detail).

(4) **De Facto Sovereignty.** Particularly in cases where the joint staff footprint is large and/or HN capacities and capabilities are especially low, the JFC may be confronted with a discrepancy between the de jure sovereignty of the HN and the de facto power differential between HN leaders and the USG presence. Past experience has shown that local populations are very perceptive to the reality of such a situation, even when IO and PA activities are directed at emphasizing an HN lead and the HN government's sovereignty.

(5) **Governance Partners.** The primary actors in the field of governance will be HN government actors. This includes formal government representatives at the national, regional/provincial, and district/local levels. Among the USG interagency, DOS and USAID are the primary actors but others include DOJ, DOC, Department of the Treasury, and the USDA. Likely international partners will include coalition national civilian agencies and IGOs such as the UN, EU, OSCE, AU, ECOWAS, OECD, and the World Bank. Finally, NGOs and private sector organizations may conduct activities either in support of or related to indigenous governance functions.

2. Encouraging Political Reform

Insurgency is a struggle for political control of a government or region, and the COIN strategy is centered on a political solution. Part of finding a political solution may involve political reform of HN governance institutions and structures. Political reform in support of COIN objectives should be focused on fostering changes that will degrade the insurgents' ability to build their narrative around perceived political grievances. Such efforts must be based on local populations' expectations of what acceptable governance should look like.

a. **Promote Local Ownership.** HN buy-in and participation in political reform is vital for successful COIN. However, neither the HN government nor its population is monolithic—some segments of local governance structures and some segments of the local population may support (or oppose) political reform based on their perceived interests in (or perceived threat from) the reform. The USG and joint force should strategically channel assistance in ways that empower political reformers. Political reform efforts must be based on a careful analysis of existing power dynamics and expected future power dynamics at the end of the COIN campaign. If local power centers—including individuals, coalitions, parties, tribes, clans, or families—are likely to resist or circumvent political reform, sustained efforts will be required to co-opt, undermine, or replace such power centers. Capacity-building efforts that fail to account for HN and local political realities and the real power dynamics operating at different levels of governance are unlikely to have the desired impact. Similarly, efforts to obtain HN buy-in have to be aimed at genuine project ownership by the targeted HN government and local governance partners rather than appearing to local populations as mere ribbon-cutting exercises. This includes involving HN partners at the front end of projects, when key political issues are defined and projects to encourage reform on these key issues are conceived and designed. Democratic reform as practiced in Western government systems may not be feasible and/or desirable by HN partners.

b. **Local Perceptions of HN Ownership.** In cases where the joint force footprint is large and/or HN government capacities and capabilities are low, it may be difficult to overcome local perceptions that the HN government is beholden to and dependent on the security and financial resources of a foreign power. This may make it difficult to obtain true HN ownership in the eyes of the local population. In such cases, the JFC, in conjunction with USG partners, considers ways to enhance local perceptions of true HN ownership. These may include increased control by HN government and local governance structures over budgets, increased control over project and program decisions, and increased use of local contractors and local patronage networks.

c. **USG Influence and Leverage.** The JFC will require a detailed understanding of the current political landscape in the operational area, taking into account both formal political structures (e.g., HN national, provincial, and local governments and the strength of linkages among them) and informal structures (such as tribes, clans, kinship networks, religious/spiritual authorities, clubs and associations, private sector figures, and criminal and insurgent networks) or a combination of the two governance structures. This analysis will center on what, if any, reforms or changes are required to the political landscape in order to achieve the COIN objective. It will have to consider who the likely winners and losers will be once political reform takes place; whether the winners are likely to act in accordance with the COIN objective; and whether losers are likely to become insurgents or spoilers. The political strategy must provide political space for the losers of reform, and the USG and joint force may have a critical role in both constraining the winners and reassuring the losers. To fulfill this role effectively, it is important to retain leverage by empowering reformers and structuring assistance in ways that will further the COIN objective.

d. **Means.** Depending on specific conditions in the operational area, the USG and joint force will be able to employ a number of tools to encourage desired political change.

(1) **Financial and Technical Assistance.** Financial and technical assistance can be leveraged by making them conditional on political changes. Projects may be designed with a view to supporting change by including and excluding particular stakeholders. USG resources can be channeled to constructive partners within the HN government and local partners.

(2) **SA and Partnering.** Direct SA may be channeled to selectively support HNSF that are constructive COIN partners both politically and militarily. Mentoring and partnering activities provide further opportunities to steer HN partners toward constructive change.

(3) **Institution Building.** Decisions on who to empower in the process will be guided by COIN objectives. The USG and joint force will have to choose carefully which institutions should be strengthened. The same applies to parts of institutions. The insurgent narrative may attack institutional weaknesses as CVs of the counterinsurgents. This could include lack of representation or responsiveness, corruption, and a lack of transparency. Political reform efforts will need to be prioritized for maximum impact on those CVs.

(4) **Motivation.** HN governance actors can undermine COIN efforts if they fail to deliver governance functions in line with popular expectations. Publicizing abusive behavior can in itself lead to changes. USG and joint force personnel should judge carefully whether HN shortcomings are the result of a lack of capacity and capability or the result of abuse. If it is a lack of HN capacity, commanders should seek to help HN partners improve in critical areas. Where HN shortcomings result from deliberate abuses, providing information to the media can be an effective tool to incentivize individuals to modify their behavior.

3. **Building Effective Governance**

HN Structures Must Be Seen to Be Delivering Effective Governance. Whenever possible, support to indigenous governance should be channeled by, with, and through HN personnel and structures. This requires political will to do so on the part of the HN government. In addition, it may be particularly challenging to alter perceptions of the HN government if the local population perceives the HN government as not being truly sovereign. Effective governance will be defined in terms of HN standards and expectations—the prevailing social contract between population and governance structures is what matters. A social contract is an unwritten but widely accepted understanding between HN government structures and the local population as to what services and rules are considered acceptable by the local population. The focus of USG and joint force support will be on generating political effects in support of the COIN objective.

a. **Determining Requirements.** The social contract between the population and governance actors determines governance requirements. The JFC needs to understand what the local population considers to be predictable and tolerable living conditions in order to determine what local governance actors and structures might be considered legitimate by the people. Both the terms of the social contract and the mechanisms by which the HN delivers may vary across the operational area.

b. **Make-Up of Local Governance Structures.** Joint forces have to understand who should participate in governance across the operational area. Various individuals and groups are likely to claim a right to participate formally or informally. The list might include ethnic groups, tribes, clans, particular families, religious leaders, political parties, and key individuals. COIN objectives will determine whether changes are required in such local arrangements. Experience has shown that the precise local political arrangement can vary considerably across an operational area. It will therefore often be necessary to reconcile locally targeted bottom-up approaches with centralized or top-down efforts at the national level.

c. **Governance Processes and Procedures.** A key challenge for counterinsurgents is how to leverage existing governance processes and procedures to weaken the insurgency. This requires a detailed understanding of what the current decision-making models are. Formal and informal governance structures are likely to feature different decision-making models. Similarly, national-level models may differ from regional or local mechanisms. The core issue is how decisions are actually made and what, if any, parts of the process are contested by the insurgency.

(1) **Political Participation.** Counterinsurgents should understand the relationship between the mechanisms for political participation and the insurgency in the HN. Exclusion from political participation is often part of the insurgent narrative. In such cases, counterinsurgents should explore ways to encourage political participation or co-opt insurgents into HN political processes. These processes may include formal structures like political parties and government ministries. A chance to compete in national and/or local elections can offer an avenue for insurgents to move away from violence and into regular politics. However, elections can also become an occasion for violent contestation, especially if insurgents and other spoilers are able to operate with relative ease and counterinsurgent security forces are unable to provide effective public security. In such an environment, elections may actually embolden insurgents to keep fighting rather than turning to peaceful politics. In addition to formal structures, informal arrangements such as patronage networks

will often provide opportunities for alternative approaches. Patronage describes the distribution of government jobs or other favors to political allies. Patrons at different levels of formal and informal governance structures will dispense largesse, resources, and/or protection to groups of clients in return for their loyalty. Depending on the power of the patron at the center of the network, clients may in turn extend patronage to other clients at lower levels (e.g., from national, to provincial, to local levels). Counterinsurgents should consider carefully if and how such informal structures can be altered to generate effects in support of COIN objectives.

BUILDING GOVERNANCE IN SPIN BOLDAK, AFGHANISTAN

The greatest impediment to formal governance in Spin Boldak is the singular lack of concern among authorities either at the provincial or national level when it comes to the district's affairs. Despite the importance of Spin Boldak to the future of Afghanistan in terms of revenue generated through customs receipts at the border (i.e., the coalition's exit strategy), real decision-making authority in the district resides with the Afghan border police commander Gen. Razziq, rather than appointed civilian officials.

In Spin Boldak, the combination of poor governance and perceived tribal preference feeds an insurgent narrative that undermines all other efforts undertaken and bankrolled by the international community, driving a wedge between the government the coalition is backing and the people they are meant to serve and placing the coalition potentially on the wrong side of the equation.

In response to the discrimination faced by Spin Boldak's substantial IDP [internally displaced person] population, which included disparate group's lacking any representation on either the District Tribal Shura or the District Development Assembly (DDA), the district support team (DST) in late 2009 determined it best not to deal officially with the Shura/DDA, until it would accept IDP membership. To do otherwise would have sanctioned the disenfranchisement of 1/3 of the population.

The heads of the Shura and DDA were adamantly opposed to cooperation (read: sharing) with groups having in their eyes no legal claims to land or rights in Spin Boldak. Their job as they saw it was to protect local interests, including their own, against all outside threats, including from fellow Afghans. Over time, however, more and more Shura members sought to participate in the advisory committee (known locally as the commission) as this was where the DST came to consult district leadership, not the Shura/DDA. In the process, local Achekzai and Noorzai elders became at least acclimatized to sitting alongside IDP and Kuchi representatives; full acceptance will take much longer. Despite the election of a Noorzai shura head in late 2010, the sense of Noorzai second class citizenship is grist for the insurgent propaganda mill, permitting the government's enemies freedom of movement through tribal areas, whether through apathy, outright support, or intimidation. In Spin Boldak, insurgent activity has been heaviest in areas furthest from the district center where the reach of government and basic services is weakest. It is perhaps no coincidence that these are primarily Noorzai regions. For Gen. Razziq and perhaps coalition military planners at Kandahar Airfield, these outlying communities are not a priority. Complicating this picture is not only the tension between the two dominant tribes but also fissures within each as individual leaders and subtribes have over the years been forced to make their own accommodation with prevailing political forces out of a sense of preservation, in many instances setting kinsmen against each other.

In many respects, the DST was operating, through the guise of the district governor, as a poor substitute for Kabul leadership. This is not a consequence of a lack of indigenous capacity as much as it is the result of a conscious decision by Afghan power brokers (and coalition leaderships) to accept the status quo in Spin Boldak, including the dominant role played by Gen. Razziq. One risk is that the MIL [military]/DST will begin to assume more and more responsibility for addressing local affairs and needs. This is a problem faced by the coalition across the country. While building local capacity is a coalition objective, so is getting the job done. For many MIL commanders, in particular, drawing up a CERP [Commanders' Emergency Response Program] package or employing base assets is sometimes the quicker means to an end which might have been better left in Afghan hands. Without Afghan authorities taking responsibility, however, sometimes this is unavoidable, particularly when dealing with grievances that feed the insurgency. The end result, though, is a coalition fix, not an Afghan one, leaving the real sources of grievance unresolved.

Case Study: Spin Boldak DST, USAID (2010)

(2) **Decision-Making Procedures.** In addition to political representation, specific decision-making procedures may feature as grievances in the insurgent narrative. Counterinsurgents should understand which key stakeholders are empowered and which ones are excluded by decision-making procedures in both formal and informal governance structures. Adjustments at one or more levels may inform different LOEs in support of COIN objectives.

(3) **Responding to the Needs of Citizens.** Unresponsive governance structures are often part of an insurgency's motives. Even if political representation per se and adjustments to decision-making procedures are difficult to implement, minor adjustments in terms of responsiveness may be able to undermine an insurgent narrative. Efforts aimed at increasing responsiveness should start with the local population's expectations of what constitutes sufficient responsiveness, and by which formal or informal institutions.

4. Security Sector Reform

SSR is primarily a means to strengthen the capabilities, capacity, and effectiveness of the HN security apparatus, which in turn improves the capabilities of the security forces to secure and protect the population from insurgent/terrorist violence. SSR also may be used to improve the security provided by local and national law enforcement organizations. Secondarily, SSR can be a step toward improved legitimacy and potentially good governance if the population feels more secure, but does not feel the hand of an oppressive police state.

For a more detailed discussion about SSR, see JP 3-07, Stability Operations.

5. Criminal Justice System Reform

Effective and acceptable delivery of justice is an essential governance function; it allows for nonviolent dispute resolution. The HN justice system encompasses an array of formal and informal institutions, groups, and individuals. These institutions can include the ministry of justice, law enforcement personnel, law schools and bar associations, and legal advocacy organizations. The groups and individuals can include members of the judiciary, legislature, corrections, and prosecutor's office; public defenders; ombudsmen; regulatory bodies; and human rights and public interest groups. The legal framework includes the constitution, laws, rules, and regulations. Peace agreements may also constitute part of the legal framework in post-conflict countries. Justice systems differ significantly across national boundaries; there may also be multiple justice systems functioning in a country. To enhance HN legitimacy, justice reform should build upon the existing legal frameworks in the HN. This may include common law, civil law, criminal codes, traditional or religious law, and international law. Foreign SSR planners must avoid imposing their concepts of law, justice, and security on the HN, except where reform is required to meet customary international law with regard to human rights. Implementing such reform, even where warranted, will doubtless entail a sophisticated political analysis on whether to undertake the change. The HN's systems and values are central to its development of justice system reform.

For more discussion on justice sector reform, see JP 3-07, Stability Operations.

6. Disarmament, Demobilization, and Reintegration

DDR attempts to stabilize the OE by disarming and demobilizing insurgents and by helping return former insurgents to civilian life. The UN and other international organizations generally view DDR efforts as post-conflict activities. **Historically, however, DDR programs are not only possible but also desirable from the earliest stages of a COIN operation or campaign, but they must be carefully tailored to the local context.** DDR efforts during an active conflict focus on inducing insurgent defection and using former insurgents to undermine the insurgency. As the program matures, DDR can potentially dissolve belligerent force structures and provide incentives for insurgent leaders to facilitate political reconciliation. A successful DDR program helps end an insurgency and establish sustainable peace, while a failed DDR effort can stall COIN efforts and strengthen the insurgency.

a. **Purpose.** The objective of the DDR process is to contribute to security and stability in post-conflict environments so that recovery and development can begin. The DDR of former combatants is a complex process, with political, military, security, humanitarian, and socioeconomic dimensions. It aims to deal with the post-conflict security problem that arises when former combatants are left without livelihoods or support networks, other than their former comrades, during the vital transition period from conflict to peace and development. Disarmament and demobilization refers to the act of releasing or disbanding an armed unit and the collection and control of weapons and weapons systems. Reintegration helps former combatants return to civilian life through benefit packages and strategies that help them become socially and economically embedded in their communities. The DDR of children associated with fighting forces should be done separately from adult DDR processes; children should be treated as victims of human rights violations and afforded protection through this process.

b. **Disarmament.** Disarmament is the collection, documentation, control, and disposal of small arms, ammunition, explosives, and light and heavy weapons of former insurgents and the population. Disarmament also includes the development of responsible arms management programs. Ideally, disarmament is a voluntary process carried out as part of a broader peace process to which all parties accede. Disarmament functions best with high levels of trust between those being disarmed and the forces overseeing disarmament. Some groups may hesitate to offer trust and cooperation or even refuse to participate in disarmament efforts. In these circumstances, disarmament may occur in two stages: a voluntary disarmament process followed by more coercive measures. The latter will address individuals or small groups refusing to participate voluntarily. In this second stage, disarmament of combatant factions can become a contentious and potentially very destabilizing step of DDR. **The HN and multinational partners manage DDR carefully to avoid disarmament becoming a catalyst for renewed violence. Disarmament may be a slow process in an ongoing COIN and realistic goals must be set.**

c. **Demobilization.** Demobilization is the process of transitioning a conflict or wartime military establishment and defense-based civilian economy to a peacetime configuration while maintaining national security and economic vitality. **Demobilization for COIN normally involves the controlled discharge of active combatants from paramilitary groups, militias, and insurgent forces that have stopped fighting.** Demobilization under these circumstances may include identifying and gathering ex-combatants for demobilization efforts. Demobilization involves deliberately dismantling insurgent organizations and belligerent group loyalties, replacing those with more appropriate group affiliations, and restoring the identity of former fighters as part of the national population. **The demobilization of insurgents enables the eventual development of value systems, attitudes, and social practices that help them reintegrate into civil society.**

d. **Reintegration.** Reintegration is the process through which former insurgents receive amnesty, reenter civil society, gain sustainable employment, and become contributing members of the local population. **It encompasses the reinsertion of individual former insurgents into HN communities, villages, and social groups.** Reintegration is a social and economic recovery process focused on the local community; it complements other community-based programs that spur economic recovery, training, and employment services. It includes programs to support resettlement in civilian communities, basic and vocational and/or basic education, family reunification, psychosocial support, health, and assistance in finding employment in local economies. It accounts for the specific needs of women and children associated with insurgent and other armed groups. Insurgents will be under extraordinary pressure from their former fighting colleagues. This pressure to return to the insurgent ranks can come in the form of intimidation, death threats and letters, physical abuse, and in many cases, death or serious injury if the reintegrated fighter does not return to the fighting ranks of the insurgents. It is vital that COIN forces provide physical security for the reintegrated fighter; protection for him/her and their families will be paramount to ensure a lasting reintegration process and an atmosphere of trust between the government and the reintegrated fighter. In some cases, relocation of the reintegrated fighter might be necessary.

e. **DDR: Importance to COIN.** The promise and nature of DDR to insurgents often plays a crucial role in undermining insurgent recruitment, increasing insurgent desertion or defection, and even achieving a peace agreement. **Insurgent defectors are enormously valuable to ongoing COIN operations, and the HN government should use them to the maximum extent possible.** DDR closely coordinates with reform efforts in all sectors, and DDR planning directly ties to SSR, determining the potential size and scope of military, police, and other security structures. The success of DDR depends on integrating strategies and planning across all related sectors.

For additional information, see JP 3-07, Stability Operations.

(1) **DDR Planning.** Planning for a successful DDR program requires an understanding of both the situation on the ground and the goals, political will, and resources with which other actors and donor organizations are willing to support. Ideally, governmental organizations and NGOs from the international community collaborate with the HN government to plan and execute DDR programs. Joint forces must be integrated in the planning of DDR from its inception and can provide invaluable support to insurgent defection operations. Effective DDR planning relies on analysis of possible DDR beneficiaries, power dynamics, and local society as well as the nature of the conflict and ongoing peace processes. Assessments are conducted in close consultation with the local populace and with personnel from participating agencies who understand and know about the HN. The DDR planning process will vary widely depending on the conflict and the lead organization for the DDR program. The following passage outlines the four possible lead organizations for a DDR program.

(a) **HN Lead.** In some cases, such as El Salvador and Nepal, HN governments have the lead with support from the UN, other multilateral organizations (such as the World Bank), bilateral donors, and multinational forces. When the HN leads the process, supporting organizations will play an advisory role, but this should not prevent the joint force from being actively engaged in the process. Joint forces can provide an array of valuable supporting actions such as security, intelligence, operational advisors, and financial assistance.

(b) **Multilateral Organization Lead.** In other cases, such as the Democratic Republic of Congo, the UN often leads DDR efforts due to its experience in the area. UN organizations, such as the UN Development Programme and the UN Department of Peacekeeping Operations, will run the program with potential assistance from additional international or national agencies. Organizations like OECD and the World Bank have experts that often provide assistance designing, initiating, and monitoring DDR programs without being the main implementers.

(c) **USG Lead.** USG departments or agencies could potentially lead DDR efforts in future conflicts. DOS has had experience in a variety of DDR programs and can play a valuable role in planning and managing the complex tasks involved. Furthermore, the DOS's historic role in leading police and internal security service reforms and USAID's historic role in development make both agencies extremely valuable partners whether they have the lead role or not.

(d) **US Forces Lead.** In some scenarios, US forces may have to lead a DDR program, particularly if the security situation on the ground is threatening. It is important to note that if US forces do lead a DDR program, commanders should request assistance from relevant offices within the UN, DOS, USAID, or other agencies with experience in DDR.

(2) **DDR Framework.** Although each individual insurgency is complex and unique, a successful DDR process requires certain elements that can be adapted to the context of each conflict. Successful DDR efforts in the past have all included aspects of each element in the framework that follows. The joint force should advise the HN to incorporate the various elements into its DDR process.

(a) **Identification and Outreach.** Accurately identifying insurgents willing to reintegrate is the first aspect of a successful DDR framework. Many unidentified insurgents may come forward on their own accord, but evaluating the propensity for reintegration in the insurgency as a whole is still a valuable process. Identifying reconcilable insurgents requires strong intelligence and individuals with a deep understanding of the insurgent network. Once reconcilable insurgents are identified, the HN must commence outreach efforts designed to persuade insurgents to defect. The joint force can use its intelligence assets to assist HN identification and outreach efforts. Former insurgents are also essential to successful identification and outreach efforts. In Malaya, the British used captured documents and evidence from former insurgents to build dossiers on a large number of communist terrorists, which led directly to the defection of an insurgent commander responsible for the entire southern region. Establishing and enhancing identification and outreach efforts provides a solid foundation for any DDR process.

(b) **Insurgent Commitment.** Insurgents will rarely defect without some incentive or assurance of their safety. The HN government's task is to identify and execute a range of methods that will result in insurgent commitments to reintegrate. A review of successful reintegration cases suggests that there are five primary methods of achieving insurgent commitment: monetary incentives, divide-and-conquer diplomacy, the bandwagon effect, coercion, and grievance-based appeasement. All successful reintegration programs included some level of monetary incentive for former insurgents, but should not be the sole, or even central, method of gaining insurgent commitment. Divide-and-conquer diplomacy involves exploiting tensions present in the insurgency such as British efforts in Oman to drive a wedge between the Islamic insurgents that were being exploited by the hard-core communist insurgents. The bandwagon effect is simply encouraging insurgent defectors to convince their comrades to join them. Threats and coercion involve either directly forcing insurgents to reintegrate or indirectly encouraging them to reintegrate by conducting effective military operations in their area or within their group. Coercive approaches can be effective, but will not work without some incentive such as monetary incentives or grievance-based appeasement. **Grievance-based approaches focus on the motivations that drove the insurgent to take up arms in the first place. Because these approaches target the source of insurgent actions, they have the greatest potential for producing lasting peace.** The HN government may need to employ all of these methods, but the final method—grievance-based appeasement—must play a central role if the government desires lasting peace. It should be noted that, no matter how effectively the DDR plan is executed, not all combatants will participate in the process. These individuals or groups must be accounted for to minimize disruptions to the overall DDR process.

(c) **Acceptance.** Acceptance is an essential part of the DDR process and involves insurgent pledges, government forgiveness, and proper vetting. Formal insurgent pledges are necessary to ensure that insurgents are serious about their decision and to prevent insurgents from taking advantage of DDR benefits. The government must reciprocate insurgent pledges by offering forgiveness and protection. Formal acceptance ceremonies demonstrate the HN government's commitment to the reintegration process while also making it clear that retaliation against former insurgents is unlawful. Effective vetting procedures such as biometric enrollment and local government involvement will reduce the likelihood of fraudulent activities associated with the DDR process.

(d) **Using Former Insurgents.** Properly using former insurgents can have the greatest potential impact on the overall COIN operation or campaign. The government can use former insurgents for intelligence, IO, combat operations, and local defense. The British used former insurgents in Malaya and Oman to provide information on insurgent activities and to prepare material for leaflets, radio broadcasts, and newspapers. The South Vietnamese placed insurgent defectors into armed propaganda teams and scout teams that would lead South Vietnamese and US troops to Viet Cong targets. In Afghanistan, former insurgents are eligible to assist local defense efforts in their area by joining the Afghan local police. The utilization of former insurgents is a proven process that led to the defection of thousands of additional insurgents in Oman, Malaya, and Vietnam.

(e) **Promoting Lasting Peace.** Persuading insurgents to rejoin the government is ultimately ineffective if the reintegrated fighters resort to violence again in the future. **The goal of every DDR program is to contribute to security and stability in a post-conflict environment, so the DDR process must include elements that will promote lasting peace.** Several DDR principles are essential to the goal of establishing lasting peace.

1. **Insurgent Reintegration.** Former insurgents, when properly protected, reintegrated, and well treated, can become positive members of their community. Conversely, unprotected, poorly prepared, or poorly treated former insurgents will become powerful IO opportunities for the insurgents. The reintegration process and programs, such as HN-led moderate ideological or religious education and job training, should be started early in the reintegration process.

2. Amnesty and Reconciliation. Reintegration also addresses the willingness of civilian communities to accept former fighters into their midst; amnesty and reconciliation are key components to successful reintegration. In this context, reintegration cannot be divorced from justice and reconciliation programs that are part of the broader transition process and may include community reconciliation initiatives, truth telling exercises, and forgiveness rituals. Successful reintegration programs tend to be long-term and costly, requiring the participation of multiple external and HN participants. The Chinese philosopher Sun Tzu wrote that a commander must: "Build your opponent a golden bridge to retreat across." While Sun Tzu intended this remark to illustrate how a cornered enemy will often fight more intensely than one with an escape route, this admonition can apply in a COIN context as well. Counterinsurgents must leave a way out for insurgents who have lost the desire to continue the struggle. Amnesty cannot be granted for war crimes. Effective amnesty and reintegration programs provide the insurgents this avenue; amnesty provides the means to quit the insurgency, and reintegration allows former insurgents to become part of greater society.

3. Grievance Resolution. Grievance resolution is the cornerstone of a reintegration program and key to keeping former insurgents on the side of the government. In many ways grievance resolution is an inexact term because the government will not be able to resolve all of the grievances of former insurgents. Even strong democratic governments are unable to solve all of their own society's grievances. The HN government must devise ways to address insurgent grievances through forums such as peace councils or judicial bodies that provide former insurgents a nonviolent platform to air their problems. When the government is willing to provide this forum it enhances its legitimacy in the eyes of the population and those who used to be opposed to the government.

4. Reinsertion. Reinsertion is the assistance offered to former insurgents and belligerents prior to the long-term process of reintegration. Reinsertion is a form of transitional assistance intended to provide for the basic needs of reintegrating individuals and their families; this assistance includes transitional safety allowances, food, clothes, shelter, health services, short-term education, training, employment, and tools. While reintegration represents enduring social and economic development, reinsertion is a short-term material and financial assistance program intended to meet immediate needs.

5. Repatriation. The repatriation of foreign nationals to their country of citizenship is governed by complex US and international legal norms and standards, legal standards that likely apply differently in each case of proposed repatriation. Any program of repatriation is likely to raise important legal issues that must be reviewed by US legal personnel.

6. Resettlement. Resettlement is the relocation of refugees to a third country, which is neither the country of citizenship nor the country into which the refugee has fled. Resettlement to a third country is granted by accord of the country of resettlement. It is based on a number of criteria, including legal and physical protection needs, lack of local integration opportunities, health needs, family reunification needs, and threat of violence and torture. Resettlement can also mean the relocation of internally displaced persons to another location within the country.

<u>7</u>. **Return.** The return of refugees and internally displaced persons to their homes is one of the most difficult aspects of COIN. If their dislocation was originally caused by ethnic or sectarian cleansing, their return risks renewed ethno-sectarian violence. Often abandoned homes are occupied by squatters, who must be removed in order to return the home to the rightful owner. Poor real estate records and immature judicial systems and laws exacerbate the return process, as ownership must be legally established prior to return. Counterinsurgents can play a key role in transporting and providing security for returnees, and often play a role in establishing temporary legal mechanisms to resolve property disputes.

7. Economic and Infrastructure Development

Economic and infrastructure development have frequently featured as the main nonlethal LOEs in recent COIN operations. Often, such efforts have featured Western templates to determine priorities and have struggled to secure the local population's buy-in. Economic and infrastructure development in support of COIN should be based on local expectations, capabilities, and capacities to ensure sustainability. Fulfilling local expectations in terms of service delivery can help bolster the legitimacy of HN governance structures, while undermining the insurgency. By contrast, efforts that do not take local conditions and expectations as their starting point run the risk of disrupting or undermining benign local governance structures, strengthening the insurgency, fostering corruption, and creating dependencies. Counterinsurgents avoid relying on infrastructure outputs as metrics in themselves. Instead, metrics should capture how economic and infrastructure development affect political and social attitudes. In a COIN context, such efforts should directly aim at undercutting the insurgent narrative. They are not synonymous with long-term development efforts that may be carried out by other USG departments and agencies, IGOs, and NGOs. However, counterinsurgents should aim to ensure that short-term stabilization measures do not undercut long-term development goals.

a. **Service Delivery.** Decisions on supporting service delivery should be based on local expectations. The social contract in the HN determines what the population expects of different governance structures in terms of service delivery. This might include water and sanitation, electricity, communication and transportation infrastructure, medical care, and education. Careful analysis of local conditions is required to determine which of these should be supported by USG or joint force efforts to achieve the COIN objective. Priority LOEs should be developed in close cooperation with HN governance structures. Popular expectations as well as the capacity of HN governance structures to absorb support will determine what can be realistically achieved. To the extent possible, actual service delivery should be carried out—and seen to be carried out—by HN structures.

b. **Partnering and Unity of Effort.** A host of USG, indigenous, and international actors may become, or already be, involved in economic and infrastructure development activities. Counterinsurgents will have to be cognizant of the full range of activities underway in the operational area. Aid programs could be leveraged to support COIN objectives. Others may actually fuel the insurgency, for example if resources are diverted toward insurgents. JFCs should use coordinating mechanisms to maximize the potential

COIN benefits of economic and infrastructure development while minimizing potential negative consequences.

    c. **Metrics and Generating Effects.** Nonlethal LOEs should aim to generate discrete effects (social, political, security) in support of COIN objectives. For example, insurgents may function as providers of economic benefits to the population through pay for participation, hand-outs, and other opportunities for extortion. Where this is the case, economic and infrastructure development LOEs should aim to replace the insurgents with more benign structures. Metrics used to measure the impact of such efforts need to be based on the desired effect. Experience has shown that simply measuring infrastructure outputs (e.g., miles of road laid, number of schools built) tells the counterinsurgents little about their effect on the insurgency. Equally important, economic and infrastructure projects are bound to produce both winners and losers. Counterinsurgents will have to be cognizant of both and plan for likely second- and third-order effects as a result.

GOVERNANCE AND PUBLIC SERVICES IN COUNTERINSURGENCY: HEARTS AND MINDS OR HARD POLITICS?

An oversimplified version of the concept of hearts and minds has driven a lot of spending in Iraq and Afghanistan. It was based on an assumption that delivering a variety of public services will win a population over to the side of the counterinsurgents. Evidence suggests that at best such programs are ineffective, and at worst contribute to instability or are diverted to fund the insurgencies. Another approach has been to run mass employment programs to keep insurgents from hiring the under-employed to emplace improvised explosive devices, provide intelligence, etc. To date, studies have actually found that higher unemployment is usually correlated with less violence.

A third suite of approaches is more nuanced and is based on appealing to interests rather than sentiment. In this account, the provision of basic services and programs to jump-start the local economy are intended to appeal to the population's calculations about their medium- to long-term interests even as the military applies combat power to secure them against insurgents in the short term.

In all these cases, counterinsurgents were responding in part to an assumption that the grievances driving passive or active support for the insurgency are material. In some cases, they were also responding to the complaints and demands explicitly articulated by the population.

Assessing the evidence across entire theaters or conflicts is difficult. A wide study of development projects in Iraq found that small-scale projects funded through Commander's Emergency Response Program seemed to be effective at reducing violence. On the other hand, a study on programming in Helmand described that in the eyes of the population, the distribution of aid was seen as reflecting the post-2001 tribal carve-up of institutions, power, and resources, and access to development funding was seen as an avenue for consolidating wealth and political power. Evidence from focus groups suggested that "development" was viewed by individuals from non-beneficiary communities as evidence of elite capture of aid processes rather than a demonstration that aid was a public good that could be extended to all. Without adequate analysis of social fault lines, the distribution of aid in such a fragmented and polarized polity often marginalized groups and increased the sense of alienation rather than giving hope of potential change. These challenges appear to have been compounded by inevitable weaknesses in oversight and program management structures within the provincial reconstruction team.

This illustrates the difficulty in disentangling whether the problems observed in recent operations are due to planning or execution. A recurrent problem for both planning and execution is related to scale. First, governance and development programs are often structured around development objectives such as improved health outcomes or increased incomes, rather than political objectives such as rewarding participation in local governance systems. As a result, they are often structured and implemented in ways that don't adequately take into account the varied local political dynamics of different regions in a counterinsurgency environment.

Second, the pursuit of broad development objectives often naturally leads to large-scale projects whose very size makes them more difficult to carefully monitor. These two factors make development projects more vulnerable to corruption and distortion. Development projects that are distorted by the dynamics of the conflict can exacerbate grievances and discredit counterinsurgents by raising and then disappointing expectations when promises aren't met, and by reproducing the patterns of political exclusion that undermined the legitimacy of the host-nation government in the first place.

As explained by the Special Inspector General for Iraq,

War, politics, and reconstruction are linked in ways that individuals within the government failed to appreciate in the opening years of the Iraq conflict. If war, as Clausewitz said, is an extension of politics by other means, so too is relief and reconstruction an extension of political, economic, and military strategy. In this regard, there is a distinct difference between pursuing reconstruction to catalyze long-term economic growth and deploying reconstruction to support a counterinsurgency campaign.

Four consistent lessons emerge from the literature:

1. Security is the top consideration for the population, but that includes long-term security as well as short-term. Groups that feel their long-term survival will be threatened under the host-nation government are unlikely to cooperate with counterinsurgents. This means that the US must pay as much attention to the threat from predatory government forces as the insurgents, even if it addresses those threats through different means.

2. After security, the representation of marginalized groups in formal and informal governance bodies is the most important element to get right. Service delivery should flow from that representation and be used as a reward for participation. However, participation will often only be possible with credible guarantees of security.

3. On the other hand, representation is not enough to maintain legitimacy and generate cooperation among the population. It has to produce tangible benefits in terms of services and programs in order to make it meaningful. Governance systems must be relevant (in terms of addressing the most urgent problems of the population), reliable (in terms of consistency over time), and effective (in terms of delivering results).

4. Enhancing government services and kick-starting economic development is best accomplished through a limited number of small-scale and highly localized projects that are carefully monitored by counterinsurgent forces to prevent corruption or diversion, exploit existing formal and informal governance mechanisms wherever possible, and are specifically designed to reinforce a narrative of inclusive politics and reconciliation rather than elite capture and zero-sum competition.

Various Sources

Intentionally Blank

APPENDIX A
CIVIL-MILITARY OPERATIONS

"While the provision of security is a necessary activity in COIN [counterinsurgency], it will not defeat an insurgency on its own. When possible, civilian and military measures should be applied simultaneously to achieve success in an integrated strategy that delegitimizes and undermines the insurgency, builds government control, and strengthens popular support. In counterinsurgency, military forces are, in a sense, an enabling system for civil administration; their role is to afford sufficient protection and stability to allow the government to work safely with its population, for economic revival, political reconciliation, and external non-government assistance to be effective."

US Government Counterinsurgency Guide, 2009

1. Introduction and Overview

a. This appendix reviews major aspects of and considerations for civil-military teaming in a COIN environment. It is intended to help CCDRs, subordinate JFCs, their staffs, interagency partners, and the full range of actors who may be present in a COIN environment understand civilian actor roles and relationships and plan for, deconflict, and enable unity of effort for activities during the conduct of COIN operations.

b. The integration of political, security, and economic activities in COIN frequently exposes military forces to a wider range of civil-dimension skills and capabilities than those military forces typically train for or inherently possess. As a result, coordination and collaboration become more important as the JFC seeks to gain unity of effort.

c. Civil-military teams are temporary organizations of civilian and military personnel which are task-oriented to provide an optimal mix of capabilities and expertise to accomplish specific planning or assessment tasks or to conduct synchronized or integrated activities at the strategic, operational, or tactical level. Civil-military teams can either be colocated or come together for designated planning or implementation functions. They provide the JFC with a means to understand the benefits of competencies that are normally external to the military. They help integrate the knowledge, expertise, and unique capabilities of DOD and civilian agencies with multinational military forces and civilian elements of multinational partners to implement an integrated COIN strategy with their HN counterparts. Civil-military teams help the JFC understand the unique roles, responsibilities, parallel relationships, and objectives of other international and nongovernmental actors and organizations that may be present in the OE, but over which neither the JFC nor the COM exercises authority.

d. **Counterinsurgents** are responsible for the population's well-being. This includes security from insurgent intimidation and coercion, sectarian violence, and nonpolitical violence and crime. To succeed, counterinsurgents must address the basic economic needs, essential services (such as sewage, water, electricity, sanitation, and health care), sustainment of key social and cultural institutions, and other aspects that contribute to a society's basic quality of life. Informed, strong leaders must focus on the central problems affecting the local populace. Given the primacy of political considerations, military forces should support civilian efforts. The changing nature of COIN means that lead responsibility shifts among military, civilian, and HN authorities, and these transitions must be planned and managed at the highest levels. However, the joint force must prepare to assume local leadership for COIN efforts, as the situation and need dictate. The overall imperative is to focus on what needs to be done, not on who does it. While this imperative can be emphasized by senior civilian and military leaders, its practice must be based on positive interpersonal relationships and execution of an integrated civil-military strategy.

2. Purpose

a. In COIN operations, employment of a whole-of-government approach is key to supporting HN efforts to build legitimacy among relevant populations. The overarching objective of civil-military teaming is to create synergies between civilian efforts and military operations in order to counter the insurgency directly and indirectly. By engaging with the political dynamics of the conflict, securing the population, addressing root causes, and fostering effective governance, counterinsurgents seek to build support for the government and marginalize the insurgency until it is no longer a threat to the state. As the HN government's willingness and capacity to govern the population and fight the insurgency rises, third-party counterinsurgents can gradually ramp down their levels of involvement. In cases where larger third-party counterinsurgent forces have been deployed, the transition to HN responsibility can present significant risks. Those risks can be mitigated through deliberate planning between civilian, military, and HN actors.

b. **COIN is normally only effective with a holistic approach that employs all HN and supporting nation instruments of national power.** Joint military efforts to secure the population may initially dominate COIN, but the other instruments of national power are essential to achieve national strategic objectives. Interagency participants in COIN operations must know each others' roles, capabilities, cultures, and terminology. COIN planning at all levels should include HN representatives and other participants. Military participants should support civilian efforts, including those of NGOs, IGOs, USG interagency partners, IPI, and other friendly actors. However, military participants should recognize that they can inadvertently put NGOs or local civilians in danger by relating to them. The *Guidelines for Relations Between US Armed Forces and Nongovernmental Humanitarian Organizations* outline the appropriate protocols for communicating with NGOs. Military participants, as required by the situation, conduct or participate in political, social, informational, and economic programs. Societal insecurity can trigger violence that discourages or precludes nonmilitary organizations, particularly external agencies, from helping the local populace. A more benign environment allows civilian agencies greater opportunity to provide their resources and expertise, thereby relieving joint forces of some of these responsibilities. Long-term development and therefore successful COIN depends on the joint force providing an environment in which civilian agencies can effectively operate, especially with respect to economic efforts.

c. **Unity of Effort and Unified Action. Unity of effort and unified action are essential for successful COIN operations.** Unified action refers to the synchronization, coordination, and/or integration of military operations with the activities of governmental and nongovernmental entities to achieve unity of effort. Unified action includes a whole-of-government or comprehensive approach that employs all instruments of national power. Achieving unity of effort is challenging in COIN due to the normally complex OE and its many potential actors—friendly, neutral, and adversarial. The military contribution to COIN must be coordinated with the activities of USG interagency partners, IGOs, and NGOs, though this coordination may take the form of communication and not structural integration.

3. Key Actors

COIN is a **USG** effort requiring interagency coordination that is normally led by a DOS COM in support of the HN government. For USG support to an HN's COIN efforts, the COM normally is the senior USG representative.

a. **Military.** While nonmilitary considerations are paramount for long-term success in COIN, the joint military contribution is essential to provide security and other support that enables other interagency partners' COIN efforts and allows progression. Joint forces contribute to unified action through unity of command and a C2 architecture that integrates strategic, operational, and tactical organizations and synchronizes or deconflicts their tasks and activities. Services play a key role in both stability operations and countering insurgency, and their efforts are most effective when synchronized. The JFC should coordinate with and draw on the capabilities of separate agencies as well as provide support, especially security, as required by other participants. To the extent that multinational forces are assigned to the JFC, the JFC is responsible for integration of those forces into the COIN effort in accordance with any national caveats associated with those forces. Caveats are restrictions upon the use of their forces which are imposed by the governments of partner nations.

b. **Interagency.** Interagency coordination is conducted among departments and agencies of the USG, including DOD, for the purpose of accomplishing an objective. In COIN, interagency coordination among the joint force and USG interagency partners is fundamental, because they, in turn, will likely coordinate with other non-US participants.

c. **Intergovernmental.** Coordination with IGOs involves the USG, led by DOS, in conjunction with the JFC, and implemented through the relevant COM and country team, working with the HN. In some cases the HN, in conjunction with the COM and JFC, may coordinate with the IGO. When working with IGOs, the JFC should use existing mechanisms of the COM and country team, DOS, USAID, and other appropriate agencies. IGOs provide leadership, capabilities, and mandate; and may lend legitimacy and credibility to governance, especially for the HN. Interorganizational coordination includes coordination with IGOs. See Chapter IV, "The Operational Environment," paragraph 8d(4), "IGOs," for more information.

d. **Multinational.** Multinational operations do not necessarily involve the USG, but are dependent upon the context. If they do involve the USG, we say we coordinate with multinational partners. If our actions involve the whole of government, then USG, led by DOS and implemented through the relevant COM and country team, working with agencies and forces from other nations, and this coordination normally occurs within the framework of an alliance or coalition. When working with multinational organizations, the JFC should use existing mechanisms of the COM and country team, DOS, USAID, and other appropriate agencies, and establish organizational relationships as close to command relationships as possible with the multinational forces. There have been occasions where the JFC was designated the multinational force commander, but did not have unity of command over the multinational force, rather the JFC will establish organizational relationships that result in unity of effort. The HN is the most important entity for multinational coordination in COIN. As with any multinational efforts, trust and agreement bind the entities conducting COIN on common goals and objectives, which is especially important between the HN and the remainder of the multinational forces. Language and cultural differences often present the most immediate challenge, and all actors must strive to overcome these challenges through communication and improving cultural awareness. Liaisons and advisors can play a vital role in these areas. Multinational forces that support an HN's COIN effort must remember that they are present by the HN's request and that COIN is ultimately the HN's responsibility. Together, the JFC and COM should enable leaders of US contingents to establish robust organizational relationships to work closely with their multinational counterparts, and to become familiar with and coordinate with agencies that may operate in their operational area. To the degree possible, military leaders should use military liaison personnel to further enable appropriate relationships and the awareness between joint forces and their multinational and HN counterparts. Interorganizational coordination includes coordination with multinational organizations.

e. **Nongovernmental**

(1) Coordination with NGOs is between elements of the USG and implemented through the relevant COM and country team, and NGOs, multinational corporations, private contractors, and private organizations of any kind to achieve an objective. When working with NGOs, the JFC should use existing mechanisms of the COM and country team, DOS, USAID, and other appropriate agencies. Absent a COM, a JFC may have to directly coordinate with NGOs, multinational corporations, private contractors, and private organizations until a US diplomatic mission is established. This can be facilitated by reachback through the GCC to relevant departments or agencies and through the use of civil-military operations centers (CMOCs). The preponderance of effort put forth by the JTF will continue to focus on creating the security conditions necessary to support the civilian administration of the host country government and establish the US diplomatic mission. Interorganizational coordination includes coordination with NGOs. Many NGOs will not wish to openly associate with the joint force and are concerned with preserving the "humanitarian space" as an overt association with the military can give the perception that they are a partner in the COIN effort, and make them less effective or subject to insurgent attack. Collaborating and coordinating with those NGOs can be difficult, however, establishing basic awareness of these groups and their activities may be important, because they sometimes play important roles in resolving insurgencies and can support lasting stability. Try to build a complementary, trust-based relationship regardless of the NGOs level of cooperation. JFC may have a civic obligation to ensure the security of NGOs to the extent that the NGO will allow. Commanders also must be aware that some illegal and potentially adversarial organizations will attempt to claim status as an NGO.

(2) Many civilian HA providers view security differently than the joint force. In fact, the HA community has an entirely different security paradigm than the joint force. For HA providers, security is based on belligerent perception of the neutrality of HA providers rather than on the lack of violence in an area or perceived strength of military forces. This security paradigm difference may impact military planning, execution, and assessment. Planners at the operational level should ensure that they are familiar with NGO operational policies and procedures that guide their efforts. See Chapter IV, "The Operational Environment," paragraph 8d(5), "Nongovernmental Organizations," for more information.

For more information on DOD guidance on working with humanitarian NGOs in hostile or potentially hostile environments, see the United States Institute of Peace's Guidelines for Relations Between US Armed Forces and Non-Governmental Humanitarian Organizations in Hostile or Potentially Hostile Environments.

f. **Multinational Corporations.** When working with multinational corporations, the JFC should use existing mechanisms of the COM and country team, DOS, USAID, and other appropriate agencies. Multinational corporations often engage in reconstruction, economic development, and governance activities. The joint force should provide support as required to the DOS economic counselor and the Foreign Commercial Service representative of DOC in the US mission to support the IDAD strategy. Even in the absence of other interagency partners on the ground, the JFC should use reachback through the GCC to consult with the appropriate agencies in Washington, DC, prior to engagement with multinational corporations. At a minimum, commanders should seek to know which companies are present in their area and where those companies are conducting business. Such information can prevent the destruction of private property.

g. **Government Contractors.** When contractors or other businesses are being paid to support military or USG interagency partners involved in COIN, the principle of unity of command applies.

h. **Private Security Contractors.** Armed contractors may provide different security services to the USG, HN, NGOs, and private businesses. Many businesses market expertise in areas related to supporting governance, economics, education, and other aspects of civil society as well. Providing capabilities similar to some NGOs, these firms often obtain contracts through government agencies. When under a USG contract, private security contractors behave as an extension of the organizations or agencies for which they work. Commanders should identify private security contractors operating in their area and determine the nature of their contract, existing accountability mechanisms, and appropriate coordination relationships. Depending on the terms of their contract, the environment in which they operate, and certain agreements the USG is a party to, private security contractors may be subject to the laws of the HN, US law, and international law. Any failure on the part of these participants could reflect negatively on counterinsurgent credibility and HN legitimacy in the court of public opinion, both nationally and internationally.

i. **IPI.** IPI is a generic term used to describe the civilian construct of an operational area to include its populations (legal citizens, legal and illegal immigrants, and all categories of dislocated civilians), governmental, tribal, commercial, and private organizations and entities. COIN principles seek to legitimize the local governing body, whether that is an informal governing body or the HN's local government. The HN must be seen as a legitimate governing body that the population supports. With this in mind, effective USG collaboration with the IPI is a key requirement for successful COIN operations.

j. **Other.** Some organizations that the joint force must coordinate with do not fit neatly into the previous categories, or have the characteristics of more than one type of the previously mentioned categories. Additionally, many other groups can play critical roles in influencing the outcome of a COIN effort yet are beyond the control of military forces or civilian governing institutions. These groups can include local leaders, informal associations, religious groups, families, and the media. Commanders must remain aware of the influence of such groups and be prepared to work with, through, or around them.

4. Command and Interorganizational Relationships

a. Military unity of command is the preferred method for achieving unity of effort in any military operation. Military unity of command is achieved by establishing and maintaining formal command or support relationships. Unity of command should extend to all military forces engaged in COIN—US, HN, and other multinational forces. The purpose of these C2 arrangements is for military forces, police, and other security forces to establish effective control while attaining a monopoly on the legitimate use of violence within the society.

b. Conducting the US interagency coordination required for COIN requires a departure from traditional military thinking. Conventional military C2 hierarchies are not appropriate for operational structures and environments where the military commander does not possess clear authority over all activities in the assigned operational area. As a result, coordination and collaboration are more applicable to achieving unity of effort.

c. While the JFC can exercise command authority over assigned and attached forces, actors outside of DOD will not reflect unity of command with one single authority and clearly defined roles and responsibilities. Like all interagency activities, effective COIN will require a deliberate effort to ensure inclusion, rather than exclusion, of legitimate stakeholders. To achieve effective teaming, the JFC and staff must have a clear understanding of the different roles, authorities, missions, culture, and processes of external stakeholders. Due to the importance of information sharing and coordination among a diverse set of military and nonmilitary actors, a rigid hierarchical command structure may not be appropriate. At various times, the JFC may draw on the capabilities of other USG departments and agencies, provide capabilities to other organizations, or merely deconflict joint force activities with those of others. The JFC may have some form of supported or supporting relationships with a wide range of civilian actors and organizations, but in some cases USG departments' and agencies' relationships with IGOs are voluntary and based upon shared goals and good will. The relationship between the JFC and the leadership of NGOs is neither supported nor supporting.

d. **Political Considerations.** As important as unity of command is to military operations, it is one of the most sensitive and difficult to resolve issues in COIN. Nations join multinational forces for various reasons. Although the missions of multinational partners may appear similar to those of the US, ROE, home-country policies, and sensitivities may differ among partners. Military leaders must have a strong cultural and political awareness of US, HN, and other multinational military partners. The participation of US and multinational military forces in COIN missions is inherently problematic, as it influences perceptions of the capacity, credibility, and legitimacy of local security forces. Although unity of command of military forces may be desirable, it may be impractical due to political considerations. Political sensitivities about the perceived subordination of national forces to those of other states or IGOs often preclude strong command relationships; however, the agreements that establish a multinational force provide a source for determining possible authorities and command, or other relationships. When operating under the control of a foreign commander, US commanders maintain the capability and responsibility to report separately to higher US authorities in addition to foreign commanders.

e. **National Mandates and Commitment.** Nations choose the manner and extent of their foreign involvement for reasons both known and unknown to other nations. The only constant is that a decision to join in a COIN effort is, in every case, a calculated political decision by each potential member of a multinational force. The nature of their national decisions, in turn, influences the overall command structure. In most multinational operations, the differing degrees of national interest result in varying levels of commitment by alliance and coalition members. While some countries might authorize the full range of employment, other countries may limit their country's forces to strictly defensive or combat service support roles.

f. **Military Capabilities.** Numerous factors influence the military capabilities of nations. The operational-level commander must be aware of the differences in the political constraints and capabilities of the forces of various nations, and consider these differences when assigning missions and conducting operations. Commanders at all levels may be required to spend considerable time working political issues related to the utilization of multinational force troops; the requirement for diplomatic skills should not be underestimated. Service CA forces provide additional staff expertise for planning and executing integrated civil-military activities. Commanders may routinely work directly with political authorities in the region, but should coordinate with the COM to ensure alignment with US foreign policy, to speak with one voice, and to avoid redundancy in engagements with key leaders. In the absence of a US diplomatic mission to the country, the commander should coordinate through the GCC to obtain guidance for any diplomatic engagements. The basic challenge in multinational operations is the effective integration and synchronization of available assets toward the achievement of common objectives. This goal may be achieved through unity of effort despite disparate and occasionally incompatible capabilities, ROE, equipment, and procedures. To reduce disparities among participating forces, minimum capability standards should be established and a certification process developed.

g. **Command Structure.** No single command structure meets the needs of every multinational command, but one absolute remains constant. As in the creation of any multinational military structure, command relationships in COIN reflect political relationships among the partners and may change according to evolving political needs.

(1) **Lead Nation.** The best command structure in COIN is a lead nation structure wherein all member nations place their forces under one leader. The lead nation command can be distinguished by a dominant lead nation command and staff arrangement with subordinate elements retaining strict national integrity. Regardless of the starting command structure, this is the goal—the HN must ultimately take the lead for COIN to be successful.

(2) **Integrated.** Multinational commands organized under an integrated command structure provide unity of effort in a multinational setting. This command structure often has a strategic commander designated from a member nation, but the strategic command staff and the commanders and staffs of subordinate commands are of multinational makeup. This is the second-best command structure in COIN. The structure is most effective when the HN is viable and has effective political and military establishments.

(3) **Parallel.** Under a parallel command structure, no single force commander is designated. The multinational force leadership must develop a means for coordination among the participants to attain unity of effort. This can be accomplished through the use of coordination centers. Nonetheless, because of the absence of a single commander, the use of a parallel command structure should be avoided if at all possible. This may often be the initial condition for supporting an HN's COIN efforts, although it is the least favored.

For additional detail, see JP 3-16, Multinational Operations.

h. Coordination and information sharing between the joint force and USG interagency partners, IGOs, and NGOs should not be equated to the C2 of a military operation. Successful interagency, IGO, and NGO coordination helps enable the USG to build international support, conserve resources, and conduct coherent operations that efficiently achieve shared goals. All friendly and neutral actors should seek to coordinate, or at least deconflict, their activities with the activities of other organizations.

For further discussion about the appropriate protocols for communicating and working in the same OE, see The Guidelines for Relations Between US Armed Forces and Nongovernmental Humanitarian Organizations.

i. In large footprint COIN operations, the physical colocation of civil-military teams is desirable, but is not essential to achieve effective civil-military teaming. Experience suggests that civilian government organizations, from both the US and potential partner nations, may not be resourced deeply enough to provide dedicated manning to all counterpart military staffs on a continual basis. In cases where physical colocation is either not feasible or desirable, the JFC must consider options for virtual teaming or situational teaming to accomplish specific planning or operational activities.

j. Importantly, the level of authority for the JFC is limited. Civilian representation to the joint force may be dedicated or part-time. Only a liaison officer, with no decision-making authority, will represent some organizations. Others may possess full authority to make commitments for their organizations. Experience indicates that many civilian organizations and most NGOs will not enter a military headquarters. They will be very cautious about potential perceptions regarding their association with the military. Inherently, the concept will develop a reliable and accessible means of communication between its members.

k. The JFC should collaborate with the COM to establish a process between the military and civilian interagency partners when there is a disagreement regarding execution of specific operations during a USG COIN effort. Interagency partners are obligated to raise issues up their individual lines of authority (chains of command) when they cannot be resolved at lower levels.

5. Planning, Coordination, and Implementation

a. Civil-military teaming provides the JFC with a means to understand and achieve horizontal integration across the multiple aspects of planning, execution, and assessment under a given COIN strategy. The four functional components of political, economic, security, and information contribute to the overall objective of enabling the affected government to establish control, consolidating and then transitioning that control from external intervening forces (e.g., US forces) to HN forces and from military to civilian institutions.

b. **US Country Team.** All USG COIN strategies, plans, programs, and activities that are undertaken to support an HN government are managed through the elements of the US country team, led by the COM. The US country team is the primary interagency coordinating structure that is the focal point for unified action in COIN. The country team is the senior coordinating and supervising body, headed by the US COM, who is normally the ambassador. Title 22, United States Code (USC), Section 3927, assigns the COM to a foreign country responsibility for the direction, coordination, and supervision of all government executive branch employees in that country except for Service members and employees under the command of a US JFC. Where a confirmed ambassador is not present, the charge d'affaires represents the Secretary of State as the senior diplomat accredited to the foreign government. The country team is composed of the senior member of each represented department or agency. In a foreign country, the COM is the highest US civil authority. As the senior USG official permanently assigned in the HN, the COM is responsible to the President for policy oversight of all USG programs. The COM leads the country team and is responsible for integrating US efforts in support of the HN. As permanently established interagency organizations, country teams represent a priceless COIN resource. They often provide deep reservoirs of local knowledge and interaction with the HN government and population.

c. **IDAD Strategy.** Where the US supports HN efforts to counter an insurgency, COIN is normally one aspect of a larger FID mission. **IDAD is the HN's plan that US FID supports; the HN does not support the US FID plan.** The IDAD strategy is the overarching strategy in a FID mission; however, this is a joint military term, and it is important to note that the HN and others may not use this term.

(1) The purpose of the IDAD strategy is to promote HN growth and its ability to protect itself from subversion, lawlessness, and insurgency. IDAD programs focus on building viable political, economic, military, and social institutions that respond to the needs

of society. The HN government mobilizes the population to participate in IDAD efforts. The ultimate goal is to prevent an insurgency or other forms of lawlessness or subversion by forestalling and defeating the threat; thus, IDAD is ideally a preemptive strategy. If an insurgency or other threat develops, IDAD becomes an active strategy to combat that threat. When dealing with an insurgency, IDAD programs focus on addressing the root causes and dealing with the actual extant insurgency.

(2) JFCs and joint planners must understand the HN's IDAD strategy if they are to plan effectively to support it. In some cases, the joint force may need to assist the HN to formulate an appropriate IDAD strategy, especially if the joint force began operations in an area of weak or no HN governance. While IDAD is the overarching strategy, the HN government below the national level needs to build the capability and capacity to support IDAD, which may necessitate civil-military support. Civil-military support may come in the form of organizations like national-level governmental assistance teams (GATs) or subnational organizations, such as the provincial reconstruction teams (PRTs) which operated in Iraq and Afghanistan.

d. **IDAD Coordination.** Military assistance is often required to provide a secure environment to enable the activities of the COM and the country team in support of the HN's goals as expressed through the IDAD strategy. The US country team, led by the COM, is the cornerstone of US coordination with the HN. The COM, the US country team, the GCC, and other JFCs are responsible for ensuring that US plans and efforts are nested within the IDAD strategy. It is important to note that there are multiple supporting actors or echelons in both the commanders' and multinational partners' FID programs.

(1) **Sovereignty.** The sovereignty of an HN must be respected. This means that the HN has the authority over the manner and pace of operations conducted within its borders. Sovereignty issues are among the most difficult for commanders conducting COIN operations. Multinational commanders—whether US, other nation, or specifically HN—are required to lead through coordination, communication, and consensus, in addition to traditional command practices. Political sensitivities must be acknowledged. Commanders and subordinates often act as diplomats as well as warriors. Within military units, legal officers and their staffs are particularly valuable for clarifying legal arrangements with the HN. To avoid adverse effects on operations, commanders should address all sovereignty issues through the chain of command to DOS and COM. As much as possible, sovereignty issues should be addressed before executing operations. Examples of sovereignty issues include aerial ports of debarkation; basing; border crossings; collecting and sharing information; protection (tasks related to preserving the force); jurisdiction over members of the US and multinational forces; location and access; operations in the territorial waters, both sea and internal; overflight rights; police operations, including arrest, detention, penal, and justice authority and procedures; railheads; and seaports of debarkation. Counterinsurgents must be particularly respectful of HN sovereignty issues that cut to the heart of governance, rule of law, and the economy. Counterinsurgents must support the HN to find their own way, exercising extreme patience, rather than directing HN actions. This can be a point of friction between military commanders who tend to focus on short- to midterm objectives and military end states and country team personnel who tend to focus on long-term issues.

(2) **Coordinating Mechanisms.** Commanders create coordinating mechanisms, such as committees or liaison elements, to facilitate cooperation and build trust with HN authorities. HN military or nonmilitary representatives should have leading roles in such mechanisms. These organizations facilitate operations by reducing sensitivities and misunderstandings while removing impediments. Sovereignty issues can be formally resolved with the HN by developing appropriate technical agreements to augment existing or UN Security Council resolutions or status-of-forces agreements. In many cases, embassy SC organizations, NGOs, and IGOs have detailed local knowledge and reservoirs of good will that can help establish a positive, constructive relationship with the HN.

(3) **Coordination and Support.** Coordinate and support down to the village and neighborhood level. All members of the joint force should be aware of the political and societal structures in their areas. Political structures usually have designated leaders responsible to the government and people. However, the societal structure may include informal leaders who operate outside the political structure. These leaders may be associated with economic, religious, informational, and family based institutions. Other societal leaders may emerge due to charisma or other intangible influences. Commanders should identify the key leaders and the manner in which they are likely to influence COIN efforts and attempt to build relationships and coordination mechanisms with them.

e. **Concept. The IDAD strategy integrates all security force and development programs into a coherent, holistic effort.** Security actions provide a level of internal security that permits and supports growth through balanced development. This development often requires change to address root causes. These changes may in turn promote temporary unrest; however, they are necessary for long-term success. The IDAD strategy must include measures to maintain conditions under which orderly development can take place. Similarly, addressing the root causes of the insurgency often includes overcoming the HN government's inertia and shortcomings. It may be difficult for US leaders to convince the HN government to reform, but these reforms are often the best way to diffuse the root causes of and support for the insurgency. An underlying assumption for the IDAD strategy is that the threat to the HN lies in insurgent political strength rather than military power. Although the counterinsurgents must contain violent insurgent actions, concentration on the military aspect of the threat does not address the real long-term danger. IDAD efforts must pay continuing, serious attention to the political claims and demands of the population and insurgents. Military and paramilitary programs are necessary for success, but are not sufficient alone.

f. **IDAD Functions.** The IDAD strategy blends four interdependent functions to prevent or counter internal threats.

(1) **Balanced Development.** Balanced development attempts to achieve HN goals through political, social, economic, and other developmental programs. Balanced development should allow all individuals and groups in the society to share in the rewards of development, thus alleviating frustration due to inequities. Balanced development should satisfy legitimate grievances that the opposition attempts to exploit. The government must recognize conditions that contribute to the internal threat and instability and take preventive measures. COIN must strive for balanced development as insurgents will take advantage of

real or perceived development inequalities, especially with IO. All civil-military development should account for the IDAD balanced development function, including the integration of entities such as GATs and PRTs.

(2) **Security.** Security includes all activities implemented in order to protect the populace from the threat and to provide a safe environment for development. Security of the populace and government resources is essential to countering the threat. Protection and control of the populace permit development and deny the adversary access to popular support. The security effort should establish an environment in which the local government can provide for its own security with limited national government support; however, this security must adhere to the current legal framework. This function also includes any SFA functions that multinational forces, including the US, provide to the HN.

(3) **Neutralization.** Neutralization is a political concept that makes an organized force irrelevant to the political process. It is the physical and psychological separation of the threatening elements from the population and includes all lawful activities to disrupt, preempt, disorganize, and defeat the insurgent organization. It may involve public exposure and the discrediting of COGs during a period of low-level unrest with little political violence, may involve arrest and prosecution when laws have been broken, or can involve combat action when the adversary's violent activities escalate. All neutralization efforts must be legal and scrupulously observe HN constitutional provisions regarding rights and responsibilities. The need for security forces to act lawfully is essential not only for humanitarian reasons but also because this reinforces government legitimacy while denying the adversary an exploitable issue. Special emergency powers may exist by legislation or decree. Government agents must not abuse these powers because they might well lose the popular support they need. Denying the adversary an opportunity to seize on and exploit legitimate issues against the government discredits their leaders and neutralizes their propaganda.

(4) **Mobilization.** Mobilization provides organized manpower and materiel resources and includes all activities to motivate and organize popular support of the HN government. This support is essential for a successful IDAD program. If successful, mobilization maximizes manpower and other resources available to the HN government while it minimizes those available to the insurgent. Mobilization allows the government to strengthen existing institutions, to develop new ones to respond to demands, and promotes the government's legitimacy. All mobilization efforts must have a plan for eventual demobilization or reintegration into the HN government and security apparatus.

g. **Assessment.** The HN and any multinational partners must continually analyze the results of the IDAD strategy. Part of the assessment process is to establish MOEs and MOPs, as well as having a methodology to provide feedback for future planning, refinement of strategy, and continued formulation of strategic national policy. While the HN should have input into all aspects of assessment, it should take the lead in determining MOEs. MOEs measure changes in system behavior, capability, or OE. MOEs in COIN predominately focus on the population. Although the HN has the best understanding of its own culture, its views have to be balanced with the views of other multinational partners to assist in providing other perspectives. Multinational partners' perspectives are especially important if the HN government is slow to reform or has had a previous record of harsh treatment against its own citizens.

h. **Campaign Plan to IDAD Transition.** Some situations may require the joint force to occupy territory and to provide governance through a transitional military authority. However, this authority should transition to civilian authority as quickly as the situation allows. This civilian authority could be a provisional governing authority or an IGO such as the UN. Authority could also transfer from a provisional civilian authority to an IGO as an intermediate transition. Ultimately, authority will be transferred to an HN when either a government in exile or new government is ready, although this transition may be a lengthy process to ensure continued effective governance. As with transitions in governance, there may be several military transitions. When ready, the HN will first assume the lead and then eventually take over military operations. This transition may be phased over time.

For more information, see JP 3-08, Interorganizational Coordination During Joint Operations; *JP 3-16,* Multinational Operations; *and JP 3-22,* Foreign Internal Defense.

6. United States Civil-Military Integration

Effective COIN requires the integration of HN and supporting nation civil and military efforts into a single holistic approach. This requires a concerted effort to ensure that interagency partners have a common understanding of the challenge and each others' roles and capabilities in addressing it.

a. **Shared Understanding of the OE.** Gaining an understanding of the environment— including the insurgents, affected population, and different counterinsurgent organizations— is essential to an integrated COIN operation. Various agencies acting to reestablish stability may differ in goals and approaches, based on their experience and institutional culture. When their actions are allowed to adversely affect each other, the populace suffers and insurgents identify grievances to exploit. Integrated actions are essential to defeat the ideologies professed by insurgents. A shared understanding of the operation's purpose provides a unifying theme for COIN efforts. Through a common understanding of that purpose, the COIN leaders can plan an operation that promotes effective collaboration and coordination among all agencies and the affected populace. Constructs like the green cell provide a building block to build a shared understanding of the affected population in the OE. This shared understanding enables coordination during planning and execution of COIN operations.

b. **Preferred Division of Labor.** It is generally preferable for civilians to lead the overall COIN operation. Even where civilians' capability and capacity do not match their expertise, they should lead in the areas of governance, economics, rule of law, etc., as policy guides and decision makers who define the role the military should and will play to support the effort. Military leaders should avoid the temptation to take over the role of decision maker in these areas despite a lack of civilian capability and capacity. Their forces may play a significant role in executing actions in these areas, but should never proceed without the guidance of civilian agency personnel as to the COA and the military role. It is important to note that civilian agencies often have the greatest capability and the joint force may have the greatest capacity; in this case the civilian agency should lead the overall effort with the joint force in a supporting role. Legitimate local authorities should receive special preference to lead or perform civilian tasks. There are many US agencies and civilian IGOs with more expertise in meeting the fundamental needs of a population than military forces have; however, the ability of such agencies to deploy to foreign countries in sustainable numbers and with ready access to necessary resources is often limited. The violence level in the area also can affect civilian agencies' ability to operate. The more violent the environment, the more difficult it is for civilians to operate effectively. Hence, the preferred or ideal division of labor is frequently unattainable. The more violent the insurgency, the more unrealistic is this preferred division of labor.

c. **Realistic Division of Labor.** Participants best qualified and able to accomplish nonmilitary tasks are not always available. Civilians will also never be available in the numbers hoped for to coordinate at all the different levels of a military operation. Commanders should therefore prioritize and moderate requests for coordination with civilians. The realistic division of labor does not always match the preferred division of labor. In those cases, military forces may be required to perform those tasks. Sometimes joint forces have the skills required; other times they learn them during execution.

(1) **Civilian Contribution.** USG interagency partners and IGOs rarely have the resources and capabilities needed to address all COIN tasks. Success requires adaptable leaders who prepare to perform required tasks with available resources. These leaders understand that long-term security cannot be imposed by military force alone; it requires an integrated, balanced application of effort by all participants with the goal of supporting the local populace and achieving legitimacy for the HN government. Military forces can perform civilian tasks but often not as well as the civilian agencies with people trained in those skills. Further, military forces performing civilian tasks are not performing military tasks. Diversion from those tasks should be temporary and only taken to address urgent circumstances. In addition, the militarization of an HN police force may discredit that police institution in the eyes of the public and, in the long term, be detrimental to the HN. Transition from a military force conducting basic policing and rule of law tasks and functions to an HN civilian-based police force must be facilitated in institutional development by professional advisors/trainers. Military forces should be aware that putting a military face on economics, politics, rule of law, etc., may do more harm than good in certain situations. The implications of the military role in these areas should be discussed at length with the country team.

(2) **Military Capability and Capacity.** In uncertain security situations, US and multinational military forces often possess the only readily available capability to meet many of the local populace's fundamental needs. Human decency, and even the law of war, may require joint forces to assist the populace in their operational areas. Leaders at all levels prepare to address civilian needs, including identifying people in their units with regional and interagency expertise, civil-military competence, and other critical skills needed to support a local populace and HN government. Even if lack of civilian capacity requires military forces to take on this mission, military leaders should consult with the country team on the proper COA to follow. Commanders should also seek awareness of NGOs that may be

operating in the region and providing for the basic needs of the population. The joint force must strive to support the population and other partners that are supporting the population.

d. **Transitions.** Regardless of the division of labor, an important recurring feature of COIN is transitioning responsibility and participation. As consistently and conscientiously as possible, military leaders ensure continuity in meeting the needs of the HN government and local populace, which is best accomplished by all efforts supporting the IDAD strategy. The same general guidelines governing battle handovers apply to COIN transitions. Whether the transition is between military units or from a military unit to a civilian agency, all involved must clearly understand the tasks and responsibilities being passed. Maintaining unity of effort is particularly important during transitions, especially between organizations of different capabilities and capacities. Relationships tend to break down during transitions. A transition should not be a single event where all activity happens at once, but rather a rolling process of little handoffs between different actors along several streams of activities. There are usually multiple transitions for any one stream of activity over time. Using the coordination mechanisms can help create and sustain the links that support effective transitions without compromising unity of effort.

e. **Coordination and Liaison.** COIN partners and other organizations have many interests and agendas that military forces cannot and should not try to control. Their local legitimacy is frequently affected by the degree to which local institutions are perceived as independent and capable without external support. Nevertheless, military leaders should make every effort to ensure that COIN actions are as well integrated as possible. Active leadership by civilian and military leaders is imperative to coordinating actions to create an effect, establish formal and informal liaison, and share information. Influencing and persuading groups outside a commander's authority requires skill and often subtlety. Commanders should also recognize that they will often be in a supporting role, and must realize that they may be on the receiving end of being influenced and persuaded by civilian agencies in charge. As actively as commanders pursue unity of effort, they should also be mindful of their prominence and recognize the wisdom of acting indirectly and in ways that allow credit for success to go to others—particularly local individuals and organizations. The joint force should remain in a supporting role to appropriate civilian agencies or groups, follow US policy and the COM's direction, and focus on supporting the IDAD strategy.

For more information, see US Government Counterinsurgency Guide, *and JP 3-16,* Multinational Operations.

7. United States Civil-Military Integration Mechanisms

There are several US civil-military integration mechanisms that facilitate unified action for COIN. These structures are often employed in other types of missions, such as peacekeeping or humanitarian relief, but they are fundamental for successful COIN. These mechanisms fall into two general areas: those that are located outside of the theater and those that are located in theater. It is important to note that these are options and may not always be present and their relationships can vary.

a. **Civil-Military Mechanisms in the US.** Key civil-military integration mechanisms located outside of the GCC's AOR include the National Security Council, special missions established in Washington, DC, to provide policy guidance for a theater (e.g., the Iraq Policy and Operations Group, and the Afghanistan Interagency Operations Group), and appointed leaders focused on a particular COIN effort.

For more information on national-level mechanisms, see JP 3-08, Interorganizational Coordination During Joint Operations.

b. **Civil-Military Integration Mechanisms in Theater.** GCCs are charged with coordinating US military policy and operations within an assigned AOR. Subordinate JTFs are assigned to conduct joint military operations within a designated operational area which may be one or more countries affected by an insurgency. The US country team, advance civilian team (ACT), JFC, executive steering committee, provincial authority, civil-military coordination board (CMCB), joint CMO task forces, joint interagency task forces, GATs, PRTs, and CMOCs are key civil-military integration mechanisms that are normally located inside the designated operational area. The more extensive the US participation is in a COIN operation and the more dispersed US forces are throughout a country, the greater the need for additional mechanisms to extend civilian oversight and assistance. Operating with a clear understanding of the guiding political aims, members of the military at all levels must be prepared to exercise judgment and act without the benefit of immediate civilian oversight and control and ultimately to reinforce HN credibility and legitimacy. At each subordinate political level of the HN government, military and civilian leaders should establish the necessary integration mechanisms. These mechanisms should include military and civilian representatives of the HN and other multinational members. Commanders should be aware of the activities of IGOs and NGOs in the theater. However, JFCs should be aware that the NGO independent, impartial, and sometimes neutral status does not bind them to working as part of a USG or multinational force, or to support the IDAD strategy.

(1) **Joint Interagency Coordination Group (JIACG).** JIACGs help CCDRs support COIN by facilitating unified action in support of plans, operations, contingencies, and initiatives. The primary role of the JIACG is to enhance interagency coordination. The JIACG is a fully integrated participant on the CCDR's staff with a daily focus on joint strategic planning. It provides a capability specifically organized to enhance situational awareness of interagency activities to prevent undesired consequences and uncoordinated activity. When activated, the JIACG will assist with the reception of the integration planning cell of the interagency management system into the staff. The integration planning cell is an interagency team that brings operation-specific capabilities to a regional military command, either a GCC or an equivalent multinational headquarters. The purpose of the integration planning cell is to support civil-military communication and integration of the civilian and military planning in order to achieve unity of effort. JIACGs include representatives from other federal departments and agencies and state and local authorities, as well as liaison officers from other commands and DOD components. **The JIACG provides the CCDR with the capability to collaborate at the operational level with other USG departments and agencies.** Representatives and liaison officers are the subject matter experts for their respective agencies and commands. They provide the critical bridge between the CCDR and

USG interagency partners; however, JIACGs can be called by different names in different combatant commands.

For additional information on JIACGs, see JP 3-08, Interorganizational Coordination During Joint Operations, *and the* Commander's Handbook for the Joint Interagency Coordination Group.

(2) **National-Level GATs.** A national-level GAT supports governance and development at the national level in an uncertain environment. GATs operate by combining civilian and military personnel for development and governance into one cohesive team. A representative from DOS is the team leader, and a military officer is normally the deputy commander. Personnel from appropriate USG agencies make up the elements focused on governance and development where DOD personnel comprise the civil security focused staffs. However, when civilian agencies lack the capacity, DOD personnel, especially reservists with civilian skills, may be used to mitigate a shortfall. GATs vary in structure, size, and mission to suit their situation; however, all GATs facilitate the plan in a collapsed state setting or the IDAD strategy in COIN that directly supports an HN. GATs extend the reach, capability, and capacity of governance and facilitate reconstruction. While the GATs are primarily concerned with addressing national-level conditions, they also work on building and improving communication and linkages between the central government and regional/local agencies.

(3) **Subnational GATs.** PRTs, embedded PRTs, and district support teams (DSTs). DSTs are examples of subnational civil-military teams which were formed to address unique aspects of COIN operations and campaigns in Iraq and/or Afghanistan. These teams were designed to improve stability in a given area by helping build the legitimacy and effectiveness of an HN local or provincial government in providing security to its citizens and delivering essential government services. PRTs vary in structure, size, and mission. PRTs extend the reach, capability, and capacity of governance and facilitate construction. While PRTs and DSTs are primarily concerned with addressing local conditions, they also work on building and improving communication and linkages among the central government and regional and local agencies.

(4) **ACT.** An ACT may be formed to implement the USG strategic plan for reconstruction and stabilization through development and management of the interagency implementation plan (IIP), under the leadership of the COM. The ACT stands up at the USG field headquarters, typically the embassy. When established, it is the integrating civilian counterpart of the JTF at the country level. The ACT is comprised of a combination of USG personnel already in the country and other agency personnel deployed to the country from agency headquarters or elsewhere.

(5) **Executive Steering Group (ESG).** The COM and a JFC can jointly form an ESG. The ESG may be composed of the principals from the joint force, the US embassy, NGOs/IGOs present in the operational area, and other organizations as appropriate. Lacking another similar forum, the ESG can provide high-level outlet for the exchange of information about operational policies as well as for resolution of difficulties arising among the various organizations. The ESG plays a policy role and is charged with interpreting and coordinating

operational area aspects of strategic policy. A commander at any echelon may establish an ESG to serve as a conduit through which to provide information and policy guidance to participating agencies. The ESG may be charged with formulating, coordinating, and promulgating local and theater policies required for the explanation, clarification, and implementation of US policies. The ESG should either be co-chaired by the JFC and COM or assigned outright to either individual, depending on the nature of the US mission and possibly based on the security situation.

(6) **Regional Authority.** Direction and coordination of PRTs is conducted by a national-level interagency steering committee, under the supervision of the COM and JFC (for US-led PRTs) or a multinational executive committee (for multinational force-led PRTs). This body will also conduct liaison with the HN national government to support PRT operations. Both embassy and joint force personnel staff the steering committee. Regional authorities may be established with regional commanders overseeing a number of PRTs to ensure coordination between provinces and with national-level objectives. The regional authority coordinates the deployment and operations of all US PRTs in the operational area, including ensuring that PRTs have a long-term vision nested with either the campaign plan or the IDAD strategy, whichever is appropriate at the time. If an ACT has been established at the country level, a decision to deploy field advance civilian teams (FACTs) to subnational regions or provinces may follow. FACTs, which are an element of the ACT and are managed by its headquarters, are responsible for implementing plans pertaining to their particular geographic AOR and for informing revisions of the overall USG strategic plan and IIP. They are also responsible for coordinating planning with any US military entities operating in their AOR, in order to achieve the objectives in the IIP. FACTs are primarily local, on-the-ground operational entities, but their role in assessments, plan revisions, and subnational field-level planning is also important.

(7) **CMCB.** If established, a CMCB is the JFC's vehicle for coordinating CMO support. Membership is typically restricted to key representatives from the joint force staff sections. A senior member of the staff, such as the deputy commander or chief of staff, serves as chairperson of this board. If a CMOC has been established at the subordinate level, the CMOC director would be a key member of the board and also may serve as its chairperson. During COIN multinational operations, the commander should normally include multinational partners on the board unless there are compelling reasons not to. The type of C2 structure and the level of staff integration in the joint force should drive the decision to establish a coordination board and determine its membership. Depending on the situation, the commander should include selected members from the US country team on the board.

(8) **Joint Civil-Military Operations Task Force (JCMOTF).** The JFC may establish a JCMOTF to improve CMO in support of COIN operations. The JCMOTF can provide the JFC a subordinate command to exercise necessary control and coordinating support when the size and scope of the COIN mission is beyond organic CMO capabilities. The JCMOTF should be functionally organized around an existing command structure with augmentation. The JFC designates the JCMOTF commander. A JCMOTF is composed of units from more than one Service and is formed to carry out CMO. Although the JCMOTF is not a CA organization, there may be a requirement for strong representation of CA. Because of their expertise in dealing with NGOs, IGOs, and USG interagency partners, they will

greatly enhance the opportunity for success in COIN. By design, Army, Navy, or Marine Corps CA assets can provide the base structure to create a JCMOTF. In rare instances, and depending on resource availability, a JCMOTF could be formed as a standing organization.

For more information, see JP 3-57, Civil-Military Operations.

(9) **USAID Office of Civilian Military Cooperation (CMC).** CMC seeks to optimize application of USAID's unique development expertise to shape USAID/DOD cooperation in steady state, prevention, stabilization, transition, reconstruction, and HA activities to strengthen HN effectiveness. Representing the spectrum of the agency functions, CMC provides the focal point for USAID interaction with US and foreign militaries in formalized relationships through coordinated planning, training, education, and exercises. Program areas of common interest include COIN as well as HA, conflict prevention and mitigation, disaster management, countering violent extremism, post-conflict stabilization and reconstruction, and SSR.

Intentionally Blank

APPENDIX B
AUTHORITIES IN COUNTERINSURGENCY OPERATIONS

1. Overview

a. Law and policy govern the actions of US forces in all military operations, including COIN. A legal basis must exist for US forces to conduct operations. This legal basis influences many aspects of a COIN operation, specifically ROE, how US forces organize and train foreign forces, the authority to spend funds to benefit the HN, and the authority of US forces to detain and interrogate. Under the Constitution, the President is the Commander in Chief of the US Armed Forces. Therefore, orders are issued by the President through SecDef to a CCDR for a COIN operation. This appendix summarizes some of the laws and policies that bear upon COIN operations. No summary provided here can replace a consultation with the unit's supporting staff judge advocate.

b. **Leadership in Support of HN COIN.** In general, operations encompass six distinct, but often overlapping phases: shape (0), deter (I), seize initiative (II), dominate (III), stabilize (IV), and enable civil authority (V). The military is the lead organization for the seize the initiative and dominate phases with civilian agencies and departments often designated the lead organizations for the other four phases. Whenever possible, civilian agencies should lead COIN efforts, especially when the mission is for US support to HN COIN efforts. However, the changing nature of COIN means that lead responsibility shifts among military, civilian, and HN authorities, and these transitions must be planned and managed at the highest levels. Military participation in COIN is focused on establishing security, assisting in SSR, and supporting other stability operations as required. Although JFCs should be prepared to lead COIN efforts if required, the JFC must normally focus military operations in support of a comprehensive effort led by the COM. Military forces should also be prepared to work in informal or formal integrated civil-military teams that could include, and in some cases be led by civilian agencies, foreign governments, IGOs, NGOs, and members of the private sector with relevant skills and expertise.

2. Title 10 Authority

Military Leadership in Support of COIN. There are cases in which DOD, through Title 10 authority, is the lead organization for COIN operations. When COIN efforts are part of large-scale IW, and/or when the US does not have an established diplomatic presence in an AOR, the GCC is the lead authority and the JFC should focus military operations as part of the GCC's comprehensive plan. The President or SecDef give the deployment and execution order. Transition to civilian authority or HN authority occurs at the direction of the President, usually when an HN governing authority and diplomatic presence is established.

3. Rules of Engagement

ROE are directives issued by competent military authority that delineate the circumstances and limitations under which US forces will initiate and/or continue combat engagement with other forces encountered. Often these directives are specific to the operation. The standing ROE establish fundamental policies and procedures governing the actions to be taken by US commanders and their forces during all military operations outside US territory except for law enforcement and security functions performed on US facilities. When working with a multinational force in COIN operations, commanders must coordinate the ROE thoroughly. All ROE must comply with the law of war. ROE in COIN are dynamic. Commanders must regularly review ROE for their effectiveness in the complex COIN environment. Training counterinsurgents in ROE should be reinforced regularly.

4. Field Authorities in Counterinsurgency Operations

a. In a COIN operation where the military and civilian agencies share the same OE, tensions may rise over a number of issues. Various agencies acting to reestablish stability may differ in goals and approaches based on their institutional authorities and culture. While the overall goal is unified action, at times, varying degrees of coordination and communication between the wide degree of actors, and unclear roles, especially as they pertain to the legal authorities agencies leverage, may lead to the substantial incongruence between desired and actual COIN. Complicating matters, the range of operations employed by the military and civilian organizations during IW (FID, SFA, COIN, CT, stability operations, and UW) are tied to an array of legal authorities, each with its own rules that limit where, how, and when a capability can be applied. Understanding the legal authorities each actor can leverage is an integral component to understanding the OE.

b. **Memorandums of Agreement and Memorandums of Understanding.** The relationships and authorities between military and civilian agencies are usually given in the document directing an agency to support the operation. Commanders exercise only the authority those documents allow; however, the terms in those documents may form the basis for establishing some form of relationship between commanders and agency chiefs.

5. Assistance Authorities and Counterinsurgency

DOD is usually not the lead USG department for assisting foreign governments, including the provision of SA—that is, military training, equipment, and defense articles and services—to the HN's military forces. DOD contribution may be large, but the legal authority is typically one exercised by DOS. DOS delegates some of these authorities to DOD (foreign military sales, foreign military financing, international military education and training leases).

a. **FID.** US forces have limited authority to provide assistance to foreign governments. Without receiving a deployment or execution order, US forces may be authorized to make only limited contributions in support of an HN's COIN effort. If the Secretary of State requests and SecDef approves, US forces can participate in this action. The request and approval go through standing statutory authorities in Title 22, USC. Title 22 contains the Foreign Assistance Act, the Arms Export Control Act, and other laws which authorize SA, developmental assistance, and other forms of bilateral aid. The request and approval might also occur under various provisions in Title 10, USC. Title 10, USC, authorizes certain types of military-to-military contacts, exchanges, exercises, and limited forms of humanitarian and civic assistance in coordination with the COM for the HN. In such situations, US military personnel work as administrative and technical personnel. They are part of the US diplomatic

LARGE FOOTPRINT MISSION: WHO'S IN COMMAND?

In the counterinsurgency operations in Iraq and Afghanistan, unity of command was one of the most sensitive and difficult challenges to overcome. A microcosm of this problem could be found in the civil-military units including provincial reconstruction teams (PRTs), regional commands, and district support teams (DSTs). In Iraq, PRTs were led by senior Department of State officials, and military members of the team (as well as all other US Government civilians) were, in theory, under the senior civilian's command. However, due to Title 10, US Code, restrictions, in practice military members could only report to the deputy PRT lead who was a military officer. Only the deputy PRT lead could rate the performance of military members on the PRT, even though the command was supposed to be civilian led. While some PRT commanders were able to overcome the distinct command and control and reporting chains required by statute (their success was based on the interpersonal relationships that these commanders established with their interagency partners), others struggled to achieve unity of action.

In Afghanistan, the regional command, PRTs, and DSTs were headed by a military commander who had an equal ranking senior civilian representative, typically from the Department of State. The PRT commander did not command civilian personnel on the team. According to Title 22, US Code, authorities, that task was reserved for the ranking senior civilian on the team who was in charge of all other chief of mission personnel serving at the PRT. In Afghanistan, command relationships were further complicated when US military and civilian personnel served on International Security Assistance Force partner-led civil-military teams.

Commanders need to be aware that there are times when US codified authorities actually create barriers to achieving unity of command. Because of the authorities involved, emphasis is placed on the personality of the commander and his/her ability to reach out to civilian partners and coalition partners to devise systems and processes that may not be able to achieve unity of command, but accomplish unity of effort. In Afghanistan, a board of directors model was employed in Regional Command East in an effort to get all members of the team working in synch. In complex, large footprint operations where there are a number of different US Government departments and agencies, coalition forces and coalition civilians, nongovernmental organizations, intergovernmental organizations, and contractors operating in the same operational area, the best scenario for command is for commanders to ensure that they gain an understanding of the purposes, goals, and restrictions under which their interagency partners (and other partner organizations) are operating. Absent such an understanding, the military and non-military efforts may frustrate and interfere with one another because the military and civilian organizations are functioning under separate statutory obligations that may lead to conflicting guidance and direction.

Various Sources

mission, pursuant to a status-of-forces agreement or pursuant to an exchange of letters. This cooperation and assistance is limited to liaison, contacts, training, equipping, and providing defense articles and services. It does not include direct involvement in operations.

b. **SFA.** DOD is usually not the lead governmental department for assisting foreign governments, even for the provision of SFA—that is, military training, equipment, and defense articles and services—to the HN's military forces. DOD contribution may be large, but the legal authority is typically one exercised by DOS. With regard to provision of training to a foreign government's police or other civil interior forces, the US military typically has no authorized role. The Foreign Assistance Act specifically prohibits assistance to foreign police forces except within carefully circumscribed exceptions, and under a Presidential directive, and the lead role in providing police assistance within those exceptions has been normally delegated to DOS's Bureau of International Narcotics and Law Enforcement Affairs. However, the President did sign a decision directive in 2004 granting authority to train and equip Iraqi police to the Commander, US Central Command. Similarly, the President signed a decision directive in 2009 granting authority to US Central Command to support the North Atlantic Treaty Organization Training Mission–Afghanistan.

c. All training and equipping of foreign security forces must be specifically authorized. Usually, DOD involvement is limited to a precise level of man-hours and materiel requested from DOS under the Foreign Assistance Act. The President may authorize deployed US forces to train or advise HNSF as part of the operational mission. In this case, DOD personnel, operations, and maintenance appropriations provide an incidental benefit to those security forces. All other weapons, training, equipment, logistic support, supplies, and services provided to foreign forces must be paid for with funds appropriated by Congress for that purpose. Examples include the Iraq Security Forces Fund and the Afghan Security Forces Fund of fiscal year 2005. Moreover, the President must give specific authority to DOD for its role in such train and equip efforts. There are instances when the President signs a decision directive that gives the commander, under policy guidance from the COM, the authorization to organize, train, and equip HN forces, including police as discussed above. Absent such a directive, DOD lacks authority to take the lead in assisting an HN to train and equip its security forces.

For more information, see JP 3-22, Foreign Internal Defense.

6. Counterdrug Authorities and Counterinsurgency

a. While the JFC should not assume that all COIN operations involve a counterdrug component, cases have arisen (Afghanistan and Colombia) in which a nexus exists between insurgents and illicit narcotics trafficking. Therefore, based on the determination of the OE, use of specific DOD counterdrug authorities may be required in coordination with COIN activities.

b. The statutes listed in the annual national defense authorization act identify the purposes for which DOD may expend funds appropriated for DOD drug interdiction and counterdrug activities. Each use of these authorities or funds requires a determination, based on the facts specific to that proposed use, that the funds will be expended for the purpose of counterdrug activities. These activities include measures taken to detect, interdict, disrupt, or curtail any activity reasonably related to drug trafficking. Once the determination is made, the activity may proceed, assuming the activity complies with other applicable authorities.

c. **Transfer of Detainees to the HN.** There are certain conditions under which US forces may not transfer the custody of detainees to the HN or any other foreign government. US forces retain custody if they have substantial grounds to believe that the detainees would be in danger in the custody of others. Such danger could include being subjected to torture or inhumane treatment.

For more information on transferring detainees, see DODD 2310.01E, The Department of Defense Detainee Program, *and consult the legal advisor or staff judge advocate.*

d. **DOD Civilian Personnel and Contractors.** Modern COIN operations involve many DOD civilians as well as civilian personnel employed by government contractors. The means of disciplining such persons for violations differ from the means of disciplining uniformed personnel. These civilians may be made subject to general orders. They are also subject to US laws (e.g., Title 18, USC, Sections 7, 2441, and 3261), and to the laws of the HN. Civilians may be prosecuted or be subjected to adverse administrative action. Determining criminal jurisdiction over civilians involves an analysis of many factors including status the civilian has (e.g., contractor personnel, DOD civilian, HN civilian) as well as agreements with the HN (e.g., status-of-forces agreements, exchange of notes). Under certain limited circumstances, Uniform Code of Military Justice authority may be exercised over DOD civilians, contractor employees, and other persons serving with or accompanying armed forces during declared war or contingency operations, or the DOJ may prosecute civilians under the Military Extraterritorial Jurisdiction Act. The daily oversight and supervision of contract personnel is governed by the contract, and the contracting officer oversees contract performance. DOD directives contain further policy and guidance pertaining to US civilians accompanying forces conducting COIN operations. For more information on civilian personnel accompanying US forces, see Secretary of Defense Memorandum of March 10, 2008, *UCMJ Jurisdiction Over DOD Civilian Employees, DOD Contractor Personnel, and Other Persons Serving With or Accompanying the Armed Forces Overseas During Declared War and in Contingency Operations*. For more information on contractor personnel accompanying US forces, see DODI 3020.41, *Operational Contract Support (OCS)*, and consult the staff judge advocate.

Intentionally Blank

APPENDIX C
EXAMPLE COUNTERINSURGENCY QUALIFICATION STANDARDS OUTLINE

1. Receive Basic Individual Country-Specific COIN Education

1.1 Receive COIN Overview

1.2 Explain Insurgency Fundamentals

1.3 Explain COIN Fundamentals

1.4 Explain Information and Intelligence in COIN

1.5 Explain COIN Operations

1.6 Understand Country Perceptions

1.7 Understand Basic Language Phrases

1.8 Understand the Culture's Political, Economic, Social, Belief, and Environmental Dimensions

2. Understand the Operational Environment

2.1 Develop an Understanding of a District/Province Area

2.2 Understand Civil Dispute Resolution Mechanisms

2.3 Understand Governance at the District/Province Level

2.4 Understand the Country National Security Force in the AOR

2.5 Understand Essential Services at the District Level

2.6 Understand Economic Development at the District Level

3. Conduct Relief in Place

3.1 Outgoing Unit Conducts a Relief in Place

3.2 Incoming Unit Conducts a Relief in Place

4. Conduct Decentralized Operations

4.1 Establish Combat Outpost

4.2 Conduct Combined COIN Patrols

4.3 Execute Battle Handover Following SOF-DA

4.4 Protect the Force

4.5 Conduct PR

4.6 District-Level Information Gathering

4.7 Conduct Raids

4.8 Avoid Civilian Casualties

4.9 Conduct Joint Fires

4.10 Conduct I2 Operations Activities

5. **Partner with National Security Forces (NSF)**

5.1 Unit Prepares for Partnering

5.2 Assess NSF Partner Unit

5.3 Conduct Security Vetting of Security Forces

5.3 Train NSF Partner

5.4 Conduct Partnered Operations

5.5 Build NSF Partner Unit Sustainment Capabilities

6. **Conduct Information Operations**

6.1 Develop Local IO Plan

6.2 Conduct Individual Engagement

6.3 Conduct Key Leader Engagements

6.4 Understand Population's Perceptions Toward Government, NSF, Multinational Forces, and Insurgents

7. **Create Conditions for Stability**

7.1 Conduct District Stability Framework

7.2 Support Government Development Programs

7.3 Conduct Key Leader Engagements

7.4 Facilitate Integrated Operations in Support of District Development

7.5 Execute Commanders' Emergency Response Program

7.6 Protect Freedom of Movement

8. Conduct Detainee Operations

8.1 Detain Individual By, With, and Through NSF

8.1.1 Notification (e.g., to the International Committee of the Red Cross)

8.2 Conduct Detainee Handling

8.3 Train Female Enablers for Site Exploitation and Searches

8.4 Conduct Site Exploitation

8.5 Understand and Comply with Judicial Procedures

8.6 Collect Criminal Evidence and Testimonials to Support Country Judicial Process

8.7 Conduct Field Detention Site Operations

8.8 Transfer Detainee to Government Custody

9. Develop a Learning Organization

9.1 Establish Information-Sharing Ethos

9.2 Manage Information Effectively

9.3 Conduct Training in the OE

Intentionally Blank

APPENDIX D
PRECEPTS FOR COUNTERINSURGENCY

The following tactical precepts are taken from recent experience. They complement the operational tenets mentioned in Chapter III, "Fundamentals of Counterinsurgency," paragraph 3, "Tenets of Counterinsurgency," and can be tailored to accommodate unique COIN circumstances as general guidelines.

1. Secure and serve the population. The decisive factor in COIN is the local population. The people may be a COG. Only by providing them security and earning their trust can the HN government and joint forces prevail.

2. Live with the people. The joint force must position joint bases and combat outposts as close as feasible to those that we're seeking to secure as feasible. Decide on locations with input from our partners and local citizens based on intelligence and security assessment input.

3. Support justice and honor. Whenever possible, help the populations to retain or regain their honor. Treat people with dignity and respect; that will win friends and discredit enemies. Act quickly and publicly to deal with complaints and abuses. Never allow an injustice to stand unaddressed; never walk away from a local person who believes he or she has been unjustly treated.

4. Confront impunity. Protect the people from all enemies. These include known combatants, inadequate governance, corruption, and abuse of power. Empower the legitimate government by protecting the people from malign actors and other terrorists.

5. Pursue the enemy relentlessly. Partner with joint and multinational partners to fix the enemy and do not let the enemy go. When the enemy fights, make the enemy pay. Seek out those that threaten the population.

6. Fight hard and fight with discipline. Hunt the enemy aggressively but only use the firepower needed to win a fight. More enemies will be created when civilians are killed and their property is damaged. That helps the insurgent and is counterproductive.

7. Identify and confront corrupt officials. Help the HN government achieve the aim of fighting corruption with all means possible. Work with trusted partners and within the chain of command to spotlight networks of malign actors. Act with HN officials and multinational partners to confront, isolate, pressure, and defund malign actors—and, where appropriate, refer malign actors for prosecution.

8. Hold what is secured. Together with HN partners, create a plan to develop an area once secure. The people need to know that they will not be abandoned. Prioritize population security over short-duration disruption operations.

9. Foster lasting solutions. Help HNs create good governance and enduring security. Avoid compromises with malign actors that achieve short-term gains at the expense of long-term stability.

10. Money is an important tool when used in the right hands. Pay close attention to the impact of spending and understand who benefits from it. And remember, the joint force will be associated with who it funds. How money is spent is often more important than how much is spent.

11. Be a good guest. Treat the people and their property with respect. Perceptions are drawn from all actions: driving, patrolling, helping the community, etc. View the joint forces' actions through the eyes of the people. Alienating civilians sows the seeds of defeat.

12. Build relationships. Earn the people's trust by talking to them. Inquire about social dynamics, frictions, local histories, and grievances. Hear what they say. Be aware of others in the room and how their presence may affect the answers given. Cross-check information and get the full story. Avoid knee-jerk responses based on first impressions. Do not be a pawn in someone else's game. Spend time and listen.

13. Walk. Stop by, don't drive by. Patrol on foot whenever possible and engage the population.

14. Act as one team. Work closely with international and HN partners, civilian as well as military.

15. Partner with HNSF. Live, eat, train, plan, and operate together. Depend on one another. Hold each accountable at all echelons down to troop level. Coach your HN partners to excellence. Respect them and listen to them. Be a good role model.

16. Promote local reintegration. Together with HN partners, identify and separate the "reconcilables" from the "irreconcilables." Identify and report obstacles to reintegration. Help the HN address grievances and strive to make the reconcilables part of the local solution.

17. Be first with the truth. Beat the insurgents and the malign actors to the headlines. Get accurate information to the chain of command, to HN leaders, to the people, and to the press as soon as possible. Integrity is critical to this fight. Avoid spinning the story and do not make things out to be better than they actually are. Acknowledge setbacks and failures, including civilian casualties, and then state how the HN and multinational force will respond and what was learned. Advance the strategic narrative.

18. Fight the information war aggressively. Challenge disinformation. Turn the enemies' extremist ideologies, oppressive practices, and indiscriminate violence against them. Help negate the insurgent narrative.

19. Live our values. Stay true to values that US Armed Forces hold dear. This is what distinguishes the US Service member from the enemy. It is often brutal, physically demanding, and frustrating. Everyone experiences moments of anger, but do not give in to dark impulses or tolerate unacceptable actions by others.

20. Transition with continuity. From day one, start building the information that will be provided to successors. Share information and understanding in the months before

transitions. Strive to maintain operational tempo and local relationships throughout transitions to avoid giving insurgents and malign actors a rest. Maintain continuity throughout any period of transition.

21. Win the battle of wits. Learn and adapt more quickly than the enemy. Be cunning. Outsmart the insurgents. Share best practices and lessons learned. Create and exploit opportunities.

22. Exercise initiative. In the absence of clear orders, commanders should utilize commander's intent and other guidance received while attempting to get clarification.

23. Integrate civilian-military teams. COIN requires unified action. Embedded civilian-military teams such as PRTs can now operate directly alongside military units, adding new capabilities, skills, and funds to the COIN effort. Those teams bring political and economic expertise to the brigade and regimental combat teams with whom they serve, operate under force protection rules that allow them to accompany our military forces on operations, and conduct extended engagement with local communities. To exploit military and civilian capabilities to their fullest potential, fully integrate the civilian partners into all aspects of COIN operations—from inception through execution.

24. Fight for intelligence—all the time. Tactical reporting, from civilian and military agencies, is essential: there are thousands of eyes out in an area—all must act as scouts, know what to look for, and be trained and ready to report it. Also, units should deploy analytical capacity as far forward as possible, so that the analyst is close—in time and space—to the supported commander. The presence of the joint for multinational force, living alongside the people, may result in a plethora of unsolicited tips about the enemy. Units must be prepared to receive this flood of information. Intelligence staffs and commanders must learn how to sort through reports, separating the plausible from the fictitious, integrating the reports with other forms of intelligence, and finally recognizing and exploiting a break into the enemy network.

25. Make the people choose. Some in the civilian population will want to sit on the fence and avoid having to choose between the insurgents and the government. They attempt to protect themselves by supporting the strongest local power; however, this makes them vulnerable to enemy intimidation. Get the populace off the fence—and on the side of the national government. Once the population has chosen to support the government, they will become vulnerable to the insurgents, and protecting the population becomes a priority.

Intentionally Blank

APPENDIX E
REFERENCES

The development of JP 3-24 is based upon the following primary references:

1. General

a. *The National Security Strategy of the United States of America.*

b. *National Defense Strategy of the United States of America.*

c. *National Military Strategy.*

d. *National Military Strategy for Cyberspace Operations.*

e. National Security Presidential Directive-44, *Management of Interagency Efforts Concerning Reconstruction and Stabilization.*

f. DOD, *Sustaining US Global Leadership: Priorities for 21st Century Defense,* January 2012.

g. DOD Financial Management Regulation Volume 12, Chapter 27.

h. DOS Foreign Affairs Manual 7112.1.

i. DODI 3000.05, *Stability Operations.*

j. DODD 3000.07, *Irregular Warfare (IW).*

k. Foreign Service Act of 1980 (Public Law 96-465, October 17, 1980).

2. Joint Publications

a. JP 1, *Doctrine for the Armed Forces of the United States.*

b. JP 2-0, *Joint Intelligence.*

c. JP 2-01.3, *Joint Intelligence Preparation of the Operational Environment.*

d. JP 3-0, *Joint Operations.*

e. JP 3-05, *Special Operations.*

f. JP 3-07, *Stability Operations.*

g. JP 3-08, *Intergovernmental Coordination During Joint Operations.*

h. JP 3-12, *Cyberspace Operations.*

i. JP 3-13, *Information Operations.*

j. JP 3-13.2, *Military Information Support Operations.*

k. JP 3-13.3, *Operations Security.*

l. JP 3-16, *Multinational Operations.*

m. JP 3-22, *Foreign Internal Defense.*

n. JP 3-26, *Counterterrorism.*

o. JP 3-31, *Command and Control for Joint Land Operations.*

p. JP 3-40, *Countering Weapons of Mass Destruction.*

q. JP 3-50, *Personnel Recovery.*

r. JP 3-57, *Civil-Military Operations.*

s. JP 3-61, *Public Affairs.*

t. JP 4-0, *Joint Logistics.*

u. JP 4-02, *Health Services.*

v. JP 5-0, *Joint Operation Planning.*

3. Service Publications

a. AFDD 2-0, *Global Integrated Intelligence, Surveillance, and Reconnaissance.*

b. AFDD 3-2, *Irregular Warfare.*

c. AFDD 3-22, *Foreign Internal Defense.*

d. FM 3-24/MCWP 3-33.5, *Counterinsurgency.*

e. Marine Corps Doctrinal Publication (MCDP) 1-0, *Marine Corps Operations.*

f. MCDP 1-2, *Campaigning.*

g. MCDP 5, *Planning.*

4. Department of State Publications

United States Government Interagency Counterinsurgency Initiative, *US Government Counterinsurgency Guide,* January 2009.

5. Central Intelligence Agency Publications

Guide to the Analysis of Insurgency, 2012.

6. General

a. *Village Stability Operations and Afghan Local Police: Bottom-Up Counterinsurgency* (Headquarters, Combined Joint Special Operations Task Force—Afghanistan).

b. Aitken, Rob. "Cementing Divisions? An assessment of the impact of international interventions and peace-building policies on ethnic identities and divisions," *Policy Studies* (2007) Vol. 28, No. 3, pp. 247-267.

c. Arreguin-Toft, Ivan. "How the Weak Win Wars: A Theory of Asymmetric Conflict," *International Security* (Summer 2001), Vol. 26, No. 1, pp. 93-128.

d. Asprey, Robert B. *War in the Shadows: The Guerrilla in History, Volumes I and II.* William Morrow and Company, 1994.

e. Barak, Oren. "Dilemmas of Security in Iraq," *Security Dialogue,* Vol. 38, No. 4, December 2007.

f. Biddle, Stephen, Jeffrey A. Friedman, and Jacob N. Shapiro. "Testing the Surge: Why Did Violence Decline in Iraq in 2007?" *International Security,* Vol. 37, No. 1 (Summer 2012), pp. 7-40.

g. Brass, Paul. *Theft of an Idol* (Princeton, NJ: 1997, Princeton University Press).

h. Brubaker, Roger, Mara Loveman, and Peter Stamatov. "Ethnicity as Cognition," *Theory and Society* (2004), Vol. 33, pp. 31-64.

i. Byman, Daniel. *Understanding Proto-Insurgencies.* Santa Monica: RAND Corporation, 2007.

j. Cassidy, Robert M. *Counterinsurgency and the Global War on Terror: Military Culture and Irregular Warfare.* Westport: Greenwood Publishing Group, Inc., 2006.

k. Celeski, Joseph D. JSOU Report 05-2: *Operationalizing COIN.* Hurlburt Field: Joint Special Operations University, 2005.

l. Christia, Fotini. *The Closest of Enemies: Alliance Formation in the Afghan and Bosnian Civil Wars.* PhD Thesis. 2008. Harvard University.

m. Collier, Paul, Anke Hoeffler, and Dominic Roehner. "Beyond Greed and Grievance: Feasibility and Civil War," *Oxford Economic Papers* (2009), Vol. 61, No. 1, pp. 1-27.

n. Counterinsurgency (COIN) Intelligence, Surveillance, and Reconnaissance (ISR); Operations Defense Science Board Task Force on Defense Intelligence, Office of the Under Secretary of Defense for Acquisition, Technology and Logistics, February 2011.

o. Connable, Ben. "Military Intelligence Fusion for Complex Operations," RAND, 2012.

p. Derleth, R. James W., and Jason S. Alexander. "Stability Operations: From Policy to Practice," *PRISM Journal,* Vol. 2, No. 3 (June 2011).

q. Fearon, James, and David D. Laitin. "Ethnicity, Insurgency, and Civil War." *American Political Science Review* (2003). Vol. 97, pp. 75-90.

r. Fishel, John T., and Max G. Manwaring. *Uncomfortable Wars Revisited.* Norman: University of Oklahoma Press, 2006.

s. Fitzsimmons, Michael. *Governance, Identity, and Counterinsurgency: Evidence from Ramadi and Tal Afar* (March 2013) Strategic Studies Institute, Army War College.

t. Flynn, Michael, James Sisco, and David Ellis. *"Left of Bang": The Value of Sociocultural Analysis in Today's Environment.*

u. Flynn, Michael T., and Charles A. Flynn. "Integrating Intelligence and Information," *Military Review* (January-February 2012).

v. Flynn, MG Michael, Matt Pottinger, and Paul Batchelor. "Fixing Intel: A Blueprint for Making Intelligence Relevant in Afghanistan," Center for New American Security (January 2010).

w. Galula, David. *Counterinsurgency Warfare.* London: Praeger, 1964.

x. Glatzer, Bernt. 2001. "War and Boundaries in Afghanistan: Significance of Local and Social Boundaries," *Weld des Islams*, Vol. 41, No. 3, pp. 379-399.

y. Gordon, Stuart. 2011. *Winning Hearts and Minds? Examining the Relationship Between Aid and Security in Afghanistan's Helmand Province.*

z. Horne, Alistair. *A Savage War of Peace: Algeria 1954-1962.* Harper Perennial Modern Classics. 2002.

aa. Humphreys, Macartan, and Jeremy Weinstein. "Who Fights? The Determinants of Participation in Civil War," *American Journal of Political Science*, Vol. 52, No. 2, April 2008, pp. 436-455.

bb. Ignatieff, Michael. *The Warrior's Honour: Ethnic War and the Modern Conscience* (1998: Toronto, Penguin Books).

cc. Isaac, Jeffery C., Stephen Biddle, Stathis N. Kalyvas, Wendy Brown, Douglas A. Ollivant. 2008. "The New US Army/Marine Corps Counterinsurgency Field Manual as Political Science and Political Praxis," *Perspectives on Politics* (June 2008), Vol. 6, No. 2, pp. 347-360.

dd. Hale, Henry. "Explaining Ethnicity," *Comparative Political Studies,* Vol. 37, No. 4, May 2004, pp. 458-485.

ee. Hammes, Thomas X. "Countering Evolved Insurgent Networks," *Military Review* (July-August 2006), pp. 20-21.

ff. Hoffman, Frank G. *Conflict in the 21st Century: The Rise of Hybrid Wars.* Arlington: Potomac Institute for Policy Studies, 2007.

gg. Kalyvas, Stathis. *The Logic of Violence in Civil War.* New York: Cambridge University Press, 2006.

hh. Kalyvas, Stathis. 2008. "Ethnic Defection in Civil Wars," *Comparative Political Studies,* Vol. 41, No. 8 (August 2008), pp. 1043-1068.

ii. Kilcullen, David. *The Accidental Guerilla* (Oxford: 2009, Oxford University Press).

jj. Kilcullen, David. "Intelligence," in *Understanding COIN, Doctrine, Operations and Challenges,* ed. Thomas Rid and Thomas Keany (New York: Routledge, 2010), p. 161.

kk. Lamb, Robert D. *Microdynamics of Illegitimacy and Complex Urban Violence in Medellin, Colombia.* 2010. PhD Thesis. School of Public Policy, University of Maryland.

ll. Long, Austin. *On Other War—Lessons from Five Decades of RAND Counterinsurgency Research.* Santa Monica: RAND Corporation, 2006.

mm. Long, Austin, Stephanie Pezard, Bryce Loidolt, and Todd C. Helmus. *Locals Rule: Historical Lessons for Creating Local Defense Forces for Afghanistan and Beyond.* 2012. RAND.

nn. Long, Austin. "The Anbar Awakening." *Survival* (2008), Vol. 50, No. 2, pp. 67-94.

oo. Manwaring, Max G. *A Contemporary Challenge to State Sovereignty: Gangs and Other Illicit Transnational Criminal Organizations in Central America, El Salvador, Mexico, Jamaica, and Brazil.* Carlisle: Strategic Studies Institute, 2007.

pp. McCary, John A. "The Anbar Awakening: An Alliance of Incentives," *The Washington Quarterly* (January 2009), Vol. 32, No. 1, pp. 43-59.

qq. McFate, Montgomery, and Steve Fondacaro. "Reflections on the Human Terrain System During the First Four Years," *PRISM Journal,* Vol. 2, No. 4 (September 2011).

rr. Metz, Steven. *Rethinking Insurgency.* Carlisle: Strategic Studies Institute, 2007.

ss. Mockaitis, Thomas R. *The Iraq War: Learning from the Past, Adapting to the Present, and Planning for the Future.* Carlisle: Strategic Studies Institute, 2007.

tt. Myerle, Jerry, Megan Katt, and Jim Gavrilis. *Counterinsurgency on the Ground in Afghanistan: How Different Units Adapted to Local Conditions* (2010), Center for Naval Analyses.

uu. Olson, Wm. J. "War Without a Center of Gravity: Reflections on Terrorism and Post-Modern War," *Small Wars and Insurgencies,* Vol. 18, No. 4 (December 2007).

vv. Posen, Barry. "The Security Dilemma and Ethnic Conflict." *Survival* (1993), Vol. 35, No. 1, pp. 27-47.

ww. Rosenau, William. *Subversion and Insurgency.* Santa Monica: RAND Corporation, 2007.

xx. Simonsen, Sven Gunnar. "Addressing Ethnic Divisions in Post-Conflict Institution-Building: Lessons from Recent Cases," *Security Dialogue* (2005), Vol. 36, No. 3, pp. 297-318.

yy. Smith, General Sir Rupert. 2005. *The Utility of Force: The Art of War in the Modern World.* United Kingdom: Allen Lane.

zz. Tilly, Posen. "War Making and State Making as Organized Crime," in *Bringing the State Back In,* ed. Peter Evans, Dietrich Rueschemeyer, and Theda Skocpol (Cambridge: Cambridge University Press, 1985).

aaa. Trinquier, Roger. *Modern Warfare: A French View of Counterinsurgency.* New York: Praeger, 1964.

bbb. Weinstein, Jeremy. *Inside Rebellion.* Cambridge University Press. 2006

ccc. White, Nathan "Developing US Intelligence Capabilities for Population-Centric Counterinsurgency and Stability Operations: Learning from Iraq and Afghanistan" in "Unity of Mission," ed. Jon Gunderson and Melanne Civic, Center for Complex Operations, Forthcoming publication.

ddd. Wood, Elisabeth Jean. *Insurgent Collective Action and Civil War in El Salvador* (New York: Cambridge University Press, 2003).

eee. Zedong, Mao. *On Guerrilla Warfare.* London: Cassell, 1965.

fff. Zimmerman, Rebecca S., Alton V. Buland, Todd C. Helmus, Bryce Loidolt, *"If You've Seen One VSP, You've Seen One VSP": Understanding Best Practices in Village Stability Operations.* September 2010. Commander's Initiative Group—Combined Forces Special Operations Component Command—Afghanistan.

ggg. Zimmerman, Rebecca, "Know Thine Enemy," *SAISPHERE* (January 3, 2011).

APPENDIX F
ADMINISTRATIVE INSTRUCTIONS

1. User Comments

Users in the field are highly encouraged to submit comments on this publication to: Joint Staff J-7, Deputy Director, Joint Education and Doctrine, ATTN: Joint Doctrine Analysis Division, 116 Lake View Parkway, Suffolk, VA 23435-2697. These comments should address content (accuracy, usefulness, consistency, and organization), writing, and appearance.

2. Authorship

The lead agent for this publication is the US Army. The Joint Staff doctrine sponsor for this publication is the Operations Directorate (J-3).

3. Supersession

This publication supersedes JP 3-24, 05 October 2009, *Counterinsurgency Operations*.

4. Change Recommendations

a. Recommendations for urgent changes to this publication should be submitted:

TO: JOINT STAFF WASHINGTON DC//J7-JE&D//

b. Routine changes should be submitted electronically to the Deputy Director, Joint Education and Doctrine, ATTN: Joint Doctrine Analysis Division, 116 Lake View Parkway, Suffolk, VA 23435-2697, and info the lead agent and the Director for Joint Force Development, J-7/JE&D.

c. When a Joint Staff directorate submits a proposal to the CJCS that would change source document information reflected in this publication, that directorate will include a proposed change to this publication as an enclosure to its proposal. The Services and other organizations are requested to notify the Joint Staff J-7 when changes to source documents reflected in this publication are initiated.

5. Distribution of Publications

Local reproduction is authorized, and access to unclassified publications is unrestricted. However, access to and reproduction authorization for classified JPs must be IAW DOD Manual 5200.01, Volume 1, *DOD Information Security Program: Overview, Classification, and Declassification,* and DOD Manual 5200.01, Volume 3, *DOD Information Security Program: Protection of Classified Information.*

6. Distribution of Electronic Publications

a. Joint Staff J-7 will not print copies of JPs for distribution. Electronic versions are available on JDEIS at https://jdeis.js.mil (NIPRNET) and http://jdeis.js.smil.mil (SIPRNET), and on the JEL at http://www.dtic.mil/doctrine (NIPRNET).

b. Only approved JPs are releasable outside the combatant commands, Services, and Joint Staff. Release of any classified JP to foreign governments or foreign nationals must be requested through the local embassy (Defense Attaché Office) to DIA, Defense Foreign Liaison/IE-3, 200 MacDill Blvd., Joint Base Anacostia-Bolling, Washington, DC 20340-5100.

c. JEL CD-ROM. Upon request of a joint doctrine development community member, the Joint Staff J-7 will produce and deliver one CD-ROM with current JPs. This JEL CD-ROM will be updated not less than semi-annually and when received can be locally reproduced for use within the combatant commands, Services, and combat support agencies.

GLOSSARY
PART I—ABBREVIATIONS AND ACRONYMS

ACT	advance civilian team
AFDA	Air Force doctrine annex
AFDD	Air Force doctrine document
AFSOF	Air Force special operations forces
AOI	area of interest
AOR	area of responsibility
ARSOF	Army special operations forces
ASCOPE	areas, structures, capabilities, organizations, people, and events
AtN	attack the network
C2	command and control
CA	civil affairs
CAO	civil affairs operations
CBRN	chemical, biological, radiological, and nuclear
CC	critical capability
CCDR	combatant commander
CCIR	commander's critical information requirement
CMC	Office of Civilian Military Cooperation (USAID)
CMCB	civil-military coordination board
CMO	civil-military operations
CMOC	civil-military operations center
COA	course of action
COG	center of gravity
COIN	counterinsurgency
COM	chief of mission
CONOPS	concept of operations
COP	common operational picture
CR	critical requirement
CT	counterterrorism
CTF	counter threat finance
CTP	common tactical picture
CV	critical vulnerability
CWMD	countering weapons of mass destruction
DA	direct action
DCO	defensive cyberspace operations
DDR	disarmament, demobilization, and reintegration
DOC	Department of Commerce
DOD	Department of Defense
DODD	Department of Defense directive
DODI	Department of Defense instruction
DOJ	Department of Justice

DOMEX	document and media exploitation
DOS	Department of State
DST	district support team
ESG	executive steering group
EW	electronic warfare
FACT	field advance civilian team
FID	foreign internal defense
FM	field manual (Army)
GAT	governmental assistance team
GCC	geographic combatant commander
HA	humanitarian assistance
HN	host nation
HNSF	host-nation security forces
I2	identity intelligence
IDAD	internal defense and development
IED	improvised explosive device
IGO	intergovernmental organization
IIP	interagency implementation plan
IO	information operations
IPI	indigenous populations and institutions
ISI2R	identify, separate, isolate, influence, and reintegrate
IW	irregular warfare
JCMOTF	joint civil-military operations task force
JFC	joint force commander
JIACG	joint interagency coordination group
JIPOE	joint intelligence preparation of the operational environment
JOPP	joint operation planning process
JP	joint publication
JPASE	Joint Public Affairs Support Element (USTRANSCOM)
JTF	joint task force
LOE	line of effort
LOO	line of operation
M&E	monitoring and evaluation
MARSOF	Marine Corps special operations forces
MCDP	Marine Corps doctrine publication
MCWP	Marine Corps warfighting publication
MISO	military information support operations
MOE	measure of effectiveness

MOP	measure of performance
MSO	maritime security operations
NAVSOF	Navy special operations forces
NGO	nongovernmental organization
NSF	national security forces
OE	operational environment
OECD	Organisation for Economic Co-operation and Development
OODA	observe, orient, decide, act
PA	public affairs
PEO	peace enforcement operations
PMESII	political, military, economic, social, information, and infrastructure
PNT	positioning, navigation, and timing
PO	peace operations
PR	personnel recovery
PRT	provincial reconstruction team
ROE	rules of engagement
SA	security assistance
SATCOM	satellite communications
SC	security cooperation
SCHBT	shape-clear-hold-build-transition
SecDef	Secretary of Defense
SFA	security force assistance
SOF	special operations forces
SR	special reconnaissance
SSR	security sector reform
TFC	threat finance cell
TTP	tactics, techniques, and procedures
UGA	ungoverned area
UN	United Nations
USAID	United States Agency for International Development
USC	United States Code
USG	United States Government
UW	unconventional warfare
WMD	weapons of mass destruction

counterguerrilla operations. Operations and activities conducted by armed forces, paramilitary forces, or nonmilitary agencies against guerrillas. (JP 1-02. SOURCE: JP 3-24)

counterinsurgency. Comprehensive civilian and military efforts designed to simultaneously defeat and contain insurgency and address its root causes. Also called **COIN.** (Approved for incorporation into JP 1-02.)

disaffected person. None. (Approved for removal from JP 1-02.)

governance. The state's ability to serve the citizens through the rules, processes, and behavior by which interests are articulated, resources are managed, and power is exercised in a society, including the representative participatory decision-making processes typically guaranteed under inclusive, constitutional authority. (JP 1-02. SOURCE: JP 3-24)

insurgency. The organized use of subversion and violence to seize, nullify, or challenge political control of a region. Insurgency can also refer to the group itself. (Approved for incorporation into JP 1-02.)

irregular forces. None. (Approved for removal from JP 1-02.)

paramilitary forces. Forces or groups distinct from the regular armed forces of any country, but resembling them in organization, equipment, training, or mission. (JP 1-02. SOURCE: JP 3-24)

subversion. Actions designed to undermine the military, economic, psychological, or political strength or morale of a governing authority. (JP 1-02. SOURCE: JP 3-24)

subversive political action. None. (Approved for removal from JP 1-02.)